Lawyer and Client: Who's in Charge?

Lawyer and Client: Who's in Charge?

Douglas E. Rosenthal

RUSSELL SAGE FOUNDATION   NEW YORK

PUBLICATIONS OF RUSSELL SAGE FOUNDATION

Russell Sage Foundation
230 Park Avenue, New York, N.Y. 10017

For Erica

Contents

List of Tables and Figures

Acknowledgments

Dozens of individuals helped me to shape, conduct, and complete this book. I hope they know of my gratitude although they are too numerous to name. Special appreciation goes to the clients I interviewed (whose anonymity I am obliged to preserve), to Leland Tolman and Presiding Justice Harold Stevens of the Appellate Division First Department, who authorized my access to a sample of closing statements; to David Caplovitz, Harold Lasswell, Mark Lebow, Norman Landau, Cecil J. Badway, Howard Lester, Abraham and Jacob Fuchsberg, Robert Kagan, Murray Teigh Bloom, and Joseph Lobenthal for their informative assistance; to Charles E. Lindblom, David Danelski, James David Barber, Quinton Johnstone, Richard Michaelson, and especially my dear wife Erica, who read various versions of the manuscript and made many constructive suggestions; to Lindblom, Robert Dahl, and Sir Isaiah Berlin, teachers whose influence on my ideas has been greater than they know; to my parents; to the Trustees and staff of Russell Sage Foundation who provided financial support and a stimulating and congenial work environment, the Russell Sage Program at Yale Law School with which I have been associated, and to Jean C. Yoder and William Bennett of Russell Sage Foundation who guided the book's production; to Andrew Dolan and William Repsher who helped me with the legal research and made numerous suggestions; to Meira G. Pinsleur who prepared the index; and to Ellen Harrigan, my aunt Beth Muir, Margaret Castelluzzo, Elaine Mozur, and Terry Blum who helped prepare the manuscript. I wish to thank Lindsey Churchill and Stanton Wheeler who have given constant and valued assistance, advice, friendship, and support. Finally, I am grateful to Jay Katz who has intensively involved himself with this study from its earliest beginnings. His intellectual support and friendly encouragement have improved it vastly.

Introduction

The traditional professions of law, medicine, and science are in trouble with the public and with themselves. As this is written, lawyers are asking and being asked why so many of those implicated in the immoral and illegal activities of the Watergate affair are lawyers; how widespread is the corruption of lawyers? Physicians and surgeons are being confronted with evidence that many existing health care services, even for the middle class, are inferior, and that much of the surgery which is performed is unnecessary; and government sponsored scientific research, heretofore thought proper, is being challenged for incidents of inhumanity, as in the Tuskegee Syphilis Study,[1] and bias, as in the national census surveys, which allegedly underreport the residents of inner-city ghettos.[2]

It seems that many people, professionals and laymen alike, have been responding to these troubles by one-sided conclusions: either that professionals have not been asserting enough control over the policies and practices of the professions or that professionals cannot be trusted to serve the public interest unless put under some form of strict public control. According to many, the problems of the professions, if they are going to be solved at all, must be solved by the professions themselves without public interference. According to some others, professionals should be stripped of some of their existing power and representatives of the public should be in charge of the provision of professional services. To one side the greatest dangers are socialism, anarchy, and watered-down standards; to the other side they are arrogance, indifference, and unfulfilled promises. This book represents an attempt to find a constructive middle ground between these two hostile camps and to suggest a new way of looking at professional services which emphasizes the possibilities for dealing with the problems of the professions by processes of cooperation between professional and layman. The answer it suggests to the question of the title is that

---

[1] *Final Report of the Tuskegee Syphilis Study Ad Hoc Advisory Panel* (Washington: U.S. Department of Health, Education and Welfare, Public Health Service, April 1973).

[2] *New York Times,* April 29, 1973.

neither lawyer nor layman should be in charge, but that professional service should be a matter of shared responsibility.

The most frequent and direct point of contact between the professional and the layman, and the focus of this book, is the professional-client consulting relationship in which individual professionals help individual lay clients solve their complex personal problems. This is not the only point of contact, of course. Neither are all clients individuals (some are business organizations or other institutions) nor laymen (e.g. doctors get sick), nor are all professionals individual practitioners. Professionals and clients also interact in numerous non-consulting settings such as on the governing boards of hospitals, on supervisory governmental agencies and in legislative bodies. But these more complicated forms of and settings for interaction are beyond the scope of this inquiry.

It is possible to identify a reasonably consistent and persuasive model for the proper conduct of one-to-one professional-client relationships which holds that client welfare and the public interest are best served by the professional's exercise of predominant control over and responsibility for the problem-solving delegated to him rather passively by the client. This viewpoint, which is referred to here as the traditional approach, is shared by many professionals, clients, and sociologists specializing in studies of the professions. While the professions have been sharply criticized for abusing this responsibility, I am not aware of any effort systematically to articulate a model for predominant client control in the relationship, and such is not my intention. Rather, I have tried to explicate and then test a model for the conduct of professional-client relationships which assumes that client welfare and the public interest are best served where clients participate actively in dealing with their problems and share control and decision responsibility with the professional. This middle ground viewpoint is referred to here as the participatory approach.[3]

Both approaches tap deeply felt moral values. The traditional model stresses respect for professional knowledge, competence, and integrity. The participatory model stresses respect for the motivation, common sense, and integrity of the lay client.

The primary purpose of this book is to articulate and then to test, in a specific and realistic situation, the validity of the two views of the proper professional-client relationship. The specific case study situation for making the test is the lawyer-client relationship in making a personal injury claim.

The test of the two models made with respect to one type of professional-

---

[3] See the discussion in Chapter 1, pp. 7-13, and the sources cited therein.

client relationship with respect to one type of client problem suggests that the traditional view of the professional's proper role is descriptively incorrect and normatively inappropriate. Clients who participate actively in the conduct of their claim get significantly better results than clients who passively delegate decision responsibility to their lawyer. The book concludes with a set of proposals for restructuring the professional-client relationship so as to promote both the productivity and dignity of the professions and the well-being and dignity of laymen.

A secondary, but not insignificant, goal of this book is to understand the dynamics of personal injury claims making under a liability system of compensation, thereby helping people who are injury victims to be more sophisticated consumers of personal injury legal services. When they think of the law as it may apply to them, most laymen tend to think of personal injury claims as the most important part of the lawyer's practice.[4] There is a good reason for this. One in every five registered vehicles in the United States will be involved in an accident during this year.[5] Automobile accidents alone kill more than 55,000 and disable more than 2 million people annually. Nonvehicular accidents occurring at places of employment or public places disable an additional 4 million people annually.[6] Under the traditional common law system of claims compensation, the injured party to recover compensation must be able to prove that someone else was liable (i.e. legally at fault) for negligently causing the accident.

New York State has just adopted a limited form of no-fault insurance for automobile accidents.[7] Under this compensation system, the injured party may recover compensation without having to prove that another was liable for causing the accident. The adoption of this plan will probably lessen, but not end, the important role played by personal injury law in our legal system and the role played by lawyers dealing with clients in personal injury law. New York's new no-fault law removes liability claims only with respect to automobile accidents, rather than claims arising from other types of personal injury, and applies only to less serious automobile accident claims where damages do not exceed the low ceiling amount of $500. This book contains no appraisal of the

---

[4] *Missouri Bar Prentice-Hall Survey* (Jefferson City: The Missouri Bar, 1963), p. 36.

[5] Statistic supplied by the Insurance Information Institute, 110 William Street, New York City.

[6] *Accident Facts* (Chicago: The National Safety Council, 1968 ed.), p. 3. "Disabled" means beyond the day of the accident.

[7] *McKinney's Session Laws News of New York,* March 10, 1973, pp. 9–18 and A–95.

relative merits of alternative accident compensation systems. The reader will find an extensive literature on this subject elsewhere.[8]

A third, though lesser goal of this book, is to begin to develop measures for the objective appraisal of legal performance. Such an appraisal raises formidable difficulties[9] but I have tried to show that it is worth attempting if we are to gain reliable information about the adequacy of existing professional services. One of the lessons of this appraisal is that failures of professional performance are less a matter of improper training or inadequate professional policing—though these are relevant factors—than of the complexities inherent in the problems for decision and the institutional pressures that push against a satisfactory result. No group of individuals are villains in this study. I am critical, rather, of a set of traditional ideas about the way professionals and clients should properly deal with each other. This book develops the argument that what is most wrong with the performance of the negligence bar and personal injury claimants in particular, and the professions and laymen in general, is largely attributable to the way that most participants in most professional-client consulting relationships view what they are doing and how they should be doing it.

This book has been influenced by the perspective of three disciplines. From the vantage of political science comes the interest in the real and apparent conflict between democratic control by lay citizens and authoritative policy direction by specialists. It is a classical problem of politics, and perhaps, in a democratic society, *the* classic problem. At issue in professional-client interaction are acts of influence and claims to authority—the subject matter of political science. From the vantage of sociology and social psychology comes a concern for understanding the often subtle mechanisms and components of social interaction which occurs between clients and their professional consultants, and the insights provided by a considerable literature in the sociology of

---

[8] Those interested in learning about and appraising various no-fault insurance plans are encouraged to read Jeffrey O'Connell, *The Injury Industry* (Urbana: University of Illinois Press, 1971). A more technical discussion may be found in Guido Calabresi, *The Costs of Accidents: A Legal and Economic Analysis* (New Haven, Conn.: Yale University Press, 1970). More modest changes in the existing liability claims system are advocated in the following two reports: Committee on Law Reform, "Report on the Comparative Negligence Rule" (New York: Association of the Bar of the City of New York, January 1953); and Institute of Judicial Administration, "Recovery of Interest as Damages in Personal Injury Cases" (New York, 1957).

[9] These difficulties are discussed in Edward Suchman, *Evaluative Research* (New York: Russell Sage Foundation, 1967), chap. II. See also Avedis Donabedian, "Evaluating the Quality of Medical Care," *Milbank Memorial Fund Journal,* 44 (July 1966): 166–206.

professions, especially studies of the doctor-patient relationship. Manifestly, this is also a legal inquiry. It is about the principles and policies that should govern professional-client relationships. To make sound laws we need to know about actual legal consequences and the accuracy of the law's underlying social assumptions. The law of professional responsibility is no exception.[10]

The data for this analysis are drawn from several sources. Characterization of the two professional-client models is drawn from social science literature on the professions and on decision making and from statements by professionals and laymen. The experiences and attitudes of clients come from a sample of 60 Manhattan residents who were plaintiffs in relatively serious personal injury claims for which they received some compensation during 1968. An evaluation of these claims was made by a reviewing panel of three experienced negligence attorneys and two non-attorney insurance claim adjusters. The attitudes and experiences of negligence lawyers come primarily from interviews with 20 lawyer informants and from writings by and about lawyers. These data are supplemented by information gained from questionnaires mailed to 48 of the attorneys who represented the sampled clients. The legal doctrine of professional responsibility is taken from *The Code of Professional Responsibility, Opinions of the American Bar Association Committee on Professional Ethics,* reported legal opinions, and law journal articles.

The book is divided into six chapters, with two appendices. Chapter 1 sets forth the two contradictory general theoretical models of the professional-client consulting relationship. Chapters 2 through 5 explore the six elements of the traditional model as reflected in personal injury legal practice. Chapter 2 reports the findings that active clients get better case results and that ineffective legal service is not uncommon. Chapter 3 describes the nature of personal injury problems and decisions and demonstrates that in important ways these problems and decisions are nonroutine, subjective, and involve open choices accessible to lay understanding. Chapter 4 examines the conflicts of interest between lawyer and client that appear to make "disinterested service" exceedingly difficult in personal injury claims. Chapter 5 is a consideration of the barriers limiting the access of laymen to effective legal service in personal injury claims and the role of "the organized bar" is maintaining these barriers, among other things denying clients information relevant to the informed choice of lawyers. In Chapter 6 the traditional model of professional-client relation-

---

[10] Lester Mazor, "Power and Responsibility in the Attorney-Client Relation," *Stanford Law Review* 20 (June 1966): 1138.

ships in general is reevaluated in the light of these findings with respect to the lawyer-client relationship in personal injury claims, and it is argued that the lessons drawn from this specific case study are more broadly applicable to other problems involving the interaction of professionals and their lay clients. Appendix A explains the research methodology and Appendix B reproduces the rules of the New York Appellate Division, First Department, relating to attorneys' representation of personal injury claims (which are referred to in the text at several points). They are quoted in detail to assist the reader.

Chapter One: Traditional and Participatory Models of the Professional-Client Relationship

There are two ideas about the proper distribution of power in professional consulting relationships. The traditional idea is that both parties are best served by the professional's assuming broad control over solutions to the problems brought by the client. The contradictory view is that both client and consultant gain from a sharing of control over many of the decisions arising out of the relationship. The traditional view has been more systematically elaborated as part of a larger theory of professional service—especially by sociologists specializing in the study of professionalization in medicine.[1] This view is traditional in the sense that it has been the prevailing view since the time of Hippocrates.[2] Even Plato, who argued that free men are entitled to

---

[1] Citations are necessarily selective. For a more extensive bibliography see: Wilbert E. Moore and Gerald Rosenblum, *The Professions: Roles and Rules* (New York: Russell Sage Foundation, 1970), and the essays included in H. M. Vollmer and D. L. Mills, eds., *Professionalization* (Englewood Cliffs, N.J.: Prentice-Hall, 1966). Among the more influential monographs are the following: Max Weber, *Law in Economy and Society,* edited by Max Rheinstein (Cambridge, Mass.: Harvard University Press, 1954), introduction and pp. 198–233; Emile Durkheim, *The Division of Labor in Society* (New York: Free Press, pb. ed., 1964), preface to the second edition; Florian Znaniecki, *The Social Role of the Man of Knowledge* (New York: Columbia University Press, 1940); A. M. Carr-Saunders and P. A. Wilson, *The Professions* (Oxford: Clarendon, 1933); L. J. Henderson, "Physician and Patient as a Social System" (1935), reprinted in Vollmer and Mills, *Professionalization,* p. 199; Everett C. Hughes, *Men and Their Work* (New York: Free Press, 1958); Talcott Parsons, "The Professions and Social Structure" (1939), in *Essays in Sociological Theory,* rev. ed. (New York: Free Press, 1964); Erving Goffman, "The Medical Model and Mental Hospitalization: Some Notes on the Vicissitudes of the Tinkering Trades," in *Asylums* (New York: Doubleday Anchor Books, 1961), p. 321.

[2] In the "Precepts," Hippocrates concerns himself with the difficulties posed for physicians in manipulating patients made uncooperative by their illnesses; *Hippocrates,* The Loeb Classical Library (London: Heinemann, 1962 ed., translated by W. H. S. Jones), vol. 1, pp. 303–333.

the care of physicians who spend time hearing their patients out and explaining and justifying their diagnosis and proposed remedies, viewed the physician as retaining the position of dominance, using the art of persuasion as a technique of control.[3] According to traditionalists, a profession is to be distinguished from a mere trade or occupation by its primary devotion to public service rather than to personal gain for the individual practitioner. Medicine, the law, natural science and the ministry are the most obvious professions. Many would also accord this prestige status to architecture, the military, education, and the social sciences. Some would extend the list to a broad range of consumer service occupations.[4] The examples in this chapter will be confined to the legal and medical professions. The traditional approach to professional control is rooted in and implied by this concept of a profession. Sociologist Howard Becker has characterized what I call the traditional approach in the following terms:

> Professionals, in contrast to members of other occupations, claim and are often accorded complete autonomy in their work. Since they are presumed to be the only judges of how good their work is, no layman or other outsider can make any judgment of what they can do. If their activities are unsuccessful, only another professional can say whether this was due to incompetence or to the inevitable workings of nature or society by which even the most competent practitioner would have been stymied. This image of the professional justifies his demand for complete autonomy and his demand that the client give up his own judgment and responsibility, leaving everything in the hands of the professional.[5]

Becker is the only student of the professions, so far as I have been able to discover, who has presented (in the article from which the quotation is taken) a systematic challenge to the traditional approach, and I know of no one who has formulated an alternative model stressing client participation in control either as realistic behavior or as an ideal, although Eliot Freidson has conducted an interesting case study of patients' participating somewhat actively

---

[3] See "Laws," Book Four in *The Dialogues of Plato* translated by Benjamin Jowett (New York: Random House, 1937), vol. 2, pp. 491–492.

[4] See generally, Kenneth Lynn, ed., "The Professions," *Daedalus* 92 (Fall 1963). For a more restrictive view, consult Harold Wilensky, "The Professionalization of Everyone?" *The American Journal of Sociology* 70 (September 1964): 137.

[5] Howard Becker, "The Nature of a Profession," *Education for the Professions* (Chicago: The National Society for the Study of Education, 1962), pp. 38–39. For similar expressions of this viewpoint, see Carr-Saunders and Wilson, *The Professions,* p. 284; and Talcott Parsons, *The Social System* (London: Tavistock Publications, 1952), p. 441.

in a prepaid medical insurance program in the Bronx, New York.[6] A few debunkers have written exposés of inadequate professional service, but these have tended to be dismissed as emotional and one sided.[7] The more scholarly have cautioned against facilely conferring professional status upon marginal occupations; these warnings suggest by negative implication, that in the hard-core professions of law and medicine, the traditional approach is appropriate.[8] Throughout the sociological literature, particular traditional elements have been questioned or qualified in passing, as "vicissitudes," "ambivalences," or exceptions meriting recognition but not undue emphasis.[9] Where doubts have been raised as is increasingly happening, they have not led to the systematic proposing of an alternative.[10]

For formulation of an alternative one must go outside of sociology to the fields of psychiatry and the psychology of bureaucratic organizations. The first presentation of an alternative approach designed for the doctor-patient relationship, but more broadly relevant to other forms of professional practice, was made in 1956 by psychiatrists Thomas Szasz and Marc Hollender. They proposed three basic models of the doctor-patient relationship and argued that each was appropriate under certain circumstances and inappropriate under others.[11] Model No. 1 is the active doctor and the inert patient unable to respond to interaction, as when anesthetized in surgery. Model No. 2 is the guiding doctor and the cooperating patient—analogous to the relationship prescribed by the traditional professional rationale:

---

[6] Eliot Freidson, *Patients' Views of Medical Practice* (New York: Russell Sage Foundation, 1961).

[7] Illustrative are Fred Rodell, *Woe unto You Lawyers* (New York: Pageant Books, 1957); Fred J. Cook, *The Plot Against the Patient* (Englewood Cliffs, N.J.: Prentice-Hall, 1967); Howard Lewis and Martha Lewis, *The Medical Offenders* (New York: Simon & Schuster, 1970).

[8] Wilensky, "The Professionalization of Everyone?"

[9] Two places where these tensions are discussed explicitly are in Goffman, "The Medical Model and Mental Hospitalization"; and Robert Merton and Eleanor Barber, "Sociological Ambivalence," in *Sociological Theory, Values and Sociocultural Change: Essays in Honor of Pitirim Sorokin,* ed. E. A. Tiryakian (New York: Harper Torchbooks, 1967).

[10] Recent source materials collected by Katz do provide the basis for studying the traditional model and for developing a systematic alternative to it. Jay Katz, *Experimentation with Human Beings* (New York: Russell Sage Foundation, 1972), pp. 185–235.

[11] Thomas Szasz and Marc Hollender, "A Contribution to the Philosophy of Medicine: The Basic Models of the Doctor-Patient Relationship," *Archives of Internal Medicine* 97 (1956): 591.

The more powerful of the two parties [doctor, professional, employer] will speak of guidance or leadership and will expect cooperation of the other member of the pair [patient, client, employee]. The patient is expected to "look up to" and "obey" his doctor. Moreover, he is neither to question nor to argue or disagree with the orders he receives.[12]

Model No. 3 is mutual participation in a cooperative relationship in which the cooperating parties have relatively equal status, are equally dependent, and are engaged in activity "that will be in some ways satisfying to both [parties]."[13]

The contribution of Szasz and Hollender is in suggesting for the first time that even in the "purest" profession, medicine, the traditional rationale of exclusive professional control was neither the only possible basis for consulting interaction nor necessarily the best basis for all therapeutic situations.

It is no accident that the joint authors are psychiatrists. In psychoanalytic theory a great deal of attention has been given to the norms of therapist-patient interaction in individual psychotherapy. Most psychoanalytically-oriented psychiatrists now take the view that effective psychotherapy requires for its success an active acceptance of personal responsibility by the patient.[14] The patient collaborates with the therapist in identifying the problems to be treated and shares in decisions about the nature and extent of the treatment to be undertaken. In other words, the preferred psychotherapeutic model of interaction is one of mutual participation rather than one of guidance-cooperation. There has not been, however, a consensus on the proper extent of patient control. One school, under the influence of clinical psychologist Carl Rogers, has taken the relatively extreme position that the most effective therapy takes place in an atmosphere in which it is assumed that the client is capable of making all decisions for himself, with the therapist's task being to provide the "client with the opportunity of making responsible choices."[15] Most psychiatrists who favor a considerable degree of patient (client) participation reject this defini-

---

[12] Ibid., p. 587. The model for No. 2 is the parent-child relationship. This antecedent also is acknowledged in a paper by Talcott Parsons and Renee Fox, "Illness, Therapy and the Modern Urban Family," in *Patients, Physicians and Illness*, ed. E. Gartley Jaco (New York: Free Press, 1958).

[13] Szasz and Hollender, "A Contribution to the Philosophy of Medicine," p. 587.

[14] See Daniel Freedman and Frederick Redlich, *The Theory and Practice of Psychiatry* (New York: Basic Books, 1965); also Jay Katz, "The Right to Treatment—An Enchanting Legal Fiction?" *The University of Chicago Law Review* 36 (Summer 1969), pp. 755–783.

[15] Carl R. Rogers, *Client-Centered Therapy* (Boston: Houghton Mifflin, pb. ed., 1965), p. 51.

tion of the therapist's task. They point out that the psychotherapist knows more about the "wider context" of the patient's illness than the patient knows himself and that this knowledge must be used to lead (control) the patient to the point where he can assume effective responsibility.[16] Nevertheless, while the extent of client control remains at issue, psychoanalytically-oriented psychiatrists tend to agree that client participation per se is constructive rather than harmful.

A further development of the client-participation idea has been described in connection with the proper structure and policies for governing mental hospital wards. In at least one hospital, a conscious attempt has been made by both staff and patients to share the power of ward government more equitably in the hope that active patient participation will directly promote mental health. A study of this ward, done jointly by political scientist Harold Lasswell and psychiatrist Richard Rubenstein, concludes that a greater sharing of decision has in fact promoted the self-confidence and self-respect of many of the patients without producing administrative chaos, although power was not shared to the extent anticipated.[17] The extent to which norms suitable for the psychiatrist-patient relationship are relevant to other less "intimate" and "subjective" consulting-client relationships will be considered later.

Another branch of social science in which the potential benefits of lay participation in expert decision making have been explored is industrial relations. While there are important structural differences between the professional-client and the employer-employee relationships, many of the same arguments and assumptions underlie rationales for power distribution in both. Influential in this field was a psychologist—Kurt Lewin. He designed experimental situations to test the benefits of a high degree of worker participation in industrial decisions. He and his associates found that participation has less impact, pro or con, on productivity, than on the sense of psychological well-being of workers. As with the Lasswell and Rubenstein study, it was found that the appearance of participation frequently masked subtle forms of control by the

---

[16] Merton Gill, Richard Newman, and Frederick Redlich, *The Initial Interview in Psychiatric Practice* (New York: International Universities, 1954), pp. 82–83.

[17] Harold Lasswell and Richard Rubenstein, *The Sharing of Power in a Mental Hospital* (New Haven, Conn.: Yale University Press, 1966); see for example "the locked-closets incident," p. 222 ff. For a finding in partial conflict, see Robert N. Rapoport, *Community as Doctor: New Perspectives on a Therapeutic Community* (London: Tavistock Publications, 1960), p. 221: "democratization and communalism may bring less therapeutic success than a 'marked positive orientation to salient staff members, especially high status staff.'"

authorities. Lewin's work has been carried on by others, notably Tannenbaum, and the results remain controversial.[18]

Clearly the two conflicting approaches—hereafter to be called the traditional and the participatory—raise a hard issue. Does the professional-client relationship work better when there is primarily professional control or when there is a partnership of control between professional and client? In this book an answer will be offered, based on an empirical test. At this point it will help to look more closely at the two approaches, especially at the assumptions used to justify each.

Underlying each approach is a relatively consistent, usually implicit model of how professionals and clients should interact and the justifications for these forms of interaction. Not only does each model lead to different positions on the larger issue of power but to different ideas about how the professional-client relationship should be conducted in specific details. These disagreements can be seen in the contrasting answers that a supporter of each approach would give to the following six questions:

1. How active should clients be in trying to understand their problem and in trying to influence its solution?
2. Do professionals usually give effective service?
3. Do client problems have a single best routine and technical solution inaccessible to lay understanding?
4. Do professionals give disinterested service?
5. Are high professional standards set and maintained by professional associations and the courts?
6. How accessible is effective professional service to paying clients?

In Table 1.1, the two contrasting sets of answers are stated as six basic elements of each model.

Some readers may quarrel with the relevance of particular questions and answers, and with the associations made among various answers within the same set. The following discussion will try to justify the appropriateness of these six elements.

------

[18] A brief report on this work is made by Michel Crozier in *The Bureaucratic Phenomenon* (Chicago: University of Chicago Press, 1963), pp. 203–208. Two excellent longer reviews are by Arnold S. Tannenbaum, "Participation," *Social Psychology of the Work Organization* (Belmont, Calif.: Wadsworth Publishing Co., 1966), chap. 7; and Victor Vroom, "Industrial Social Psychology" in *Handbook of Social Psychology,* 2d ed., eds. Gardner Lindzey and Elliot Aronson (Reading, Mass.: Addison-Wesley, 1969), vol. 5, pp. 227–240. See also Peter Blau, *The Dynamics of Bureaucracy* (Chicago: University of Chicago Press, 1955), pp. 202–206.

Table 1.1: The Two Models Contrasted

Question	Traditional Answer	Participatory Answer
1. Proper client behavior?	It consists of little effort at understanding; passive, trusting delegation of responsibility; and following of instructions.	It involves an active, skeptical effort to be informed and to share responsibility, making mutually agreeable choices.
2. Effectiveness of professional service?	Ineffective professional service is rare.	Ineffective professional service is common.
3. Nature of professional problems?	They are routine and technical, having a best solution inaccessible to lay understanding.	They involve open, unpredictable individualized choices, understandable to a layman, for which there is no single best answer.
4. Disinterested service?	Professionals can and do make the client's interest their own.	Disinterested professional service is virtually impossible.
5. Professional standards?	High standards are set and maintained by the professions themselves and by the courts.	Standards are neither clearly set nor effectively enforced by either the professions or the courts.
6. Accessibility of effective professional service to paying clients?	Effective professional service is accessible to all paying clients.	Many paying clients have difficulty finding effective professional service.

HOW ACTIVE SHOULD CLIENTS BE IN TRYING TO UNDERSTAND THEIR PROBLEM AND IN TRYING TO INFLUENCE ITS SOLUTION?

According to the traditional theory the client who is passive, follows instructions, and trusts the professional without criticism, with few questions or requests, is preferable and will do better than the difficult client who is critical and questioning.[19] It is of paramount importance that the interaction

---

[19] Talcott Parsons, "Social Structure and Dynamic Process: The Case of Modern Medical Practice," *The Social System*, p. 437. Parsons, "Research with Human Subjects and the 'Professional Complex,'" *Daedalus* 98 (Spring 1969): 358, fn. 5. See more generally, Samuel Bloom, "The Role of the Patient," *The Doctor and His Patient* (New York: Russell Sage Foundation, 1965), pp. 98–118.

between client and professional be stable and free of conflict.[20] This stability requirement is one of the justifications cited for demanding complete client confidence in the professional consultant. Without such confidence the client may disrupt the consultation and undercut the effectiveness of the professional's service. It has been argued by Moore and Tumin that client trust in unvarying professional competence and the certainty of a good outcome is necessary whether or not trust actually is warranted.[21] This assumes, gratuitously, that the public can be kept in the dark if it turns out that professional performance is in reality poor. Most writers who accept the necessity of client trust do not rely on Moore and Tumin's argument.[22] The less cynical view is that most professional performance is in reality of sufficient competence to justify public trust.

The participatory theory promotes an active strategy assuming that it is primarily the client's own responsibility to grapple with the problem.[23] Instead of delegating responsibility to the professional and leaving the decisions to him while being kept only minimally informed, the participating client seeks information to help him define his problem and what he wants to accomplish, rather than waiting to be told how to proceed. Periodically he reviews and reevaluates the steps already taken, and the professional's performance, by questioning and by appraising the consistency and accuracy of the professional's answers. He is aware that there are open choices to be made in solving his problem and expects to have his concerns reflected in the choices made.[24]

The passive client, on the other hand, reacts much as described by a doctor recalling his own behavior at a time when he was seriously ill:

---

[20] Charles Kadushin, "Social Distance between Client and Professional," *The American Journal of Sociology* 67 (1962): 517–531.

[21] Wilbert E. Moore and Melvin M. Tumin, "Some Social Functions of Ignorance," *American Sociological Review* 14 (December 1949): 789.

[22] Which is appropriately criticized by Harold Wilensky, *Organizational Intelligence* (New York: Basic Books, 1967), preface pp. x–xi.

[23] The idea of problem-solving strategies is explained by Robert Thomson, *The Psychology of Thinking* (London: Penguin Books, 1959), p. 70. Thomson draws much from the work of Jerome Bruner et al., especially, *A Study of Thinking* (New York: Science Editions, 1965), chap. 4. For one interesting experimental study of complex personal decision-making see: Orville Brim, David Glass, David Lavin, and Norman Goodman, *Personality and Decision Processes* (Stanford, Calif.: Stanford University Press, 1962).

[24] This conception of an active strategy is based on the model of rational decision set out by David Braybrooke and Charles E. Lindblom, *A Strategy of Decision* (New York: Free Press, 1963). A shorter statement may be found in Lindblom, *The Policy-Making Process* (Englewood Cliffs, N.J.: Prentice-Hall, 1968), chap. 4.

> There is a remarkable disparity between the agitated subjectivity of the patient in recounting his symptoms and the detached objectivity with which he regards the steps in treatment. He hires the doctor to attack the disease much in the manner of a Renaissance king hiring Swiss mercenaries, and although he is painfully aware that he also furnishes the battleground, it rarely occurs to him that he might engage himself in the battle.[25]

The passive client's delegation of responsibility and control detaches him from the problem solving process. Only repeated or dramatic evidence of professional nonperformance or misconduct leads to an active reevaluation of the delegation—and the decision whether or not to fire the first professional and delegate responsibility to a second one.

Of course, the active strategy is costly. From the client, it demands energy, intelligence, and judgment. From the professional it demands patience and tolerance built on recognition of an obligation to earn the client's cooperation. The passive strategy makes fewer demands on both parties, but if the professional in fact makes a mistake, it may not be noticed in time to be corrected.

Traditionalists find the notion of an active strategy naïve and possibly dangerous. Take away the professional's role of decision responsibility and the client is more likely to be frightened and resentful. Traditionalists are convinced in fact that people would reject an active problem-solving role even if it were offered to them by an unusually self-sacrificing and foolhardy professional. While participationists concede that most people presently do not push to assert an active role, they contend that clients have never received any real encouragement. On the contrary, they say, clients have been socialized by the traditional theory to think it mistrustful to want influence—mistrust being an illegitimate client response. In the participationist view, if clients don't want decision-making responsibility once it has been effectively offered to them, they can knowingly waive it. But even the chance to forego participatory opportunities is an improvement over the norm of nonparticipation. Traditionalists respond with skepticism about the capacities of most people to make *knowing* waivers. The traditional model implies that there are only two choices for a client: complete trust or uncompromising hostility. The participating model rejects such a clean-cut distinction. In the words of Miss Schiff (a pseudonym, as are all the sample clients' names), a young schoolteacher client in the sample, "I think basically that most people can be trusted but because most people can be trusted doesn't mean that one should trust people blindly." It has been argued that in fact people never do fully trust strangers, even if they are pro-

---

25 Paul Williams in *When Doctors Are Patients,* eds. Max Pinnar and Benjamin Miller (New York: Norton, 1962), pp. 225–226.

fessionals,[26] and that, as with a treaty negotiation between suspicious diplomats, stable and efficient collaborative effort can be maintained between mutually suspicious professionals and clients for extended periods about matters of great delicacy and importance.[27]

DO PROFESSIONALS USUALLY GIVE EFFECTIVE SERVICE?

Traditionalists believe that passive client trust is warranted by the consistently high standards of performance of virtually all certified professionals. As part of a broad and impressionistic survey of the legal profession conducted after World War II, Phillips and McCoy concluded that,

> on the whole, the service which the Bar renders to the community is immeasureable. That it should be rendered with so little justified criticism is a splendid tribute to the maintenance of lofty standards by men whose only restriction is their own conscience and whose only guide is the high tradition of their profession.[28]

Similar judgments about the medical profession are even more common.[29] However, reports with less reassuring conclusions about the adequacy of existing legal and medical service are occasionally made.[30] Is the American Medical Association, for example, correct in being substantially satisfied with present surgical practice, or is Paul R. Hawley, former director of the American College of Surgeons, correct when he says that *"one-half* of the surgical operations in the United States are performed by doctors who are untrained or inadequately trained to undertake surgery?"[31] With the stakes so high and the disparity so great, it is astonishing how little is known about the true calibre of various

---

[26] "The self-system of the stranger is always viewing the other person as an enemy and taking due precautions against the other person on this basis." Harry Stack Sullivan, *The Psychiatric Interview* (New York: Norton, 1954), p. 139.

[27] This has been a central theme in the writing of Charles E. Lindblom; see *The Intelligence of Democracy; Decision-Making through Partisan Mutual Adjustment* (New York: Free Press, 1965).

[28] Oriel Phillips and Philbrick McCoy, *Conduct of Judges and Lawyers: A Study of Professional Ethics, Discipline and Disbarment* for the *Survey of the Legal Profession* (Los Angeles: Parker & Co., 1952), p. 84.

[29] Illustrative is Oswald Hall, "The Informal Organization of the Medical Profession," *Canadian Journal of Economics and Political Science* 12 (1946): 32.

[30] Illustrative for the legal profession is Quintin Johnstone and Daniel Hopson, *Lawyers and Their Work* (Indianapolis, Ind.: Bobbs-Merrill, 1967), pp. 7–10.

[31] Quoted in Charles Kramer, *The Negligent Doctor* (New York: Crown, 1968), p. 15.

professional services.[32] To the extent that professional failure is not rare, it becomes more urgent for clients to make the effort to participate actively in solving their problem. On the other hand, if professional problem solving is effective in virtually all situations, client activity to monitor, appraise, and supplement professional conduct is less necessary.

DO CLIENT PROBLEMS HAVE A SINGLE BEST ROUTINE AND TECHNICAL SOLUTION ACCESSIBLE TO LAY UNDERSTANDING?

A majority of claimants in the client sample reacted to the threatening uncertainties raised by their claims by looking to their lawyer for authoritative direction. An outgoing retired rabbi interviewed said, for example, "If the lawyer is competent, he knows with certainty what can be done with the law." The rabbi is expressing the idea that most of the uncertainty, the openness of problems in which there is no unvarying set of circumstances to be dealt with in a standardized way and involving disparate personal values (that may dictate contrary choices) has been largely removed from the law. This is manifestly the assumption of a sociologist who studied the work of lawyers in matrimonial cases:

> Legal problems can be thought of as having more or less built-in guidelines for practitioners. . . . An attorney's job would seem to be fairly well structured in tort actions. . . . He usually strives for a financial verdict or settlement most beneficial to his client. . . . Extremely difficult questions may remain, but there are at least broad (technical) criteria that a lawyer can take for granted.[33]

But actually, in his research into matrimonial cases O'Gorman found the client's own uncertain feelings made things unusually open, unstructured and nonroutine for a legal problem. A variation of this belief in certainty concedes that uncertain knowledge and open choices are difficulties in the professions, but only in those fields which are at the "creative frontiers" of new and changing knowledge. By implication while, say, outer-space law is an atmosphera incognita, much less is uncertain within the terrain of well-established legal knowledge of a field such as torts.[34]

---

[32] The two published empirically rigorous evaluations of medical performance of which I am aware are discussed in Chapter 6, p. 148.

[33] Hubert O'Gorman, *Lawyers and Matrimonial Cases* (New York: Free Press, 1963), pp. 99–100.

[34] This borrows and paraphrases the idea of Fox as applied to medical uncertainty. Renee Fox, *Experiment Perilous* (New York: Free Press, 1959), pp. 28–29.

The participatory theory stresses the uncertainty of the criteria and procedures of professional practice, the dependence of a best course of action on what is important to the client as much as on some objectively right remedy. T. H. Weldon, the political philosopher, has distinguished between "difficulties" which occur and have to be coped with, but for which there is no objectively right answer, and "problems" which occur and which can be solved in terms of a best answer.[35] Traditionalists hold that professional questions are "problems" in Weldon's usage; participationists believe that professional questions are more often "difficulties."

If professional problems are essentially closed as traditionalists claim, client delegation is more justifiable. However, if they are essentially open, client delegation limits the client's justifiable influence over the critical choices to be made. Similarly, if professional problems are essentially capable of routinization and the accurate prediction of various outcomes, the client is best served by putting himself in the hands of the professional who has mastered the standard responses. However, if they are in important ways nonroutinized, unpredictable problems, the client has a greater stake in seeing that his individual needs are being met.

The traditional theory rests heavily on the need for trust because it is believed that lay clients do not have and cannot feasibly obtain sufficient knowledge for even partial self-diagnosis and remedy. As Alexander Pope observed, "a little learning is a dangerous thing"; the client who thinks he knows better will inflict greater harm upon himself by rejecting good advice than by accepting it unquestioningly. Participationists are more optimistic. One study of the medical knowledge of a sample of outpatients in a hospital clinic has been reported. The researchers found that the patients

> were quite poorly informed about their own condition when they came to the clinic and about ten common diseases. . . . [and] they gave little evidence of conscious, aggressive demand for information about their condition from the physician; but there appeared to be an unformulated, latent desire for more information among the majority . . . physicians apparently cannot judge very accurately the level of medical knowledge in a patient population. The direction of their error was rather consistently to underestimate patient's knowledge.[36]

---

[35] T. H. Weldon, *The Vocabulary of Politics* (London: Penguin Books, 1953), pp. 75–83.

[36] Lois Pratt, Arthur Seligmann, and George Reader, "Physicians' Views of the Level of Medical Information among Patients," in *Patients, Physicians and Illness*, p. 222.

Participationists are suspicious about the professionals wittingly or unwittingly maintaining client uncertainty and client feelings of incompetence as a means of increasing their own indispensability—their power over the client. For example, Davis has discussed the behavior of doctors who did not want to have to meet the demands for time, effort, and involvement which they felt a sample of Baltimore parents would make if they knew that their children almost certainly faced permanent crippling by polio. To avoid these demands, and thus better control the interaction with the parents, they told the anxious parents that the outcome of the polio was still in doubt—that it was too early to think about the possibilities of permanent impairment.[37]

Many traditionalists would not deny that professionals frequently avoid informing their clients, but they feel that most clients prefer it this way. As they see it, clients want simple, reassuring answers. They are afraid of knowing too much lest some news be bad news.[38] Illustrative of traditional thinking is the following advice offered to lawyers by the Wisconsin Bar Association:

> Get at the client's problem immediately and stick to it. Don't bother to explain the reasoning processes by which you arrive at your advice. The client expects you to be an expert. This not only prolongs the interview, but generally confuses the client. The client will feel better and more secure if told in simple straightforward language what to do and how to do it, without an explanation of *how* you reached your conclusions.[39]

The participationist counters that people have a greater capacity for confronting reality than they are given credit for—especially when the risks of avoiding reality are made clear to them.[40]

The traditional model assigns the determination of how much information the client should be given about his problem and the possible ways of dealing with it to the discretion of each professional. The professional's judgment may be based on a case-by-case assessment of what each client wants to hear, how much trouble the client is likely to make for the professional in added de-

---

[37] Fred Davis, "Uncertainty in Medical Prognosis: Clinical and Functional," in *Society and Self,* ed. Barton Stoodley (New York: Free Press, 1962), p. 174.

[38] Robert Kahn and Charles Cannell, "A Medical Interview," in their *The Dynamics of Interviewing* (New York: Wiley, 1957), chap. 10, pp. 258–259.

[39] Reprinted in Joseph Goldstein and Jay Katz, *The Family and the Law* (New York: Free Press, 1965), p. 87.

[40] This is a major theme in Eric Fromm's *Escape from Freedom* (New York: Holt, Rinehart, and Winston, 1958). Fromm deplores what he sees as a fallacious trend toward deifying expert authority with the result that people become both naive and cynical at the same time (p. 250).

mands, how much time and energy it is worth spending on the case, how easy it is to communicate with the client, and related factors.

A participatory view of the problem-solving relationship gives explicit and extensive disclosure a central place. Since it is the client who will have to live with the outcome, he should be informed about the risks and benefits of alternative courses of action even if the choice is obvious to the professional and even if the client does not fully comprehend what he is being told. It is not enough to leave the amount of disclosure to the discretion of the professional. The client should be entitled to this information as a matter of course.[41] This information will not only provide psychological reassurance,[42] but will provide a basis for the client's appraisal of the professional's competence to help him. Furthermore, it can be used as a means for sharing decision responsibility with the client. Full disclosure will facilitate the client's ratification of the action taken, thus minimizing the grounds for subsequent client grievances. The discipline of having to hear and understand the information will help the client to feel less estranged from the profession and professional jargon.

Professionals are required, as a matter of law, to exercise the skill and knowledge normally possessed by members of that profession in good standing in similar communities.[43] A wide range of behavior is permitted under this rule. Within the past decade, a new rule has been added to the definition of the doctor's duty to his patient—the rule of informed consent. Under this rule, the participatory principle of meaningful disclosure of risky choices assumes legal status. Where, for example, a patient is diagnosed as suffering from cancer of the breast and the cancer is removed by surgery, there is a postoperative choice of localized radiation therapy or watchful waiting for any manifestations of continuing malignancy. Cobalt radiation treatments carry an attendant risk of serious bodily injury. If the doctor proceeds with radiation treatments without

---

[41] Some of the responsibilities of physicians to their patients in the light of participatory assumptions have been raised in an article by Jay Katz, "The Education of the Physician Investigator," *Daedalus* 98 *Ethical Aspects of Experimentation with Human Subjects* (Spring 1969): 485–497.

[42] The need for reassurance has been most extensively explored in relation to surgical procedures which threaten life and limb. See, for example, Bernard Kutner, "Surgeons and Their Patients: A Study in Social Perception," in *Patients, Physicians and Illness,* pp. 384–397; and Irving Janis, *Psychological Stress* (New York: Wiley, 1958). There has been almost no investigation of the psychological needs of legal clients. A notable exception is Harrop Freeman, *Legal Interviewing and Counseling* (St. Paul, Minn.: West, 1964). Freeman, however, fails to explore the issue of disclosure in legal counseling.

[43] *Restatement of Torts 2d* (St. Paul, Minn.: American Law Institute, 1965), 299A, pp. 73–76.

disclosing these risks to the patient and injury occurs, and if disclosure of the risks is the type of disclosure that a reasonable medical practitioner would have made under the same or similar circumstances, and if the patient can find a doctor willing to testify in court to this effect, the patient has grounds for a successful malpractice lawsuit.

The rule requiring the patient's informed consent to high risk medical procedures was enunciated by a Kansas court in the case of *Natanson* v. *Kline*.[44] It is now the law in most states. So far, courts have been reluctant to find breach of a disclosure duty where doctors can show that they made a disclosure comparable to the disclosure made by other physicians in similar situations.[45] Some courts have also adopted the traditionalist viewpoint that the doctor is free not to disclose risky choices where the emotional strain of informed consent, in the doctor's view, would impair the process of recovery.[46] Thus, the conflict between the doctor's right to determine the best interests of the patient, and the patient's right "to be master of his own body,"[47] leaves the doctrine an open field for further elaboration. How the doctrine develops should depend in large part on the validity of the traditional as against the participatory theory.

It would seem that many traditionalists are prepared to accept that client participation makes more sense in situations where the client faces choices that can dramatically alter his life. But in the law these kinds of choices are thought of by many to be less prevalent, the one exception being the criminal law where the absence of certain forms of client participation in the accused's interaction with police, witnesses, the judge, the jury, and his attorney, raises issues about the client's being denied his constitutional right to a full and fair trial.[48] This

---

[44] 186 Kan. 393, 350 P.2d 1093 (1960), *rehearing denied with clarifying opinion,* 187 Kan. 186, 354, P.2d 670. This is a leading case in that area, but not the earliest.

[45] This limitation on the informed consent rule is discussed and criticized by Eleanor Glass in her Note, "Restructuring Informed Consent: Legal Therapy for the Doctor-Patient Relationship," *Yale Law Journal,* 79 (1970): 1533–1576.

[46] See, for example, *Salgo* v. *Leland Stanford Jr. University Board of Trustees,* 154 Cal. App. 2d 560 (1957), 17 P.2d 170.

[47] "It can be argued that one is always solicitous to protect his own person or property and can be trusted better than any other to define his own best interests. The requirement of consent enables him to contract in reference to his own health. It puts a curb on surgical enthusiasm for procedures and experimentation. Nor can one overlook the fact that mental acquiescence and cooperation of the patient has strong therapeutic implications and may decide the issue of success or failure. In the last analysis, however, the paramount right of the patient to accept or reject surgery rests squarely on the bedrock of self-determination." Hubert W. Smith, "Antecedent Grounds of Liability in the Practice of Surgery," *Rocky Mountain Law Review,* 14 (1942) at 237.

[48] Lester Mazor, "Power and Responsibility in the Attorney-Client Relation," *Stanford Law Review,* 20 (June 1968): 1120–139.

reflects on the high value we put on freedom from enforced detention. The truth is that there may well be many other dramatically stressful legal situations. For instance, may not some men burdened through much of their adult life by civil wage garnishment (the judicially sanctioned deduction of a portion of a person's wages to meet his debts) suffer more than if they had been sentenced for a crime to a finite period of imprisonment?

DO PROFESSIONALS GIVE DISINTERESTED SERVICE?

The concept of disinterested service is a hallmark of the traditional model. The competent professional is able to see what is in the best interests of his client—and to make those interests his own. Disinterested service has two elements. Simultaneously, the professional must free himself from self-interested temptations that conflict with the client's cause; and he must strongly defend the client against outside interests that threaten him. Neutral detachment is not enough.[49] Sometimes these two elements may conflict, as in the case of contingent fees. While the contingent fee encourages what some see as an excessively mercenary attitude of gain at the client's expense, many clients feel that it insures their receiving energetic and disinterested service against third parties. Mrs. Reed, a sampled client whose case we will examine in Chapter 2, said, "I trusted my lawyer implicitly. I had no doubts that he had my best interests [in mind] because he was getting a percentage [of my claim]."

Critics of the traditional theory find it serving an important ideological function for the professional: to justify his freedom from criticism and control. The theory encourages both popular respect for the professions and practitioner self-respect: public relations and self-esteem. Participationists are suspicious that traditionalists may be engaging in self-delusive propaganda more than in realistic analysis. They feel traditionalists give insufficient attention to the possibility of the professional's bias in determining the client's interest. This is a major concern of psychoanalytic theory in the analyst-patient relationship. It is referred to as the twin problems of transference and countertransference. Somewhat simplified, transference is the patient's reacting to the professional based on attitudes learned in dealing with other persons who were important in his past. Superficial similarities between the professional and these earlier

---

[49] Talcott Parsons has been criticized for construing professional disinterest as "affective neutrality," though he should be credited with the insight that excessive zeal at too early a stage may impair accurate diagnosis. See George Reader and Mary Goss, "The Sociology of Medicine," in *Sociology Today: Problems and Prospects,* eds. Robert Merton et al. (New York: Harper Torchbooks, 1965), vol. 1, p. 224.

persons influence, without his awareness, the patient's behavior in the interaction. By uncovering these attitudes and behavior patterns, and by making the patient recognize them for what they are, the analysis is advanced. Countertransference is the same process with the roles reversed—the professional's unconscious needs which are triggered by the client and by having to deal with him.[50] Even psychoanalysts who have experienced a long and intensive training analysis (aimed at making them sufficiently self-aware to help others effectively) experience countertransference toward their patients. The point relevant to a participatory theory is that the professional has self-interests, of which he himself may be unaware, that may compete with the objective interests of his clients. Without sufficient self-awareness, the professional is not likely to be disinterested. Traditionalists doubt that these unconscious needs play a significantly negative part in interaction between mature adults over nonpsychiatric "technical" matters.

The issue of disinterested service is allied closely with the nature of client problems. If problems are largely open questions with risks and benefits that depend greatly upon the client's subjective ideas and feelings, the client himself can be assumed to know best his own interest. If client problems are largely closed questions with reasonably predictable outcomes that can be weighed according to widely shared criteria of value, and if this weighing process demands largely noncommunicable specialized knowledge, the competent professional can be assumed to know best the client's interest. The further issue is whether or not the competent professional can sufficiently free himself from the competing claims of self, family, colleagues, and other clients to pursue the client's interest, however identified. The traditionalist says yes; the participationist is skeptical.

ARE HIGH PROFESSIONAL STANDARDS SET AND MAINTAINED BY PROFESSIONAL ASSOCIATIONS AND THE COURTS?

Traditionalists are impressed with the way legal and medical professionals are "socialized into the world of work"—the way they are trained in the norms

---

[50] A suggestive interpretation of the lawyer-client relationship from the perspective of a psychiatrist is found in Andrew Watson, "The Lawyer and His Client: The Process of Emotional Involvement," *Psychiatry for Lawyers* (New York: International Universities, 1968), chap. I. For a more technical discussion, see D. W. Orr, "Transference and Countertransference," *Journal of the American Psychoanalytic Association* 2 (1954): 621–670.

of ethical and skilled practice and meet self-imposed high standards.[51] One book introducing the layman to the law states:

> The standards of the American lawyer are high. He must meet rigid character and educational requirements established by the courts in order to become a member of the legal profession, and in daily practice he must conform to a rigorous code of principles and practice.[52]

These rigorous standards are thought to be vigorously enforced by self-policing within the "professional community": the certification of competency by examination; the certification of moral fitness by a reviewing panel; the continuing postcertification review of professional conduct by colleagues and professional associations; and, where necessary, the relatively extreme sanctions of censure, suspension, and removal of the professional license.[53] These relatively extreme sanctions are rarely invoked.

> The rarity of extreme sanctions means either that rules are poorly enforced or that occupational socialization and informal reinforcements serve in most cases. With some possible exceptions—abortion may be one, for the law is more severe than many members of the community would support—the probability is high that socialization works.[54]

In recent scholarship, the traditional view has been disputed. Davis and Blake have argued that social rules themselves are frequently in conflict, that feared sanctions frequently conflict with and prove less influential than social rules, and that for many of the circumstances of life and work, specific social guidelines do not exist.[55] Jerome Carlin has conducted research suggesting that certain social pressures within the professional community of New York City lawyers actually reinforce unethical conduct; Carlin's findings have been replicated by Kenneth Reichstein in a concurrent study of the Chicago Bar, and

---

[51] A concise statement on this point is contained in Wilbert E. Moore, "Occupational Socialization," in *Handbook of Socialization Theory and Research,* ed. David Goslin (Chicago: Rand McNally, 1969), chap. 21, p. 862 ff.

[52] George Coughlin, *Your Introduction to Law* (New York: Barnes & Noble, 1967), p. 1.

[53] See William J. Goode, "Community within a Community: The Professions," *American Sociological Review,* 22 (1957): 194–200. But see also Goode, "The Protection of the Inept," *American Sociological Review* 32, pp. 5–19 (February 1967). The latter article argues that professional communities insulate the incompetent from public view and do not screen incompetent practitioners from professional ranks. To my knowledge, Goode has not tried to reconcile, in print, this contradiction.

[54] Moore, "Occupational Socialization," p. 882.

[55] Kingsley Davis and Judith Blake, "Norms, Values and Sanctions," in *Handbook of Modern Sociology,* ed. Robert Faris (Chicago: Rand McNally, 1964), chap. 13, pp. 456–484.

disputed by Joel Handler, at least as applied to nonmetropolitan areas of the midwest.[56] If in fact there is a high degree of unethical and incompetent conduct among professionals, it argues for more active client scrutiny and involvement in the hired professional's performance.

HOW ACCESSIBLE IS EFFECTIVE PROFESSIONAL SERVICE TO PAYING CLIENTS?

Two studies of how patients find doctors report the existence of "lay referral systems," relatively structured social contacts with lay influentials which paying patients use to identify medical problems, find doctors, and appraise their ability.[57] The concept of a lay referral system implies that clients know enough about how to find professional help to obtain it when they need it. Access to effective service is traditionally recognized as a problem mainly for the nonpaying poor.[58] Whether clients have adequate access to effective service is tied to the general question about competency among certified professionals. Many traditionalists say that,

> Today the requirements for becoming a lawyer in most states are quite stringent. You may be *quite sure* [italics mine] that the man you are dealing with has the minimum qualifications.[59]

If they are right, virtually any lawyer approached can be relied upon to give at least adequate service.

The contrary view is not only that adequate minimum qualifications are not often met, but that the problem of access is primarily one of clients' not being informed about when and to whom to go for help.

> This is . . . attributable in part to lack of lawyer visibility: some in need of help do nothing because they do not know where to turn. It also results from persons being unaware that they have a legal problem until it is too late, basically a problem in client education.[60]

---

[56] Jerome Carlin, *Lawyers' Ethics* (New York: Russell Sage Foundation, 1966), chap. 8, 9. Kenneth J. Reichstein, *"The Professional Ethics of Lawyers: A Situational Approach,"* Ph.D. dissertation, Department of Sociology, Northwestern University, 1964. Joel Handler, *The Lawyer and His Community* (Madison: University of Wisconsin Press, 1967).

[57] Freidson, *Patients' Views of Medical Practice,* pp. 133–168. Charles Kadushin, *Why People Go to Psychiatrists* (New York: Atherton, 1969), "Summary of Findings," pp. 307–318.

[58] Jerome Carlin, Jan Howard, and Sheldon Messinger, *Civil Justice and the Poor* (New York: Russell Sage Foundation, 1967), pp. 46–59.

[59] William Capitman, *Everyone's Legal Adviser* (New York: Avon, 1961), p. 25.

[60] Johnstone and Hopson, *Lawyers and Their Work,* p. 9.

A survey of New Haven residents made before World War II revealed that they only seek outside legal help in 11 percent of the situations where lawyers could have provided preventive legal advice and in 47 percent of the situations where legal troubles were manifest.[61]

Even if a layman knows that he should consult a professional, what criteria of selection does he use? Traditionally, a professional's reputation among his colleagues has been considered the most effective criterion a client can use to choose a consultant.[62] There is a widespread assumption that the higher a professional's status within the professional community, the more ethical and competent he is likely to be.[63]

A second possible criterion of selection is specialization. Many traditionalists and participationists agree with Christensen that,

> specialists can provide legal services superior in quality to those performed by generalists. Other things being equal, any given service, legal or otherwise, can be better performed by one who devotes his entire time and attention to that kind of service than by one who spreads his talents and attentions over a broad field.[64]

Some believe, however, that specialization, at least in law, is less important. In this view, basic legal skills can be applied effectively in the various legal problem areas.

Assuming that valid criteria for assessing professional competence exist, there remains the difficulty of making knowledge of professional competence

---

[61] Charles Clark and Emma Corstvet, "The Lawyer and the Public: An A.A.L.S. Survey," *Yale Law Journal* 47 (1938): 1272–1293. A more recent study indicates that except with respect to buying and selling property, middle-class citizens are no more likely to seek legal assistance than poorer citizens. Leon Mayhew and Albert J. Reiss, Jr., "The Social Organization of Legal Contacts," *American Sociological Review* 34, no. 3 (June 1969): 313. See also Preble Stolz, "The Legal Needs of the Public, A Survey Analysis," *Research Contributions of the American Bar Foundation,* no. 4, Chicago (1968); Barlow F. Christensen, *Lawyers for People of Moderate Means* (Chicago: American Bar Foundation, 1970), chap. 4; Elliot Cheatham, *A Lawyer When Needed* (New York: Columbia University Press, 1963), chap. 4, pp. 59–86. Even though most people regularly experience legal problems, a 1962 survey reports that only 20 percent of the primarily middle-class respondents (21/108) reported that they consulted lawyers regularly: Comment, *Yale Law Journal* 71 (1962) p. 1227.

[62] Rodolfo Alvarez and Wilbert E. Moore, "Information-Flow within the Professions: Comparisons of Law, Medicine and Nursing," in *On Record: Files and Dossiers in American Life,* ed. Stanton Wheeler (New York: Russell Sage Foundation, 1969), pp. 95–139.

[63] Carlin, *Lawyers' Ethics,* p. 76; Jerome Carlin, *Lawyers on Their Own* (New Brunswick, N.J.; Rutgers University Press, 1962), chap. 2.

[64] Christensen, *Lawyers for People of Moderate Means,* p. 83.

accessible to the lay public. Most laymen do not have ready access to information about the intracolleague reputations of professionals. Moreover, while doctors are permitted to list their fields of specialized competence in professional directories, the American Bar Association has steadfastly refused to permit lawyers to do the same.[65] Many traditionalists have not been overly concerned with clarifying the criteria of professional competence and disseminating information about competent professionals to the public. Educating the public about the effective utilization of professional services has not traditionally been seen as a major responsibility of professions. This, of course, is related to skepticism about what the public wants to know and is capable of understanding.[66]

With the participatory approach, it is important that clients have access to information relevant to choosing among professional consultants. Yet, given both the problems that a layman has in determining an expert's professional reputation and in appraising the appropriateness of that reputation, it is recognized that important criteria accessible to the client in the choice of a professional are responsiveness to the client's wants and a manner that shows promptness, clear thinking, attention to details, and knowledgeability in responding to questions. Liking a professional and feeling at ease with him is part of this assessment.

CONCLUSION

By now the reader will see that there is a consistent relationship among the elements of each model. If professional problems are routine and technical both in the sense of having a best answer and in the sense of being beyond lay understanding, if professionals can be relied upon to give effective and disin-

---

[65] See Glenn Greenwood and Robert Frederickson, *Specialization in the Medical and Legal Professions* (Mundelein, Ill.: Callaghan, 1964).

[66] But see the *Code of Professional Responsibility* (Chicago: American Bar Association, 1969), Ethical Consideration 2–1, p. 5. "The need of members of the public for legal services is met only if they recognize their legal problems, appreciate the importance of seeking assistance, and are able to obtain the services of acceptable legal counsel. Hence, important functions of the legal profession are to educate laymen to recognize their problems, to facilitate the process of intelligent selection of lawyers, and to assist in making legal services fully available." The assertion of this responsibility is a departure from the *Canons of Ethics* (Brooklyn, N.Y.: Edward Thompson Company, 1963), which had set the basic norms of legal conduct prior to 1969. Disciplinary Rule 2-105(A)(4) p. 27 specifically permits lawyers who have been properly certified by the authority having jurisdiction over them under state law, to hold themselves out as specialists to the extent permitted by that authority. See *infra*, p. 137.

terested service, if virtually all professionals are competent and if their continuing competence is assured by professional self-policing, then clients do not
need more information about their problems or about the skills and strategies
of their consultants, and they are best served by passive and trusting delegation
of decision responsibility to the professional.

But what if the client cannot rely upon effective service through professional self-policing, or professional disinterestedness, or the certainty of professional expertise? What if most clients are capable of informed participation in
choosing and working with a professional? In that case, increasing client information about professional service and the nature of legal problems and
encouraging client participation in problem solving is likely to promote better
the client's interest.

At the present time the participatory model probably is accepted by only
a small minority of scholars, professionals, and laymen. I do not think a single
attorney questioned in researching this study accepted it. No scholar has taken
it sufficiently seriously to articulate it as a genuine alternative to the traditional
approach. The following chapters will focus on some relevant evidence for
evaluating each of the six elements of the two models.

Chapter Two: The Relationship between Client Participation and Case Result in Personal Injury Claims

The traditional model proposes that the client who participates actively in problem solving, who shares in controlling the decisions relevant to his problems, will likely end up no better off—and probably in a poorer position—than the client who passively delegates decision making to the professional. The participatory model posits the opposite result. This chapter will test the proposition that participating clients get poorer results than nonparticipating clients. To do this, we need to determine and measure meaningful indicators of client participation and case result. The data about client participation and case worth is taken from extended personal interviews with 59 Manhattan residents who brought accident claims and who were represented by an attorney. These clients had their claims terminated during 1968 and each received at least $2,000 in compensation for his accident. The criteria and procedure for sampling is set forth in Appendix A, "The Research Method."

There are many possible types and degrees of client participation once a lawyer has been approached. Some actions are more realistic and more apparently relevant to actual influence over decisions. Decision theory has stressed the relevance for any participating decision maker of actions which focus what is most important to know and do to reach a decision, of periodic reviews to reappraise and, if necessary, to correct earlier decisions in the light of subsequent discoveries, and of persistence in employing these actions.[1] These guidelines help us to begin to identify active (participating) and passive (nonparticipating) client strategies of problem solving.

---

[1] See Charles E. Lindblom, *The Policy Making Process* (Englewood Cliffs, N.J.: Prentice-Hall, 1968), chap. 4, pp. 21–27.

THE AGGREGATE MEASURE OF CLIENT PARTICIPATION AND CASE OUTCOME

The Index of Client Participation

Inspection of the interview protocols points up five distinguishable types of client activity that might seem to have an impact on decisions made in pursuing a claim. First, the injured party must seek out quality medical attention for a thorough determination of the nature and extent of injuries, for recuperation, and for making sure that there are appropriate medical expenses and related nonmedical expenses to be included in provable claim damages. Second, the client must impress his wishes and concerns about the claim upon his lawyer, seeking the lawyer's support in dealing with the client's anxieties. Third, the client must make follow-up demands upon the lawyer for his attention to discuss how he wants to be treated or wants the case to be handled. Fourth, he must help the lawyer to marshal evidence to build a solid claim which will be worth the client's extra time and energy. Fifth, the client must continually appraise his lawyer's performance according to criteria of responsiveness, thoroughness, and consistency and, if dissatisfied, do some "comparison shopping" to support the client's sense of the appropriateness of additional demands, or to find a replacement consultant. Any client who aggressively took all five of these types of actions would have initiated the search for information bearing on his problem, alerted his attorney to his special interests, received some feedback on how well the attorney was responding to these concerns, and had the opportunity for an informed intermediate review before a final settlement was irrevocably made. Any client who took none of these steps could be said to exhibit a passive problem-solving strategy. Only two of the clients sampled reported having taken all five types of action. Eight of the clients reported taking none of them. In Table 2.1, we see how frequent are the various forms of client action as reported by the interviewees (listed in rank order of frequency).

By looking at the conduct of Mr. Bates, a civil engineer and one of the two most active clients, we get a clearer idea of what each type of client activity involves. His 13-year-old daughter had been struck by a car while riding her bike in the street. There were no known witnesses except the girl and the driver. The skin around her jaw was lacerated and several teeth were dislodged. Called from his office by his wife, Mr. Bates arrived at the hospital emergency room to find his daughter receiving prompt attention from an apparently conscientious intern. The driver of the car, motivated by deep concern about the

Table 2.1: Frequencies of Types of Client Activity

Activity	No. of Clients Taking Action	Percentage of Sample
1. Seeks quality medical attention	45	76
2. Expresses a special want or concern	23	39
3. Makes follow-up demands for attention	18	31
4. Seeks second legal opinion	16	27
5. Marshals information to aid lawyer	13	22

extent of the injury, had also come to the hospital with Mrs. Bates and the daughter. Mr. Bates took advantage of this opportunity to question the driver about his version of the accident. He obtained several expressions of concern from the distressed driver that could be construed as admissions of responsibility. The girl was released from the hospital within two hours. Mr. Bates arranged for the family doctor to take an immediate look at the intern's stitching of the facial wound and was reassured by being told that the job had been done well and no permanently visible scar tissue would form. The next day, through his family physician, he arranged to have his daughter begin an extended series of dental treatments with a specialist. For this dentistry he received a bill of $1,900. Mr. Bates related,

> The dentist told me that the bill was padded since it would be paid for by the insurer. I said nothing until I found that the insurer is lousy and wouldn't settle for a fair amount. Then I went back to the dentist and told him I was only paying him $1,000. He took it.

The dentist suggested that Mr. Bates use the dentist's brother as his attorney in making the claim. Though Bates had used another attorney with whom he had been well pleased in making a prior personal injury claim, he decided that there might be some advantages to following the dentist's advice: better attention for his daughter and greater cooperation if the dentist was needed at a trial as an expert witness for the plaintiff. However, the brother farmed out the case to a negligence specialist who was vague about what action he was taking. After more than nine months, Mr. Bates was moved to return to the referring attorney to complain about the "run-around" the specialist was giving him:

> I never got a copy of anything the negligence specialist did. Nothing was explained. I was always chasing after him. . . . A lawyer I had had in a claim of my own shortly before, had sent me a copy of every letter he wrote to the insurance company.

Speaking to the referrer put him on his guard. The referrer warned him that the specialist is probably, as Mr. Bates put it,

> playing both ends against the middle—he had made a deal with the insurance company. The referring lawyer said it would be messy to get a new lawyer and that probably I would do as well or better with this deal being made.

The second consultation served to redouble Mr. Bates' aggressiveness. As he tells it,

> I kind of put the lawyer on the spot. He came back with a settlement offer and wanted a fee of 40 percent. I told him I will settle for my daughter if she gets cash of so much money, which cut his fee by about $300; and I told him I didn't care if he went bankrupt—that was between him and the insurance company. . . . And he went back and got the settlement. . . . One other thing that they always throw in there and that is that miscellaneous costs thing, and he had something like $300 down and I told him he was only getting $100 because I didn't see any big deal in what his expenses may have been on the case.

In contrast to Mr. Bates, many clients do very little toward making a claim beyond getting medical attention and contacting a lawyer. In a 1962 study of New York City automobile accident claims, Hunting and Neuwirth described the attorney-client relationship, as revealed by their 165 interviews with claimants, in the following manner:

> In most cases, there was little or no contact between the client and his attorney except at the time of hiring (which was in some cases accomplished by a telephone call) and at the time of final settlement. Respondents showed a complete lack of knowledge of the legal procedures involved; the great percentage did not even know whether or not a suit had been instituted. In instances where the case was still pending, the majority had no idea of the progress or current status of their suits. Some persons had not heard at all from their attorneys in two and one-half years.
> When it came to settlement, most frequently it was the lawyer who decided which offer would be accepted and when.

Hunting and Neuwirth conclude from these findings that the customary attorney-client relationship in these claims is "two strangers who deal with each other only in passing."[2]

To measure the relationship between participation and case outcome it is necessary to develop an index of client activity. Index construction is an uncertain enterprise. To be valid, the index must accurately reflect actual and preferably interrelated forms of client participation. To be a meaningful basis for

---

[2] Roger Bryant Hunting and Gloria S. Neuwirth, *Who Sues in New York City?* (New York: Columbia University Press, 1962), pp. 107–109.

testing a causal relationship between client participation and case outcome, a participation index should be limited to those forms of participation which have the greatest actual impact on outcome. The index of client participation finally selected has been limited to four types of client activity. The decision was made to discard the item, "marshals information to aid the lawyer" based on the considerations that it was more weakly related to the overall (five-item) activity measure than any other single item and that it was the least common form of participation. Each of the four items retained in the index significantly correlates with the total participation index.[3] Three of the four items intercorrelate significantly and the fourth item, "impresses wishes and concerns," significantly correlates with "makes follow-up demands for attention." It would seem, therefore, that the four-item client participation index taps varied and discrete forms of activity which, nonetheless, have some (unspecified) interrelationship.

Once the four activity items were determined, it was desirable to assess the degree of persistence or attention each client showed in pursuing those actions in which he did engage. Table 2.2 demonstrates the criteria used to dis-

Table 2.2: Criteria for Distinguishing Intensity of Client Activity

Activity	*More Significant*	*Less Significant*
1. Seeks quality medical attention	Visits specialist; takes time to recover; follow-up medical observation	Sees only general practitioner; has quick recovery with little or no medical follow up
2. Expresses a special want or concern	Puts forward explicitly and discusses in detail with attorney	Puts forward implicitly or explicitly, but in passing
3. Makes follow-up demands for attention	Is explicit and follows-up with persistence	Is not persistent, or makes demand belatedly
4. Seeks second legal opinion	From a lawyer who reviews specifics of claim	From a knowledgeable non-lawyer, and/or a lawyer who reviews claim only generally

---

[3] I have used Spearman's rho to measure the association between each of the activity items and the four-item activity index. The computation of Spearman's rho and its test of significance are explained in Hubert Blalock, *Social Statistics* (New York: McGraw-Hill, 1960), pp. 317–319. Rho for "medical attention" equals $+0.62$; for "follow-up demands" it equals $+0.71$; for "second legal opinion" it equals $+0.48$; for "impresses wishes" it equals $+0.61$; and for "marshals evidence" (associated with a five-item index) it equals $+0.33$.

tinguish between more significant and less significant forms of each type of action. Each client was scored with respect to each type of activity, with a score of 0 for not taking the action at all, 1 for taking a less aggressive (less significant) form of the action, and 2 for taking a more aggressive (more significant) form of the action. For a discussion and justification of the activity index see Appendix A, "The Research Method."[4]

With this foundation, it is possible to present a dimension of client participation from a base level of no participation to the high level of participation shown by Mr. Bates. In Figure 2.1, the client interviewees are ranked on such

Figure 2.1: Dimension of Client Participation

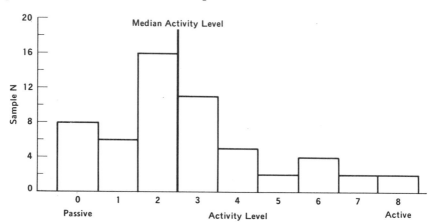

a dimension. For purposes of simplification, it is assumed at this point that each type of client activity is equally influential. As we shall see shortly, this is not strictly the case. The figure shows that the median level of client activity (2.5) is below the midpoint of the dimension. Nonetheless, the clients in this sample appear to be somewhat more active than the respondents in the Hunting and Neuwirth sample.

The Index of Case Outcome

It is relatively easy to agree on the objectives of a personal injury legal

---

[4] In total, 61 clients were interviewed. One suffered no personal injury, only property damage, and was excluded from the sample. Another client was a personal injury lawyer who handled his own claim. His case is excluded from all discussions of client activity and recovery, but is included in the summary descriptive statistics about the nature of personal injuries presented in Chapter 3.

claim: to get as much money as possible, in the shortest possible time, with the least possible feelings of unpleasantness and inconvenience, for the lowest possible fee. But it is very hard to specify and control for the "possible" with respect to each objective. Among the factors largely outside the control of the lawyer and the client that affect the value of a claim are: extent of medical costs; visibility of the victim's contribution to the causing of the accident; age, intelligence, physical attractiveness, and ethnic background of the victim and the one against whom the claim is made; and attitudes of judges and juries. Among the critical factors affecting the timing of compensation and thereby the value of the claim are: the conditions of court delay in the available jurisdictions, the relatively open or tight-fisted policy of the insurance company against which a claim is made, the degree of combativeness of the individual claim adjuster and claims attorney assigned to the case by the insurer, and the uncertainty of medical diagnosis. Among the factors affecting the client's feelings about the case are the realism of his prior expectations of what the case would involve, his notions about what others have gotten in similar cases, his tolerance for delay and uncertainty, his resiliency to the emotional demands of the adversary process, and the trust he has in his attorney and what the attorney tells him.

The custom in negligence cases is for the attorney to get a percentage of the gross recovery the client receives. Nationally, this contingent fee varies from 25 percent (for claims brought in Federal Court under the Federal Tort Claims Act) to a flat 50 percent of the total claim.[5] In Manhattan and the Bronx, the Court (Appellate Division First Department), has established a maximum fee schedule as a guideline for setting fees. In theory, to charge more than this maximum is to violate the rules of the court; to charge less is permissible. The rules give two alternative fee standards: either one-third or a sliding scale—50 percent of the first $1,000 recovered, 40 percent of the next $2,000, 35 percent on the next $22,000, and 25 percent of any amount over $25,000 of the sum recovered.[6] If an attorney expects a recovery of more than $33,000, the one-third fee is more lucrative; otherwise not. These percentages are exclusive of several legal costs (for example, court filing fees, preparation of transcripts, expert witness and special investigator fees) which the attorney can deduct from the gross recovery. This means that the client pays a prorated share (depending on the fee percentage) of service expenses over and above

---

[5] F. B. MacKinnon, *Contingent Fees for Legal Services* (Chicago: Aldine, 1964), pp. 17–24.

[6] The relevant rule is reprinted in Appendix B, p. 216.

the scheduled fee. Most clients sampled were billed in line with the fee schedule, though the less lucrative one-third frequently is charged where the recovery exceeds $4,000 and was obtained in pretrial compromise.

The four goals of greater recovery in less time with greater satisfaction for a smaller fee, tend to be mutually incompatible. For example, accident cases in New York can be brought either in the Supreme Court or in the Civil Court. The Supreme Court has jurisdiction over suits with unlimited claims, but its docket is so congested that it currently takes about three years for a case to be called to trial. The Civil Court, on the other hand, has jurisdiction over claims only up to the amount of $10,000; but cases reach trial on its docket more quickly. Similarly, it usually works out that the longer the client holds out, the larger the settlement he will be able to bargain out of the insurer. Delay in compensation is not only an expense in itself but is attended by feelings of frustration, anxiety, inconvenience, impatience with the lawyer, and general subjective client dissatisfaction. How much money received after how many months compensates for how much eroded satisfaction?[7] A good case result is not a precisely measurable or interchangeable quantum.

Most tort claim experts share a consensus view that there is an appropriate "objective" value that can be placed, approximately, on various types of liability claims. This view facilitates compromise settlements. The going values are based on prior settlements, recent jury verdicts obtained by the attorney and his associates in similar types of cases and some rules-of-the-game, such as the rule that a fair settlement in a strong case should not depart too greatly from a figure that reflects the victim's out-of-pocket expenses multiplied by three.[8] Recent jury awards within some jurisdictions outside the metropolitan area are codified and reported by national research services. Thus, it is possible to find value precedents, albeit imprecise ones, for most types of injuries.[9] Nonetheless, it remains an open question as to just how objective and consensual expert case evaluation can be.[10]

One analytical way to make use of an "objective" consensus value on case result is to have a disinterested panel of experts make a case-by-case appraisal. This was done for the 59 cases in the sample. A fact sheet was pre-

---

[7] See Chapter 3, p. 89.

[8] The three-multiplier standard has been criticized for its inflexibility. Nonetheless, many of the lawyers interviewed said that it does play a part in reaching a settlement figure.

[9] One such service is *Personal Injury Valuation Handbooks* (Cleveland: Jury Verdict Research Institute), 12 vols., looseleaf.

[10] See "Evaluating Attorney Performance" in this chapter.

pared based upon the more important determinants of any case's worth (as specified in the personal injury literature). The 59 fact sheets were submitted, independently, to each of five personal injury claim experts. The expert panel represented a balance between men who had viewed the claims process from the perspective of plaintiffs' counsel and those who had represented defendants' insurers. Two panelists were exclusively plaintiffs' attorneys: one of these was senior partner in a prestigious firm. The other was a solo practitioner. The third was presently a plaintiffs' attorney, but had been previously employed (for more than a quarter of a century) by a large national insurer. The two remaining panelists were presently employed by insurers. One of these was an attorney for a national insurer and the other had been, for many years, in charge of claims settlement for a metropolitan area mutual insurer (although not a law school graduate).[11] Each panelist was asked to put an exact dollar value on each claim—based on the given facts—at three different time periods: one year after the accident, four years after the accident (approximately pretrial), and what could be expected from a jury's trial judgment. The fact sheets did not mention the client's name, his attorney's name, the actual time it took for the case to be terminated, the lawyer's fee, or the actual dollar recovery.[12] For each case, a panel evaluation figure was computed, by averaging the five individual figures for the termination time period most closely approximating the actual time taken to dispose of the case. Thus, if the case actually was settled in 36 months, the average panel pretrial evaluation was used. The sample case results were rank-ordered according to the percentage of the mean panel evaluation represented by the actual recovery received. Thus, a client who actually recovered $3,000 on a claim valued by the panel at an average value (for all five) of $2,000 received a case result score of 150 percent. There was some variation among the five expert panelists in each of several cases. Because this is the first study of this kind, we do not know what an acceptable range of variation among case appraisals should be. Standard deviations and coefficients of variability were computed for each of the 59 cases. In two of the cases, the coefficient seemed too large to give confidence that the mean panel evaluation was an accurate reflection of an objective case value that could be ranked in relation to other cases. Only in these two cases did the coefficient of variability

---

[11] The panel included attorneys Abraham Fuchsberg, Cecil Badway, and Norman Landau. The two panelists working for insurance companies requested that their names not be used. The basis of panel selection is discussed in Appendix A.

[12] For a description of the fact sheet and the assumptions underlying it, see Appendix A, p. 206.

Figure 2.2: Case Outcome as a Percentage of the Panel Valuation

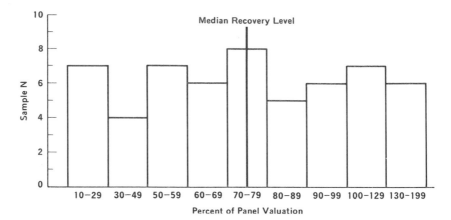

Percent of Panel Valuation

exceed the mean coefficient for all fifty-nine cases by more than 1.65 standard deviations. As a general rule, location of scores within a range of 1.65 standard deviations of the mean score is a permissible cutting point for accepting cases.[13] In Figure 2.2 the rank order of case results is reported. The nine recovery categories, though not symmetrical, reflect the most sensible clustering of the data. The index of case outcome thus is defined as the rank order of the cases from one to nine, where one represents a very poor recovery (10–29 percent) and nine represents a very good recovery (130–199 percent).

The Relationship of Client Participation to Case Outcome

We now have a rank order measure of client participation and a rank order measure of case result for the sample. If client participation does influence case result, we should expect to find a statistically significant rank order correlation between the two variables. I have used Kendall's Tau[14] to determine the rank order correlation for the 57 cases where the mean panel evaluation is acceptable and find a moderately strong positive relationship that is statistically significant. Contrary to the expectation one would deduce from the

---

[13] See Table A.5 in Appendix A, pp. 204-205, for the coefficients of variability for each case evaluation.

[14] The computation of Kendall's Tau and its test of significance are explained in Blalock, *Social Statistics,* pp. 319–324. Kendall's Tau is used here instead of Spearman's rho to take advantage of the partial Kendall's Tau in later analysis, which is not possible with Spearman's rho.

traditional professional model, participating clients not only do not get worse results, they actually get better recoveries from their legal claims.[15]

But this is only the first step in casting doubt on the traditional hypothesis. It may well be expected that client activity only masks some deeper more important explanation of a good case outcome. In fact, this is not the case. Virtually all plausibly influential causal factors were presented to the expert panel, available to be taken into explicit account by them in determining case outcome. The fact sheets for each case even included such plausible factors as any unusual personality traits apparent on first impression (such as feminine traits of male clients) and the client's occupation.

However, two potential causal factors were not taken into explicit account on the case evaluation fact sheets and, therefore, might not have been employed by the expert panel in determining case value. These factors are the social status of the client and the dollar worth of his claim.[16] An obvious explanation for some clients doing better is their social-class position. Clients who work in higher status occupations, earn more money, and are better educated, can get better legal advice, have the job and financial security to wait out protracted claims negotiations, make better impressions on lawyers, judges, and juries, and obtain better medical attention than lower-class clients. Adapting the five class index of social position employed by Hollingshead—using education level, occupational level, and income level as measures—we can rank clients according to social position.[17] This ranking is presented in Figure 2.3. The median social position for sampled clients is Class II: the upper tier of the middle class. This affirms my success in fulfilling the original intention to oversample well-to-do clients in the general population.[18] If social position significantly influences case result we would expect to find a high positive rank order correlation between the status and case result scales. Surprisingly, the two factors are not significantly related.[19] A client's high social standing does not noticeably improve his chances of receiving a good claim disposition. This re-

---

[15] Tau = +0.21. Using a two-tail test of significance (since we are not predicting the direction of the relationship) the association between client participation and case outcome is significant at the 0.01 level. This means that the chances are only 1 in 100 that the same relationship would show up in other random samplings if there was no actual relationship between client participation and case result.

[16] See Appendix A, p. 206.

[17] Ibid., p. 194.

[18] The cultural characteristics of the five classes in an urban setting are discussed in August Hollingshead and Frederick Redlich, *Social Class and Mental Illness* (New York: Wiley, 1958), pp. 66–136.

[19] Kendall's Tau = −0.027.

Figure 2.3: Social Status of the Client Sample

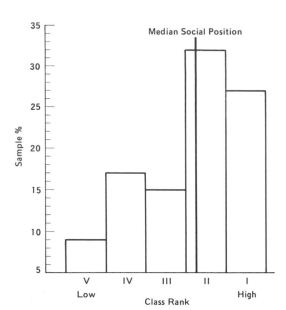

sult may be the product of implicit cues to client status presented to the panel-ists on the case evaluation fact sheet. Such implicit cues included the client's occupation and the amount of his "specials" (out-of-pocket expenses arising from the accident). More affluent clients can afford better recuperative care.

Second, not intuitively obvious, the worth of a case is a significant rival explanation to client activity of why some clients get better case results than others. Ironically (as discussed in greater detail in the next chapter), the greater the dollar amount of recovery that can be anticipated in a claim (case worth), the smaller the chances of making a good recovery.[20] A statistical pro-cedure for assessing the degree of relationship between client activity and case result, while controlling for these alternative variables one at a time, is partial correlation.[21] If client activity is not a valid independent causal variable, the partial correlation between activity and case result should move substantially toward zero from +0.21 when each of these "competing" variables is held constant. Computation of the partial Kendall correlation reveals that client

[20] Kendall's Tau between high case worth and good case result is −0.23. See Chap-ter 3, p. 77.

[21] This procedure is discussed in Sidney Siegel, *Nonparametric Statistics for the Be-havioral Sciences* (New York: McGraw-Hill, 1956), chap. 9.

activity is indeed a potent explanatory factor since no attenuation toward zero is found in either case.[22]

At the level of aggregate analysis, active client participation definitely pays off. But to see why, it is best to look separately at each type of client activity and the particular facts of contrasting cases in which this activity was significantly present or absent.

THE IMPACT OF INDIVIDUAL TYPES OF PARTICIPATION

We have focused in this analysis on five types of client activity.

Seeking Quality Medical Attention

Of the forms of client participation, seeking quality medical attention appears to have only a moderate impact upon case outcome.[23] However, to see how this form of activity can sometimes make a difference, let us consider two separate clients in the sample:

Mr. Meyer and Mr. Taub resemble each other more than most other pairs of clients. Mr. Meyer is a young author who sustained a fractured pelvis when struck by a car. Mr. Taub is a young jazz musician who broke his ankle when hit by a car running a red light. Both men are bachelors. Mr. Meyer reacted to his accident by consulting four medical specialists to get exceptional medical attention including a regimen of corrective physiotherapy exercises. Mr. Taub was X-rayed by a specialist, but the fracture was examined and set by an internist who, as far as Mr. Taub knows, was not a bone specialist. His doctor bills were about $500; Mr. Meyer's were $2,000. Mr. Meyer reacted to his injury as if it was the most important thing in his life, his primary concern. When he found the pain of getting to his third-floor walk-up apartment to be too great, he consulted with his lawyer and his landlord and arranged to take over a ground-floor apartment for three months. The extra rent was made a compensable damage. Mr. Taub, though in considerable pain, accepted the insurer's first settlement offer, with his lawyer's encouragement, only two months after the accident. He used the money to take a three-month vacation in the Virgin Islands (a noncompensable expense). There, in the warmth of the sun, he ran heavily on the ankle earlier than instructed. When interviewed 18 months later, he was still suffering ankle pains and now "regrets settling so

---

[22] The partial Kendall's Tau for client activity by recovery, holding status constant is $+0.21$. The partial Tau for client activity by recovery, holding case worth constant is $+0.23$.

[23] Spearman's rho equals $+0.14$ which is not statistically significant.

fast." Mr. Meyer's active search for specialized medical care, and his avoidance of aggravation from walking stairs, aided him to receive a better result than Mr. Taub in two senses: his health was totally restored with no disability and he got a larger claim recovery to compensate his greater expenses and considerable pain of recuperation.

Insurers often accuse unscrupulous lawyers and clients of fraudulently building a heavy claim with padded medical expenses. Some may be guilty of the charge, but not Mr. Meyer or his attorney. His attorney encouraged him to take all necessary measures to get well, and to send him the bills. He left it in Mr. Meyer's hands, as many lawyers do, to decide what care to seek. In seeking exceptional care, Mr. Meyer built up a valid claim that fully reflected the extent of his injuries. Mr. Taub, by way of contrast, did not consult medical specialists, disregarded medical instructions, and took a settlement offer prematurely—before he could possibly know the extent or permanence of his injury. His lawyer erred in encouraging the premature settlement. We can speculate that Mr. Meyer would have rejected such advice. He was too aware of the uncertainties and delayed symptoms of serious injuries.

Though many clients report that their injuries were emotionally traumatic,[24] only two—Mrs. Lombard and Miss Schiff—actively sought psychotherapy. For both, the costs of the psychotherapy were reimbursed in the settlement. A third client, Mrs. Jorry, whose daughter Helen had broken her leg in a fall, had no idea that psychotherapy could be compensated. She was one of eight clients who volunteered that their lawyers had not informed them about what expenses could and could not be included properly as special damages. The Jorrys had been sufficiently concerned about Helen's "depression" during three months of inactivity to arrange for her to take rather expensive piano lessons "as a form of therapy." These lessons could not be claimed as special damages. In not questioning their attorneys about appropriate expenses and remedial measures or in not seeking this information from other sources, the Jorrys lost the double opportunity for money and emotional restoration.

Many attorneys do not feel it is their responsibility to make this information available to their clients. They feel it is up to the client to work out what are seen as the "nonlegal" problems of adequate medical attention. This is an important point to consider. Many lawyers define the problems involved in making a claim differently from their clients. A lawyer who defines his counseling role narrowly to exclude involving himself with the medical, emotional, employment, family, and financial problems the client may face as a result of

---

[24] Chapter 3, p. 72.

his accident, may leave to the client a wide range of crucial choices. The client who assumes that the lawyer's role in the problem solving is a broad one, may anticipate attorney guidance in such "nonlegal" areas as the kind and extent of medical attention; failing to get such guidance, he may assume, often erroneously, that his response to his medical needs will have little eventual impact on the outcome of his claim. A corollary is that clients have an ample opportunity not only to participate in, but largely to control such decisions affecting their claim, broadly defined, as what doctors to see, when to return to work, when and how to pay medical bills, how to finance the period of recuperation, and how to adjust emotionally to the strains imposed by the injury.

Expressing to the Lawyer a Special Want or Concern

For most clients, anxieties about the accident's impact and about what the claims process will entail are essential to their notion of their legal problems and the lawyer's duty to them. Clients want their lawyers to reassure them and to recognize and help them deal with their concerns. With a lawyer who tends to adopt a narrowly defined role that excludes "holding the client's hand," the client who actively asserts his concerns and negotiates to have them made central, receives better service both in his subjective terms and in terms of "objective" case outcome. This form of client participation was very significantly related to case outcome.[25]

For example, Mr. Sawyer is a young executive with a large international advertising agency. His job posts him for long periods to different cities in and out of the country. Like Helen Jorry, he suffered a leg fracture below the knee when struck by a car while crossing at an intersection. Unlike Helen, he was unable to wait in readiness for a possible trial. For the better part of the first year and a half after his accident, he was working at a midwest office. He returned to Manhattan for three months, preparatory to an extended assignment in Europe. Upon arriving from the midwest, he contacted his attorney and discussed the prospects for winding up the claim. He made it clear that he probably would be unable to return for a trial on short notice. He requested the attorney to make another effort at settlement within the three-month period. The attorney had not been in touch with the insurer for the preceding six months and had anticipated no further contact until the case was called for trial. He agreed, however, to make a renewed effort in view of the client's desire for speedy termination. He got an adequate settlement the very next day.

---

[25] Spearman's rho equals $+0.25$ which is significant at the 0.05 level.

Mr. O'Shea had suffered for years from emphysema. A serious injury to his lungs in an automobile accident aggravated the condition rendering him totally disabled. Apparently he was given the opportunity to go to Arizona where he had some chance of improving his lung condition. Mr. O'Shea and his lawyer tell conflicting stories about the point at which the lawyer was informed of this prospect, and about the sense of urgency which Mr. O'Shea communicated. There is circumstantial evidence that Mr. O'Shea is noncommunicative. He did not tell his lawyer of a fall which further damaged his lungs two years after the auto accident. This information only reached the lawyer through a doctor's medical report ten months later. In any event, five years passed before the lawyer sought a special trial preference. It was granted immediately in view of the gravity of Mr. O'Shea's condition. It probably could have been obtained three years earlier. If it had, Mr. O'Shea might have gone to Arizona. He told me that the opportunity was no longer available when his case was terminated. When interviewed, he appeared to be close to death, subsisting alone in a pathetic furnished room near the Hudson River docks.

One concern worrying most clients is what to expect and how to deal with the theatrics of the adversary process. There is much in the claims process that is arbitrary and demeaning to a claimant, and many clients are aware of this from what they have heard and read and from prior litigation experiences, especially in traffic court. Some clients are active in raising and discussing these anxieties with their attorneys. They expect the attorney to tell them what to anticipate and why certain unpleasant experiences must be borne. For the client who fears the claims process, seeking and receiving this reassurance can be the difference between reacting to the pretrial examination and protracted settlement bargaining as an "uncharming game" and reacting to it as a "nightmare."

For Mrs. Lombard, there was more at stake than how to prepare for the pretrial badgering of the insurance lawyer. One of the issues being worked out in her concurrent psychotherapy was the significance of what she referred to as her stoicism, her "spartan impulses." Her case was handled in a law office with one important specialist and several young associates. She was first seen by two associates who told her to sound in the pretrial examination as if

> I was a deformed woman in constant, excruciating pain. I was offended by the way the underlings coached me trying to get me to exaggerate things. It seemed dishonest but apparently it's the way it's done. But when the top man talked to me he made it all seem reasonable. The top man was better at reacting to me, at putting things in a way that would be meaningful to me.

The lawyer talked her into exaggerating her pain under oath by acknowledging that there were special "rules" in the "game" of trial tactics. The rules say that a client must overestimate his own case and that the insurer must underestimate the claim. When it is played with moderation and restraint, it doesn't work. There is no place for understatement in the adversary process.[26] Her psychotherapy helped Mrs. Lombard accept that her anxiety about admitting pain was expressed in her exaggerated "stoicism," as much a "game" as exaggerated suffering. It facilitated a compromise with herself and with her lawyer. From the size of the settlement and from her lack of anxiety in talking about the pretrial examination, it went well.

Mrs. Forman, an attractive woman who suffered an objectively more serious injury than Mrs. Lombard (Mrs. Lombard sustained a shattered elbow, Mrs. Forman a shattered heel bone), was unprepared for the stress of the pretrial and trial exaggeration. For her it was a "nightmare":

> When the lawyer is questioning you, they twist your words; they don't let you tell the story; they interrupt; they make you out to be a liar and a fool. I just cried and cried. You can't explain what happened with just yes or no answers. Why does the atmosphere of the trial have to be so dramatic? If you are honest or tell the truth calmly, it isn't enough. That's terrible.

In her anxiety about the claim, Mrs. Forman admits to having "avoided thinking about the thing." Because she said nothing to her lawyer about her anxiety, he did not think to give her preparatory reassurance. Unprepared, she suffered.

If the client lacks independent sources of information about the claims process, he must rely upon what he can learn from his lawyer. Since many lawyers do not feel obligated to so inform the client,[27] the client will learn what to fear and how to deal with it only by active questioning. If he doesn't question, he will not be able to clarify his concerns in his own mind or know what requests of his attorney he can reasonably make. Mr. Getz, a young economist, realized that his case was too big to entrust to any but a "top negligence specialist, a big gun." He sought the help of his brother's friend, a patent lawyer, to act "as a kind of solicitor" to shop around and find the best possible attorney and "supervise and negotiate the best possible deal with him while I was still in a hospital bed." One of the things he learned from the

---

[26] Some attorneys would dispute this. As one told me, it is not overstating the pain, but meticulously and accurately recording and stating every instance of pain, that is required in effective advocacy.

[27] See Chapter 4, p. 113.

"solicitor" was that one firm was preferable if you could be sure that one of the two top partners would try your case.

> If you give them your case without saying more, they may pass it down to one of the lower-echelon lawyers to handle. From questioning him about this I decided to insist that we receive a commitment to have the bigger of the two guns represent me at trial. This we did and they gave us a slightly qualified assurance that he would.

The case was settled adequately on the eve of trial. Confidence in the trial attorney helped the client hold out to that point. A lawyer will not volunteer much of the information relevant to selecting and dealing with an attorney. To acquire it, the client must actively dig. Mr. Getz was the only interviewee using the ingenious device of explicitly enlisting an attorney to perform what in England is the solicitor's function of choosing the barrister attorney and reviewing his work with the client. In this way, Mr. Getz found an alternative source of information and reassurance.

Mrs. Silber, on the other hand, neither had an independent source of information nor sufficient contact with her attorney to ask questions and receive answers. While recuperating in the hospital, her husband contacted an attorney who had represented him in business and gave him his wife's case. When she met with the lawyer, she asked him what the fee would be. She says he replied, "Don't you worry about it, your husband and I will take care of it" and made no further mention of it again. Mr. Silber, who was also present during my interview, asserts that he and the lawyer did not at any point discuss the fee. Neither husband nor wife thought to clarify the matter. Mrs. Silber also settled her case on the eve of trial, for an offer of $2,500. She had no idea that this was a gross figure from which would be deducted her attorney's fee and legal costs. She recalls,

> I thought that since [the accident] was their fault, the insurance company would pay for my lawyer. Since I had more than $2,000 in bills I never would have accepted a settlement that came to only $500 for me. So I took it and only learned what a fool I had been when it was too late.

The lawyer was wrong not to have discussed the fee at the outset. But it is unlikely that he would have lied to Mrs. Silber if she had demanded to know the fee basis. She did not think to press her questions.

Making Follow-up Demands for the Lawyer's Attention

The single form of client participation which appears to have the greatest influence on successful case outcome is making follow-up demands for attention.[28] Some of the reasons for this can be illustrated by the case material.

Lawyers often underestimate case value. Mrs. Silber's case is an example of this. She gave the case to a man who was primarily a commercial lawyer. He correctly brought suit in the Supreme Court in Manhattan with the unlimited money damages jurisdiction. Apparently, however, the complaint and the bill of particulars did not adequately state the extent of the injury, because the calendar judge refused to give the case a trial preference, claiming it lacked $10,000 in damages. Once a preference is denied in New York Supreme Court, a case does not come to trial. At this juncture, without notifying Mrs. Silber or obtaining her permission, he farmed out the case to a young negligence specialist with a large volume of Civil Court claims. Apparently the specialist did not try to get a reconsideration of the preference refusal in Supreme Court but instead filed suit in the Civil Court. He met Mrs. Silber for the first time 16 months later, the morning her case was called. He was introduced by the referring lawyer outside the courtroom as "the man who is going to try your case." According to Mrs. Silber, "Almost the first thing he asked me was whether or not my doctor was available to come down that morning to testify in my behalf." The lawyer had not taken the time to contact her doctor in advance and have him ready as a witness. He had only a cursory familiarity with her file, which was one of about five he was carrying. After reviewing the fact sheet for this case and evaluating it, upon being told of the actual recovery, one of the panel experts commented:

> This case is a disgrace. It is worth at least $7,000. The case should have been brought in Supreme Court. If the bill of particulars had been properly drafted, it could have been made clear that this woman's heart was permanently damaged. If this had been made clear, it would not have been denied in Supreme. You have already undercut the case by having to bring it in Civil Court. The insurance company is conditioned not to recognize the seriousness of a claim in the Civil Court.[29]

One part of Mrs. Silber's problem was that neither lawyer recognized the worth of her claim. If they had, they would have taken the time to prepare the witnesses and they would have had the case restored in the higher juris-

---

[28] Spearman's rho equals $+0.28$ which is significant at the 0.02 level.

[29] §660.9(c) of the Bronx and New York County Supreme Court Rules provides for the obtaining of a trial preference in an action to recover damages "for personal injuries resulting in permanent or protracted disability." *Civil Practice Annual of New York* (New York: Bender, 1970), pp. 9–100 to 9–101.

diction court. A client with a high-value claim, who can actively persuade his attorney to take him and his case seriously, has a better chance of avoiding underestimation.

Persuasion can be either gentle or threatening. We have already seen the success with which Mr. Bates improved his lawyer's performance by applying pressure. The Rubios achieved some success with their attorney more subtly. The Rubios are Cuban refugees. A wealthy family of professionals and industrialists in pre-Castro Cuba, they lost their fortune in the flight to the United States. Mr. Rubio has the impression that their attorney initially sized them up as "ignorant Spanish-speaking people."

> In Cuba lawyers are always available and always treat you courteously and well. Here they treat you like you were a moron. You have no idea of the law. You have nothing to say and he has to handle everything. This applies to almost everything in America. People don't like to get questions. In Cuba we like to know about things. But here, if you ask people questions, they get angry and insulting.

Mr. Rubio was courteous and patient in the face of his lawyer's patronizing attitude. But he persisted in asking questions. "Little by little he [the lawyer] began to answer a little better." At the pretrial examination, Mrs. Rubio recalls that the lawyer's attention was drawn to the large and expensive diamond ring she was wearing. Thereafter he began to act noticeably friendlier as if in acknowledgment that the Rubios were a "better class of people." He later agreed to reduce his fee by 8 percent from his initial demand. After the case was settled he even called upon Mr. Rubio for some business advice.

Many lawyers are aggravated by clients who keep calling them and asking questions and making demands. They prefer being trusted to do all that is necessary in a claim without client interference. The more candid attorneys will, however, admit that it is possible, occasionally, to misplace a case file or forget about a claim. The client who persists is less likely to suffer from such an oversight. Mrs. Workman broke her hip in a fall on a newly waxed floor and required two operations to mend it. The claim was neglected by the attorney she chose to handle it. He did not even file suit. After two years, he farmed out the case, without receiving her permission, to a "big gun" negligence firm which, finally, initiated a lawsuit. Mrs. Workman had one meeting with "the big man himself. . . . He said, 'We'll take care of everything; don't worry and don't bother about it.'" She took his advice. Five more years passed and she heard nothing. Then, one day, the first attorney telephoned and said that her case had been removed from the court calendar because her second lawyer failed to make a scheduled court appearance. At this point Mrs. Workman contacted the second lawyer and threatened to take up this neglect with the bar association. He responded by getting the case restored to the court calendar and turned it over to yet a third attorney who, finally, settled the case more than eight years after the accident.

A personal injury claim is a complex process. One facet of this complexity is the enormous number of considerations which press upon the attention of both client and lawyer. Details can be missed or misunderstood. Lawyers are not infallible. Even the most experienced and skillful make errors of fact as well as judgment. If a client is active in following the details of his case and resourceful in informing himself about the elements of a claim, he may be able to catch something pertinent that the lawyer misses.

This is illustrated in the conduct of Mr. Getz, an unusually sophisticated and persistent client. His lawyer had been told by the defendant insurer that the defendant had only $20,000 in insurance coverage. By law, insurers are not required to disclose to claimants the amount of a defendant's coverage. The theory behind the law is that disclosure would encourage inflated claims. Nondisclosure is a definite defense advantage. There was no independent way Mr. Getz's lawyer could confirm the truthfulness of the information so generously provided by the insurer. Mr. Getz's lawyer was prepared to accept a settlement of $20,000 from the insurer and to seek no additional compensation from the defendant's own pocket. Mr. Getz, on the other hand, had his own reasons for feeling that the settlement should amount to more than $20,000. For one thing, he knew that the defendant came from a wealthy family. For another, after deducting the legal fee, a $20,000 settlement would not come close to compensating him for the almost one-year period he was disabled and unable to work. In conversation prior to a final settlement effort mediated by the judge assigned to try the case, the lawyer pressed Mr. Getz to accept a settlement for $20,000 plus a token surcharge of $2,000. In Mr. Getz's words,

> Reluctantly I agreed. "But would you make them sign a paper that that was the maximum amount of the insurance?" I asked. "Oh yes we would," my lawyers said. Then [X] said, "Well, let me check on that." He went into the hallway and talked with the insurer's lawyer and came back to me and said, "Well, it's a new ball game; they have more than $20,000." "How can this be?" I asked. "Well, they've always been saying that they only have $20,000 on the defendant, but it turns out there are other insurers involved too." Now I hoped that they would have checked this without me; maybe they would have. But this gave me an uneasy feeling about what would have happened if I hadn't brought this up.

Apparently Mr. Getz's lawyer, an outstanding negligence specialist, had not previously questioned the insurer (with whom he had had several prior contacts) about the existence of co-insurers. If he had asked the question at an earlier stage in the claim, and the insurer had told the truth or given an evasive answer, he would never have thought of taking just $20,000.

Dr. Stern is a garrulous dentist in his mid-sixties, a man who likes and "thinks well of everybody." He was run into by a taxi and sustained a broken leg, requiring the insertion of an artificial socket. Dr. Stern is a cheerful fatalist. He settled his case for $5,000 on his lawyer's advice that the maximum they could realistically collect out of a trial verdict would be the $10,000 of the taxi insurance bond.

> I think the law is wrong, is ridiculous the way it is with a $10,000 limit—when a person has been hurt the way I have for the rest of my life. It doesn't nearly cover my [$14,000 worth of] expenses. . . . The settlement, big deal! Well, as long as I'm alive. And everybody was so wonderful to me. My lawyer was a lovely young fellow . . . and he was a very nice fellow, the cabdriver. He came to see me at the hospital.

Unlike Mr. Getz, Dr. Stern never thought to have the lawyer check on the possibility of reaching additional assets of the two-man cab company. The lawyer was not aware, apparently, of the New York City License Bureau regulation which prevents a hack owner from selling his medallion until he has satisfied outstanding uncollected judgments against his cabs. Since medallions have a market value of more than $20,000, it is worthwhile to an owner to settle a claim for any amount appreciably less—even, say, $15,000. The lawyer knew he could, with a judgment in excess of the $10,000 insurance bond, force the judicial sale of the "beat-up taxis themselves" but he figured this wouldn't be worth the effort. In an interview for this study, he mistakenly said that there was no way to tie up a medallion. By underestimating the potential collectible assets, the lawyer advised Dr. Stern to settle for less than he should have. This is the sort of relatively obscure point that a conscientious but less experienced lawyer might not know. A persistent client might have filled the gap either by requests that the lawyer check on this matter or by seeking independent sources of information.

The lay client is handicapped in getting and evaluating information about his claim by his inexperience and by his dependence upon his lawyer's candor and directness. Though handicapped, many clients did not feel helpless. Several clients made comments similar to that of Mr. Teich:

> We are all judges of human nature. When you talk to people you can tell if they know their business or not—especially in the way they ask and answer

questions. . . . Like, if a lawyer doesn't get information at the first interview, and he needs to call two or three times to ask additional questions, he
doesn't know his job.

These clients engaged in a process of continual appraisal of that part of their
lawyer's performance which they could observe. There are four standards that
many clients use to size up their lawyers: (1) Does he have a congenial personality? (2) Is he responsive to my questions and requests? (3) Are his answers consistent? (4) Does he keep me informed about what he is doing?

It is important to most clients to like their lawyers. Mrs. Lowe agreed to
be interviewed by me because she was still so angry at her lawyer that she
wanted to "report him to someone." The lawyer met with her personally only
after the settlement had been arranged. He conducted all business over the
telephone.

> He was the rudest, the nastiest, the most inconsiderate person I have ever en-
> countered. He asked, "What happened to you?" I started to tell him and he
> interrupted, "Well, that's not important. What number stairway was it"—just
> in that tone of voice [bored and patronizing]. . . . Well I tell you I'm not
> intimidated easily but the man upset me terribly. I was happy to hang up the
> receiver. [He explained] no details, no nothing. There were a lot of things I
> didn't tell the lawyer about, I was so infuriated.

Mr. Abel's lawyer, in contrast, built up his client's confidence by being
unusually responsive. Mr. Abel said about him:

> He impressed me because he wasn't trying to be overimpressive. He didn't
> come on like a big wheel or like a hip shot [a man who shoots from the hip].
> He was considerate. He would call me from time to time to see how I was
> doing, to ask if I needed any finances for medical aid or to sustain me for my
> hours [out of work].[30] This impressed me because this he did not have to do.
> . . . I never was in his office. He always came to me. Each time he came here
> [to Mr. A's apartment]. Times I wanted to know about the proceeding of the
> case, or when we would go to court or what was going on, he would come to
> me and explain to me what was taking place . . . eh . . . like the results
> of the doctor's finding. He kept me pretty well informed by forms and ex-
> planation.

Many clients are dissatisfied with the way their lawyer behaves toward
them. Nevertheless, as with Mrs. Lowe, they accept it and neither complain

---

[30] It is a violation of the Code of Professional Responsibility for a lawyer to lend
his client money. *Code of Professional Responsibility* (Summit, N.J.: Martindale-
Hubbell, Inc., 1969), Disciplinary Rule DR 5–103(B), p. 64. The lawyer, however,
may help the client borrow money from independent lenders and may advance on guarantee the expenses of litigation, "provided that the client remains ultimately liable for
such expenses."

nor think of taking their case elsewhere. Many reasons are given for tolerating what a client sees as rude, unresponsive, or evasive professional service. Mr. Jorry was persuaded by his attorney that the attorney was doing him a favor by taking the case at all. He was manipulated to expect no better treatment. "I'm realistic enough to know there are bigger fish in the sea," he told me, "and nobody wants to bother with our type of claim." This from a man with a claim evaluated by the panel as worth more than $4,000. Most clients (37 of 59 of the sample) are unaware that changing lawyers is a relatively simple matter, even after a year or two has passed. They feel bound by an irrevocable commitment. Some take lawyer's "unpleasantness," when encountered, as a further excuse to be uninvolved in the claim. Since the lawyer gets annoyed when they make demands, there seems to be no point in making demands. As most clients accept the traditional model of the professional-client relationship they often feel guilty about any misgivings they may have. Misgivings may appear to be a violation of the imperative norm of trust in the lawyer. "Who am I to mistrust a professional? What do I know?" The nightmarish experience of Mrs. Forman was exacerbated by the declining health of her attorney as her case progressed. By the time of the trial he was critically ill; he died two months later. Mrs. Forman recalls:

> At the trial I overheard an attorney sitting in the courtroom as a spectator say, "What is that lawyer [her lawyer] doing? He is ruining the case! . . ." Later on we felt that we should have done something about getting another lawyer. Our lawyer was a very sick man at that point. But we didn't do anything because we were fools; we were afraid of hurting his feelings and we didn't trust our judgment to do this. We were embarrassed to say or do anything. . . . If I had this to do all over again, I might have done things differently—been a little more questioning. But I trusted the lawyer. I was foolish about the whole thing and avoided thinking about the thing; it was distasteful and we didn't want to have to think about it.

Seeking a Second Independent Legal Opinion

Some of the more active clients feel confident of their ability to appraise their lawyers in terms of the four "lay" criteria of congeniality, responsiveness, consistency, and keeping the client informed. When they have doubts about the quality of service they are receiving with respect to these criteria, and when these doubts are not allayed by what the attorney says or does, they seek or threaten to seek a second legal opinion. Mr. Donald found that it wasn't necessary to do more than "threaten to take the case away because [my attorney] hadn't kept in touch." The lawyer "got very angry at this, but he also got to work on the case." For one thing he finally got around to filing suit. A second legal opinion can be used either as a threat and/or as an independent source of relevant information about the claim of which the first lawyer need not necessarily be told. The second opinion can also be used as a technique of expert appraisal in itself. A lay client may not be able to articulate what it is about his first lawyer that bothers him. But, if the second lawyer has the desirable qualities the first one lacks, it will be recognizable. This experience is reported not only by clients who actively solicited second opinions on their own initiative, but by a few clients whose cases were farmed out to negligence specialists on the referring attorney's initiative. Mr. Meyer's experience is illustrative. At his initial meeting with his first lawyer, he asked him directly whether or not he was a negligence specialist. Mr. Meyer was "assured" that he was. A year later, lawyer number one informed Mr. Meyer that the case was being farmed out to another specialist because, as he remembers being told,

> "Your case has some unusual aspects which this other lawyer can better handle." It was quite obvious that the first lawyer had lied when he had said that he was a specialist. When I met the second lawyer, the difference was like night and day. He was efficient; he gave direct answers; he acted like he knew what he was doing. . . . A perfect example of the difference between the first and second lawyer is that the first time I met with the specialist, he told me about the liability question—the contributory negligence rule. This seemed to me to be so important, that I was dumbfounded that the first lawyer had never said anything about it.

Miss Schiff had some initial misgivings about her attorney's manner. "He seemed a little too sure of himself" for her liking. In their first meeting he had told her that she could realistically expect a settlement "in the neighborhood of $20,000." Almost a year later, at the pretrial examination, the insurer made an offer of $12,000, and her lawyer advised her to take it—even though it wouldn't begin to cover her expenses, and the liability issue was clearly in her favor. "At that point," she says,

> I lost confidence in his judgment. That was so opposite what *he* had said in the past. I went to a friend and asked him to find me another lawyer. He sent me to [X] who had an excellent reputation, I was told. The second lawyer seemed much better. He handled [the transfer] very well. He kept me away from the first attorney and made it clear that I didn't have to see or talk to him. . . . After the case was taken away, the first lawyer wanted some exorbitant fee for work already done. . . . He wanted much more as a fee than he had originally urged me to settle the claim for. . . . I had the creepy feeling that maybe the first lawyer was on the take. I don't know; the second lawyer never said anything unprofessional about the first lawyer. The second lawyer took care of it all.

The second lawyer settled the case for $22,500, almost twice as much as the first lawyer would have accepted.

By trusting her judgment, getting a second opinion, and changing lawyers when the second proved more satisfactory, Miss Schiff avoided the poor result reached by Mrs. Reed.

Mrs. Reed had fallen on an ice-covered, broken-up sidewalk and fractured her lower leg. A metal plate was permanently inserted. It has not healed properly and continues to cause her pain. Unlike Miss Schiff's case, the liability issue was only fair to good. The government of New York City is not liable for injuries resulting from icy pavements which the Department of Sanitation has not had a reasonable time (judicially interpreted, in general, to be more than 48 hours)[31] to clear. In addition the city contended that the fall had been caused by freshly formed ice. Nevertheless, her case was not a poor one. Mrs. Reed asserted that she tripped over the broken pavement improperly left by the city in a dangerous condition. Her lawyer had had photographs taken which showed breaks in the pavement. Her teenage son and his girl friend had witnessed the fall and were prepared to testify on her behalf. Mrs. Reed tells this story:

> I brought the girl friend down with me to see the lawyer. . . . She was 17 or 18 years old. He wouldn't interview her or take a statement or nothing. He said, "She's just a kid; who would listen to her?" He didn't want to be bothered. . . . After two years of hearing nothing from the lawyer, he called to say he had given the case to another lawyer. He didn't bother asking for my permission. . . . Three years later we [she and Mr. Reed] went down to the court for the trial. The lawyer said it [the case] didn't look so good and I should settle for what I could get. . . . It all happened so fast there was no time to consider. We went before the judge who asked if this is a settlement I want. I already had been told by the lawyer that this was the best I could get so I said "yes" to him [the judge]—even though he warned me that agreeing now would mean that I could never get any more even for a future operation. . . . So what could I do? I had no choice. The lawyer told me there was no time, I had to decide right away. He told me there wasn't even time to discuss it with my husband.

Mrs. Reed settled for $3,500. From this, the two lawyers took a 54 percent share—50 percent in fees and 4 percent as disbursements. This violates the Appellate Division Rules which permit a maximum contingent percentage of 42 percent for a $3,500 recovery. The expert panel put the true value of the claim in excess of $20,000. Mrs. Reed only received a net of $1,600. It is unlikely that she would have fared worse if she had changed lawyers.

---

[31] *Harper* v. *City of New York*, 63 N.Y.S. 2d 418 (Sup. Ct. App. Term, 1946).

Seeking a second legal opinion was, as a discrete form of activity, weakly related to successful case outcome.[32] One reason seems to have been that some of the clients only obtained casual and nonspecific second opinions—informally at cocktail parties, for example—which did not include a specific review of the details of the claim and their lawyer's actions. Furthermore, in the cases of two clients who realized poorer recoveries, their "second opinions" actually constituted firing their first attorney and giving their case to a second one. Each was more actively involved in questioning and appraising his first than his second attorney. After giving his case to the second man, each withdrew from further active involvement, feeling that he had finally found a professional to be trusted.

Marshaling Evidence to Improve the Claim

One measure a client can take to impress his attorney with the significance of his claim and, at the same time, reduce the costs to the lawyer of handling it, is to strengthen the claim by his own actions. After Mr. Stacey's son had been hit by a car, while playing in the street in front of his home, Mr. Stacey rushed to the scene of the accident and photographed the skid marks left on the pavement by the braked tires. The street is heavily trafficked. By the time the attorney could have arranged, the following day, to have a photographer sent, the tire marks probably would have been obliterated. Mr. Stacey was able to present his lawyer with relevant evidence of the car's speed at the time of impact at no cost to the lawyer. Mr. Donald, a physicist, was encouraged by both the policemen who prepared the accident report and by his attorney to press a charge of drunken driving against the driver who hit him. He took the advice and asked his lawyer to appear with him in criminal court.

> My lawyer said, "Press that case because it's to your advantage to have him found guilty." I said, "Aren't you involved in this enough to come down to the criminal court with me?" He said, "Well, that's your bit; I'm not involved." He was really no help; he didn't want to get involved. . . . Later I found out that it was not usual for people to pursue charges, but I showed up in court [anyway] three times for various hearings. It became clear that the cops were not too anxious, because the arresting officer failed to appear in court for the hearings [after the first one]. I felt sorry for the guy after nine months. He was poor, this was his first offense, and he was repentant. I dropped the drunk driving charge and he pleaded guilty to a reckless driving offense.

For his persistence, Mr. Donald handed his lawyer crucial proof of the defendant's legal liability.

---

[32] Spearman's rho equals $+0.10$ which is not significant.

As already stated, this was the least influential form of client activity. It was also the form of activity least likely to have been performed by active clients.[33] While its discrete impact may not be very great, the experiences of Mr. Stacey and Mr. Donald indicate that it can constructively supplement claims in which attorneys are not thorough about gathering evidence and claims in which important evidence may be lost by the time the client consults an attorney.

THE LIMITS OF CLIENT PARTICIPATION
IN EXPLAINING CASE OUTCOME

Client activity is consistent with obtaining better claim results and it appears to explain, in part, why some clients do better than others. It is nonetheless true that some clients who participate actively in claims making get poor results and some who are passive clients get good results. By setting a cut-off point at the median rank for client activity (between an activity score of 2 and 3), we can differentiate between active clients, with an activity score above the cut-off point and passive clients with an activity score below the cut-off. Similarly, by setting a cut-off point at the median rank for case outcome (an actual recovery equal to 70 percent of the mean of the panel evaluations), we can differentiate between cases in which good results were achieved (more than 70 percent of the panel mean recovered) and cases (with less than 70 percent recovery) in which poor results were realized. This differentiation permits us to relate client participation to case outcome. Table 2.3 shows that 75 percent of the active clients, but only 41 percent of the passive clients, get good results. We find, once again, a significant, positive statistical relationship between active client participation and good case result.[34]

Table 2.3 also shows that 7 "active" clients got poor results and that 12 "passive" clients got good results. The apparent explanation for the latter figure is that these clients were given effective representation by their attorney without client assistance, encouragement, or prodding. As to the active clients, it is appropriate to ask why client activity did not assure them a good case result.

Four of the "active" clients with poor results were minimally active, with

---

[33] Spearman's rho for the relationship between "marshalling information" and case outcome equals $+0.01$ which is not significant. The only other form of client activity with which "marshalling information" significantly correlated was "makes follow-up demands for attention." Spearman's rho equals $+0.38$ which is significant at the 0.01 level.

[34] The relationship is significant at the 0.01 level with a two-tailed Chi-square test. This test is explained in Blalock, *Social Statistics*, p. 212.

Table 2.3: Client Participation Related to Case Result

Result	Active Client	Passive Client	
Good	75%	41%	
	(21)	(12)	N = 33
Poor	25%	59%	
	(7)	(17)	N = 24
	N = 28	N = 29	N = 57

activity scores of 3. In the sense of a qualitative judgment, they can hardly be considered to have participated actively in their claims. For three of the four, the major form of activity was to seek quality medical attention. Where concerns were expressed or demands made, it was in a desultory manner. For the fourth, the major form of activity was changing lawyers but then doing almost nothing once the new lawyer was brought into the case.

As to two of the remaining three unsuccessful active clients, one was almost broke. He felt that he needed money quickly. The other had more modest goals than "getting what he was entitled to." Fundamentally, he wanted to "break even" to recover his out-of-pocket expenses once the attorney's fee and the legal costs had been deducted. He achieved this modest goal with his objectively "poor" settlement. The third client, Mr. Atwood, is himself a negligence defense attorney working as house counsel to an insurer. He hired another lawyer to handle his claim but was quite involved in his case. Mr. Atwood began to feel severe back pains more than three months after the car he was driving was hit from behind. He settled early for a low amount because he felt the chances of proving a causal relationship between the accident and the back pains was poor. He was satisfied to have his bills paid.

It should be noted that none of the active clients can be said to have done poorly because they were active. Nor was any client "sent packing" for being too bothersome. The fact of client activity does not explain poor recoveries. Rather, review of the individual sample cases suggests that the more of these forms of activity the client employs and the more persistently he employs them, the better his chances of protecting his emotional and economic interests in the case outcome. The client who is most likely to suffer is the one who has strongly motivated interests but fails to express or safeguard them—like Mrs. Forman, Mr. O'Shea, and Mrs. Silber.

While only four of all the clients in the sample appear vigorously to have pursued a fully active strategy of client participation there are, even with clients such as these, limits to the effectiveness of participation. It is always in the lawyer's power—intentionally or unintentionally—to evade requests, disregard client concerns, and fail to bring to the client's attention considerations that greatly matter to him. Second legal opinions, if not independent, or if given casually without careful attention, or if given by a man who sees things very much the same way as the first lawyer, will not fill these gaps in the client's understanding. At best, active clients can assist effective attorneys and can recognize and replace manifestly ineffective ones. Client participation, however, is no substitute for effective professional representation—as the success of some of the passive clients shows.

The participatory model does not diminish the importance of the lawyer's role in problem solving. The benefits of client activity appear to derive only from greater collaboration with the attorney, not from the client's exclusively performing the attorney's functions. In a 1959 study, Rosenberg and Sovern of Columbia University Law School estimated that about 20 percent (39,000 of 193,000) of New York claimants who seek compensation for bodily injuries each year do so without the assistance of a lawyer.[35] There is substantial evidence showing that lay clients, whether active or passive, who are represented by a lawyer get better results in their claims than persons who, with the strategy of complete self-reliance and full case control, prepare the claim themselves.[36] In a follow-up New York study, for example, it was found that 90 percent of represented claimants recovered some compensation, while the recovery rate for unrepresented claimants was 65 percent.[37] The disparity is even more dramatic in a Pennsylvania study of the same period. In 65 percent of the unrepresented claims (129 of 194) the victims received no award; the victim went totally unrewarded in only 5 percent of the represented claims (6 of 117).[38] One important explanation for this is that lawyers weed out un-

---

[35] Maurice Rosenberg and Michael Sovern, "Delay and the Dynamics of Personal Injury Litigation," in *Dollars, Delay and the Automobile Accident Victim,* a publication supported by the Walter E. Meyer Research Institute of Law (Indianapolis, Ind.: Bobbs-Merrill, 1968), "Appendix C," pp. 135–136.

[36] There is no reason, however, why experts in the claims process cannot do their own claims successfully, without independent legal representation. See e.g., Hunting and Neuwirth, *Who Sues in New York City?,* pp. 149–152.

[37] Marc Franklin, Robert Chanin, and Irving Mark, "Accidents, Money and the Law: A Study of the Economics of Personal Injury Litigation," in *Dollars, Delay and the Automobile Accident Victim,* p. 42. The authors also refer to a Temple University study with the same finding.

[38] Clarence Morris and James Paul, "The Financial Impact of Automobile Accidents," in *Dollars, Delay and the Automobile Accident Victim,* p. 15.

profitable claims.[39] Among other explanations, the following are also important: (1) laymen, unwittingly, often make damaging admissions of contributory negligence; (2) laymen often underestimate future disability and expenses they will incur when making a settlement shortly after an accident; (3) many laymen are satisfied recovering out-of-pocket expenses in claims where a lawyer would seek reparation for pain and suffering; (4) experienced trial lawyers can make a more credible threat of taking a case to trial if no adequate settlement offer is received; (5) laymen are less knowledgeable about preparing the relevant evidence of a claim; and (6) experienced lawyers can frequently get modest recoveries even with weak claims as a "favor" from the insurer to promote goodwill in future more costly claims negotiations.[40]

EVALUATING ATTORNEY PERFORMANCE

Comparison of actual recoveries with the mean panel evaluation provides one relatively "objective" empirical measure of the quality of professional service received by personal injury claimants. The conclusion does not speak well for the legal profession. In 77 percent of the cases (44 of 57), clients did worse than they should have according to the arithmetic mean of the values assigned to their claim by each of the five panelists. Even allowing for a conservative error factor of 30 percent—that is, even assuming that the panel mean is consistently inflated by as much as 30 percent above the "true" objective worth of each claim—42 percent of the clients (24 of 57) received poor recoveries.

Though claim evaluation is obviously an open question, with several plausible but inconsistent criteria, for the purposes of my analysis an expert panel evaluation is preferable as a measure of case result and attorney performance to subjective client satisfaction. The main reason for this is that the panelists explicitly take into account the full range of factors[41] affecting the worth of a claim and, therefore, its realistic recovery amount. None of the other criteria do this. A second reason is that a client's sense of satisfaction is influenced by his frequently uninformed preconceptions about what

---

[39] See Chapter 4, p. 99. Franklin, Chanin, and Mark, "Accidents, Money and the Law," p. 43, fail to take this factor into account at all.

[40] These and other considerations are well discussed in H. Laurence Ross, *Settled Out of Court: The Social Process of Insurance Claims Adjustments* (Chicago: Aldine, 1970).

[41] Excluding, of course, client activity, which is not yet a recognized relevant factor, and client status and size of claim which were taken into account, if at all, only implicitly.

to expect in a claim situation. For example, one-third of the client sample report having believed, to some degree, the stories told by friends and relatives that they would become rich or "make a lot of money" out of their claim. This piece of folk wisdom is, as this analysis shows, erroneous. When they learned that they were not going to make money, four-fifths (16 of 20) of these unwarranted optimists were dissatisfied with their case result. In some of these cases, the dissatisfaction may well have been due more to the disabused misconception than to other considerations.

Nonetheless, if the participatory model has validity, the client's idea of case worth, no matter how misguided in the eyes of the expert, deserves to be given some weight in evaluating his case outcome and his attorney's performance. According to their interview responses, roughly half of the clients (28 of 59) were satisfied with their recoveries.[42] If we consider an objectively good case result to be a score of more than 70 percent of the mean panel evaluation, then in 59 percent (33 of 57) of the sample cases, the expert panel and the clients agreed on the quality of the case result. In 42 percent of the cases they disagreed.

The most direct subjective criterion of attorney performance is the client's sense of satisfaction with the job his lawyer did for him, as distinguished from his satisfaction with the recovery itself. Two-thirds of the clients (39 of 59) expressed satisfaction with their lawyer's performance. Thus from the client's perspective, the lawyer-client relationship misfired one-third of the time.[43]

While the objective measure of a good result is analytically useful, it cannot adequately account for the full range of values sought in making a claim, nor can a simple subjective (especially an uninformed subjectivity) measure of satisfaction. This implies what will be spelled out in the next two chapters— that no one individual, neither lawyer nor client, is likely to determine definitely a single best course of professional service in a particular claim.

CONCLUSION

In this chapter we have developed criteria for measuring the extent of client participation and for evaluating the outcomes of professional-client

---

[42] Though 52 percent (15 of 29) of the more active clients were satisfied with their case disposition, compared with 43 percent (13 of 30) of the more passive clients, the relationship between activity and satisfaction is not statistically significant for such a relatively small sample, using the Chi-square test, at the 0.05 level.

[43] Conard and associates report that 40 percent of their Michigan client interviewees were dissatisfied with their lawyers: Alfred Conard et al., *Automobile Accident Costs and Payments* (Ann Arbor: University of Michigan Press, 1964), p. 289.

problem solving, in the field of personal injury claims. These criteria have been applied to a sample of relatively high-status New York City claimants who received at least $2,000 recoveries. Based on the experiences of this sample it is possible to test two of the six propositions presented (in Chapter 1) as central to the traditional model for appropriate interaction between the client and the consulting professional.

The first and most important proposition of the traditional model is that a strategy of active client participation in dealing with the problems brought to the professional will lead to worse results than a passive, trusting delegation of responsibility by the client. We have seen in the specific setting of personal injury claims that participating clients not only do not do worse than nonparticipating clients, but they actually do significantly better. The second traditional proposition, considered in this chapter, is that ineffective professional service is rare. The evidence of the client sample reveals that ineffective professional service in the sense of service leading to inadequate outcomes is not rare but, instead, is quite common.

Using case outcome as a relatively conservative and "objective" standard for appraising attorney performance, and discounting that standard by an exaggerated error factor of 30 percent, more than 40 percent of the attorneys did not perform as well as they should have. Using the subjective standard of the client's own feelings about the professional service they received, one-third were dissatisfied.

In the next two chapters we will consider other reasons why participating clients seem to do better. These reasons too, will bear on the appropriateness of the traditional model for professional-client relationships.

Chapter Three: The Nature of Personal Injury Problems

The appropriateness of any model of professional-client interaction depends on the way one views the problems which are the subject of that interaction. It has been suggested that the problems clients bring to professionals tend to be viewed in one of two ways, essentially either as (1) clear choices which professionals are trained to make with a high degree of certainty according to relatively standardized and objective criteria—choices and criteria which, furthermore, tend to be inaccessible to lay comprehension or as (2) open choices, with a high degree of uncertainty, upon which professionals are trained to focus, but which can only be made effectively when informed by relatively individualized and subjective criteria. In this chapter we will consider which is the more appropriate way to view the problems brought to attorneys by injured claimants.

To make this appraisal, let us consider the nature of personal injury problems from three vantage points: first, the claim as presented to, and perceived by, the attorney; second, the injury as experienced by the client; and third, the claims process as seen by the disinterested observer, in terms of the principal institutions (besides the lawyer and the client) which have an impact on the claimant's recovery. These institutions are the defendant's insurer, the trial judge, the trial courts, the substantive doctrine of negligence law, and the jury. From each vantage point we will find that the problems involved in bringing a claim appear much more in the nature of open, individualized, uncertain, but comprehensible choices.

THE CLAIM AS PRESENTED TO THE ATTORNEY

The claim process, once the client has come to an attorney, can be divided into ten analytical stages:

1. Determining whether or not to make a claim
2. Preliminary case preparation
3. Preliminary settlement negotiation

  4. Intermediate case preparation
  5. Intermediate settlement negotiation
  6. Final preparation for trial
  7. Settlement negotiation before the trial judge
  8. Trial
  9. Final negotiation of a settlement
 10. Appeal

All but 2 of the 60 cases sampled from the file of 1968 closing statements were settled. Of these, 38 percent (23) were settled during preliminary negotiations, usually within the first two years after the accident; 27 percent (16) were settled before the cases were called for trial. 28 percent (17) were settled on the eve of a scheduled trial; and two were settled during the course of the trial. Of the two tried cases, one ended in a jury verdict for the plaintiff and the other ended in the insurer's unsuccessful appeal of a plaintiff's verdict. During the course of these ten stages there are numerous decisions that have to be made either implicitly or explicitly by the lawyer or the client or both together. Since most claims do not reach a trial, let us focus on 12 decisions, in the order they usually are faced, that can have a significant impact on the outcome of the case during the pretrial stages.[1]

The first important decision to make is whether or not to undertake a claim at all. When the client agrees to hire the lawyer and the lawyer agrees to take the client's case, they are mutually making the choice to proceed. Among the relevant considerations for the client are: Am I willing to bear the costs in time and emotional energy imposed by a claim? Is the lawyer I have selected highly skilled? Will we get along and see things the same way? Can I do better by making the claim myself without an attorney? How hard is he likely to work for me?[2] Among the relevant considerations for the attorney are: How much work will I have to put into this claim? Does it have sufficient worth to compensate me adequately? Do I have the time and skill to handle this case so as to get a good return? Is this going to be an easy client to work with? In

---

[1] For a readable introduction to the stages and decisions of the claim process see: Jerome Carlin, *Lawyers on Their Own* (New Brunswick, N.J.: Rutgers University Press, 1962), pp. 71–91; also two articles by Wilfred Lorry entitled "Settlement of a Personal Injury Claim," in the legal periodical, *The Practicing Lawyer*, vols. 1 and 11, 1955 and 1965. I have found the following two books to be good intermediate texts: A. Harold Frost and Marvin Ausubel, *Preparation of a Negligence Case*, rev. ed. (New York: Practicing Law Institute, 1967); and Harold Baer and Aaron Broder, *How To Prepare and Negotiate Cases for Settlement* (Englewood Cliffs, N.J.: Prentice-Hall, 1967). For a comprehensive treatise I have consulted Joseph Kelner, *Personal Injury: Successful Litigation Techniques*, 3 vols. (New York: Bender, 1965).

[2] We will defer a consideration of the client's choice of a lawyer to Chapter 5.

five of the sample cases, clients report that the first lawyer they approached declined to take their case, referring them instead to attorneys who then did accept them. Four of the attorneys who turned-down the would-be clients, said that they didn't handle negligence cases and the fifth said he was too busy with other work at that particular time. All clients, on the other hand, accepted the first lawyer who accepted them.

The second decision in the claims process is almost always made implicitly—laying out the ground rules for the lawyer-client relationship. Among the relevant issues for which ground rules are appropriate are: who should call whom; how much of the details of the case should be disclosed to the client; how much time the lawyer should spend in counseling the client to deal with medical, emotional, financial, family, and work problems; and how actively the client should be involved in the subsequent decisions to be made in the claim. In a majority of cases the lawyer guides the client into viewing his case, his role, and the lawyer's task in a way that the lawyer finds most congenial. This involves encouraging the client to rely upon the lawyer's judgment and assuaging those anxieties the client reveals. It also involves discouraging the client from making demands or harboring expectations that will be difficult for the attorney to fulfill. Setting ground rules is usually a one-way process in which the lawyer guides and the client adjusts. Those few clients with the temerity to seek ground rules that reflect their concerns are sometimes able to achieve a two-way process of mutual give-and-take.

These two threshold decisions, whether to go ahead and by what ground rules, are manifestly open in nature. Clients and lawyers are individuals with distinctive wants and styles. There can be no general objective criteria spelling out precisely how each should proceed.

The third decision is the lawyer's fee. Most lawyers inform their clients that the fee is "standard" or "set by the court" (e.g., under the Appellate Division rules) and not a matter for choice. However, as we have seen, the Appellate Division fee schedule sets only a maximum contingent fee which can be (and sometimes is) reduced. Moreover, it expressly provides a choice between two alternative methods for computing the maximum permissible contingent fee. Then, too, for the financially independent client, there is also, theoretically, the option to pay the lawyer an hourly fee for his work time rather than a contingent percentage of the final recovery.

The fourth set of decisions is raised in the preliminary preparation of the case. Lawyers are advised by the handbooks to get a detailed statement from the client about the accident at the initial interview. The client is to be warned to refer all inquiries from claim adjusters to the attorney, to make no statements and sign no papers without the lawyer's advice. He is to be instructed to keep accurate records of all expenses—not just medical expenses—arising from the accident and he is to be encouraged to keep a diary of dates on which anything of importance takes place regarding treatment, experiences of pain, or other effects of the injuries, and the work days and earnings he has lost. After meeting with the client, the lawyer is urged to review whether or not the case raises any novel legal issues; if so, these should be researched. The lawyer or a trusted associate should make a personal inspection of the accident site and arrange to have photographs taken of the accident scene, property damage, and the observable personal injuries, to preserve and dramatize the evidence. Witnesses should be located and interviewed. Police, motor vehicle, hospital, and doctor's reports should be obtained and reviewed. If these are incomplete, the lawyer should have the client examined by a doctor who is prepared to appear, if necessary, at a trial as an expert medical witness. If there is any question of who owns and is responsible for the maintenance of property involved in an accident, ownership should be checked. The availability of defendant assets should be confirmed, where possible, through credit services and by directly questioning the insurer.

All of this makes sense in the abstract. But lawyers have to make concrete calculations about how best to spend a limited amount of their time. A conscientious lawyer would go bankrupt if he tried to be so punctilious in the preparation of every case brought to him. Thus the realistic decision has to be made—what corners can be cut in which cases? Efficient techniques of office organization, record keeping and economies of scale certainly increase the scope and thoroughness an attorney can bring to case preparation. Nonetheless, limits are imposed on the attention provided by even the most efficient operations.

In Chapter 2 we looked, with the advantage of hindsight, at several examples of active clients who picked up the slack, as with Mr. Donald pursuing his criminal charge without his lawyer's aid and Mr. Getz' pushing for confirmation of the defendant's $20,000 insurance limit. With the passive clients, the destructive omissions were not cured. Dr. Stern's lawyer did not check the law about taxi medallions. The Jorrys were not told how to record expenses. Mrs. Silber's lawyer had not prepared her doctor to give expert testimony.

There is no consensus among attorneys about criteria or techniques for cutting corners. Each man develops his own work style for coping with the uncertainty of these open choices. By treating these as technical and routine choices lawyers underestimate the part that judgment, guesswork, convenience, and habit play.[3] Furthermore, by making open choices appear closed, the lawyer justifies excluding the client from the decision-making process. A passive client will accept the rationale that these are minor matters of technical detail that need not concern him. As we have seen these "minor" matters can be of decisive importance to the case outcome. Finally, as we shall see in the next chapter, the way claim preparation choices are made is influenced by a conflict of interest between the lawyer and the client.

Once the initial preparation is completed, the fifth decision is when to begin a lawsuit. In some insurance companies, the settlement policy of the claims adjusters is different from the policy of the trial attorneys. Sometimes the two sets of employees are divided into separate departments—with the nonlawyer adjusters responsible for negotiations prior to the filing of a lawsuit, and the defense attorneys responsible for negotiations once the defendant is served with a summons and complaint (the opening move in bringing a lawsuit). Occasionally, the adjusters are easier to do business with than the attorneys. In those situations it may pay to hold off the service of process. On the other hand, as we shall see, insurers have an interest in stalling settlements for as long a period as possible. The sooner a suit is begun, the quicker it can be placed on the trial calendar, minimizing the delay before trial. In 24 percent (14 of 59) of the sample cases, no suit was filed before a settlement was made.[4] Most clients in these cases had no knowledge of whether or not suit had been filed. Very few clients say that they were consulted about the time to sue. For clients who are especially anxious about expediting recovery, it is an important decision. One attorney commented that most delayed filings reflect a lawyer's desire to postpone extra work and extra expense. Drafting a complaint can be time consuming. There are fees for filing and fees for service of process. It can add up to $100 in overhead. Whether the expense is worthwhile is almost always left within the exclusive province of the lawyer. As with these other decisions under discussion, it need not be.

A sixth decision is the amount of money for which to sue. The pleadings—the plaintiff's complaint (which must include the amount of damages sought), the defendant's answer, the plaintiff's bill of particulars—freeze the facts and the

---

[3] Unreflective routinization of nonroutine tasks has been referred to as the "trained incapacity" of certain workers. Robert Merton, "Bureaucratic Structure and Personality," in his *Social Theory and Social Structure,* rev. ed. (New York: Free Press, 1957), pp. 197–198.

[4] This percentage is drawn from the lawyers' reports in the closing statements. It is predicated on the assumption that the lawyers made accurate reports. See Appendix A, p. 187.

contentions asserted by the parties. After an early opportunity to amend the pleadings, the parties are foreclosed from subsequent alterations. One problem this raises for the plaintiff is picking an amount of damages to claim which will be neither so inflated as to antagonize a judge, nor so undervalued as to foreclose adequate recovery if there are serious undiscovered injuries which only later come to light: Lawyers are always warned to make an inflated claim for damages. Sometimes they fail to inflate sufficiently. Undiscovered injuries are an uncertainty lacking probabilistic measure. A client such as Mr. Meyer may have some better sense of the possible extent of his injuries—as the one suffering them—than his lawyer. A client who avoids confronting the seriousness of his injuries—like Mr. Taub—may make a poorer assessment than his attorney.

A related decision is in which court suit should be brought. In the Supreme Court there is no limit on the money damages that may be awarded. But a suit will not be granted a general trial preference (which is tantamount to its never being called for trial), if it is adjudged to be for an injury of insufficient severity. The main guideline for appraising sufficient severity is whether damages include disability. This too is an open question of judgment. There are other relevant complicating considerations. In Manhattan the calendar delay is presently much shorter in the Civil Court than in the Supreme Court. Nonetheless, as the expert panelist commented with respect to Mrs. Silber's case, insurers (and judges too) in the Civil Court are conditioned to minimize damages claimed—and there is always the inflexible recovery limit of $10,000 even if one successfully carries through to a jury verdict.

Another set of considerations has to do with convenience to the lawyer and client of the place of venue (the county of the court in which suit is brought). Suit, in many circumstances, may be properly brought in either of two or more counties. The New York Civil Practice Law and Rules (CPLR) sets limits on the choices to be made, according to the residences and business offices of the parties (including the insurer) and the place of the accident—among other criteria;[5] although, in many cases this still leaves alternatives. If suit is brought in Manhattan, where the accident took place and where the defendant's office is located, it may be more convenient for the attorney with a Manhattan office. But the plaintiff may live in Suffolk County and so may his doctor, his leading witness. Yet another consideration is the partiality of juries in different locales. Urban juries are considered to be more generous to plaintiffs than rural juries. If the plaintiff is Jewish there are likely to be more Jews on a jury in Brooklyn; if he is a Catholic, there are more Catholics in Queens.

---

[5] *CPLR* (New York: Bender, 1965), Article 5, "Venue," pp. 500–512.

The next decision to be made after suit has been filed, is whether or not to seek a jury trial. It is generally believed that in New York plaintiffs can expect a better award from a jury than a judge. But if time is of the essence, a nonjury trial can be obtained in as little as a quarter of the time. The plaintiff's decision to waive the right to a jury trial may be vetoed by the insurer, who also has the right to demand a jury trial.[6] Nonjury tort trials do take place, but not as frequently as jury tort trials.

Another crucial decision was highlighted in Mr. O'Shea's case: the question of a special trial preference to avoid the calendar delay which results even after one has obtained a general trial preference. An attorney may submit a motion for a special preference where he can support either the contention that delay will likely result in the death of the plaintiff before he can have a trial or, that delay will reduce the client to a condition of poverty resulting in his becoming a public charge. The question of whether, and when, to seek the preference was only relevant in two of the sample cases, that of Mr. O'Shea and Mr. Wilkins. Mr. Wilkins is an ex-prize fighter who was receiving welfare at the time of his accident.

All of these choices can be made within a few months after the accident or at an intermediate period thereafter. The next set of decisions are raised by the prospect of settlement negotiations and the need to adopt a settlement strategy. Among the relevant settlement choices are the following: at what level to set the initial settlement demand; at what time to make the first approach for discussion; what degree of belligerence to manifest; how much of one's evidence and strategy to disclose to the insurer; and how much time to allow between negotiating conversations.[7] Here again, almost always, these open choices—for which there are no hard and fast answers—are left to the lawyer's judgment without occasion for his explaining or justifying the choices he plans to make. The one choice in which all of the sample clients participated was whether or not to accept a settlement offer and, if so, how much to accept. In most cases, the lawyer's influence over the client's notion of what is acceptable is very great.[8]

The next decision is raised by anticipation of the examination before trial (EBT). The EBT is a spontaneous confrontation of witnesses which discloses to each party the evidence upon which the other plans to rely at trial. It is usu-

---

[6] Ibid., Article 41, "Trial by Jury," Section 4102.

[7] The most detailed discussion of these questions is to be found in Philip Hermann, *Better Settlements through Leverage* (Rochester, N.Y.: Aqueduct Books, 1965).

[8] Roger Bryant Hunting and Gloria S. Neuwirth, *Who Sues in New York City?* (New York: Columbia University Press, 1962), p. 108.

ally held in the office of the plaintiff attorney with a stenographer present who prepares a verbatim transcript. The plaintiff's attorney questions the defendant and the defense attorney then questions the plaintiff. Witnesses, if any, are then examined. This testimony, called depositions, focuses the issues in controversy and provides a useful basis for subsequent settlement negotiations. How carefully should the plaintiff be prepared for the EBT? Should the lawyer spend a great deal of time reassuring the client, letting him know what to expect and suggesting ways he might properly react—as did Mrs. Lombard's lawyer? Or, can the impact of the EBT be minimized on the assumption that the client will take it in his stride? For many clients this approach apparently worked. For one client, whose case is discussed later,[9] it did not. How are the lawyer and the client to know what is the appropriate preparation?

The final matter which should be decided is the proper approach to the pretrial settlement negotiation (which is supervised by the judge). What should the client be told? Clearly more than Mrs. Silber had been told, but how much more? How should the lawyer deal with a "Solomonic" judge who is not above coercing a settlement on his terms? How should the plaintiff's lawyer deal with the badgering and harrassment by the insurer's attorney and how should the client respond to it? Once again, routine, clear-cut answers are wanting; yet many of these choices are relevant to the success or failure of any personal injury claim, not just in the actual dollar recovery, but in the clients' ability to cope with the often stressful impact of their accidents.

THE INJURY AS EXPERIENCED BY THE CLIENT

How well injury victims cope with accidents and their aftermaths is not only a relevant measure of a successful claim, but it can itself have a significant impact on making a claim. The less an accident disrupts the victim's life, the sooner he recovers and life returns to normal, the more the claims process is simplified. Many of the issues raised for decision will be matters of relative indifference to the claimant for whom life has returned to normal. Even if the dollar compensation is not recovered to the extent and in the time anticipated, the claimant has invested little. Any sense of lost opportunities is more easily put aside in a daily routine in which injury and litigation is relatively rare. Issues of responsibility and choice only tend to count where the victim's life will not return to normal, where he will fail to make a full and/or rapid recovery of his health and his economic and social well-being as it was prior to the accident.

Conversely, the possibility, timing, and ultimate amount of remuneration

---

[9] Mrs. Federman, *infra* p. 84.

that can be gained in a claim can assist or impair that recovery of health and well-being. So too can the way that the claim is handled by the attorney.

In the previous chapter, several illustrations were presented of the ways in which the personal needs or concerns of clients affect their response to the claims process and make it appropriate that there be adjustments by the lawyer in the way he informs the client and even in the way the principal choices of the claim are made. To the extent the client brings significant personal needs to the lawyer-client relationship, he reduces the lawyer's ability to routinize the interaction between them and to standardize the goals and techniques for preparing and settling a claim. The clients subjective desires become a major source of the criteria for problem solving.

Let us consider the impact of their accidents upon the personal injury victims of this study. Most of the accidents that lead to lawsuits arise from automobile collisions—rear-end collisions, head-on collisions, and pedestrian knockdowns. Other common types of accidents for which claims are made include falls outside the home, injuries from falling objects, injuries incurred in the use of defective products or services, and injuries from unintended fires and explosions. The clients interviewed in this study experienced the full range of these accidents (Table 3.1).

Table 3.1: Types of Accidents Experienced By Interviewees

Type	Incidents	Percentages
1. Rear-end vehicle collision	11	18.3
2. Head-on vehicle collision	9	15.0
3. Pedestrian knockdown	11	18.3
4. Injured passenger	10	16.7
5. Fall	11	18.3
6. Injury by falling object	5	8.3
7. Product or service injury	2	3.3
8. Gas explosion and fire	1	1.7
	60	99.9

In their Michigan survey of auto accident victims, Conard and his associates proposed three common sense criteria for identifying a serious injury:

1. The occasion for hospital and medical expenses of $500 or more
2. The need for hospitalization (for three or more weeks)
3. Some degree of permanent physical impairment (or death)[10]

---

[10] Alfred Conard, et. al., *Automobile Accident Costs and Payments* (Ann Arbor: University of Michigan Press, 1964), pp. 159–160.

By the first criterion, 85 percent (51 of 60) of the sample cases involved serious injury to the interviewee, the spouse, or child. Half (31 of 60) involved at least overnight hospitalization and about one-third (22 of 60) led to some permanent disability or disfigurement.[11] Approximately half of the victims (28 of 60) interviewed said that the accident had a considerably unsettling impact on their lives. For them, the accident experience is not quickly forgotten and readjustment was neither quick nor easy.

A serious accident can be a terrifying experience. One wants it to be over and forgotten, but its repercussions drag on. Mrs. Rubio was riding on the turnpike with her family when the car spun and she felt herself being thrown forward and then snapped backward. For a long moment she didn't know what happened, but then she groped for the door and stumbled onto the pavement. Free for no more than a few seconds, she looked back in horror to see the car burst into flames and realized that she and her husband and son were almost killed. She stood on the turnpike, with cars driving by and cried convulsively. For two years thereafter she was unable to get into a car without becoming nauseated.

Mr. Teich was taking a vacation with his wife. While the Teichs were riding in the crowded elevator of the resort hotel in which they were staying, the cable broke and the force of the resulting fall drove Mr. Teich to the floor. When he tried to lift himself up, he was unable to stand. He looked at his wife and saw her doubled up with pain. It took ten agonizing minutes to be rescued. Even in accidents where there is less drama and less serious physical injury, one of the first reactions for almost every victim is "My God, I could have been killed." Even with a quick recuperation, the victim does not forget that he has had a narrow escape.

During the course of several client interviews, I could see much of the emotional strain being reexperienced. Respondents twisted handkerchiefs, used accelerated yet halting speech patterns, exploded in outbursts of anger and sometimes tears. Initially, Miss Schiff, the pretty school teacher, had not wanted to be interviewed at all. "I don't want to remember the horrible thing," she said over the telephone. After discussing these concerns for several minutes she changed her mind. Miss Schiff had been a passenger in the front seat of a convertible. Her head had been thrust through the windshield by the force of a collision with an oncoming car. She had several pieces of glass removed

---

[11] Accidents resulting in death were excluded from the present sample. A fourth criterion of substantial injury was used in defining the client sample: making an actual recovery of at least $2,000. By this criterion, all 60 interviewees were substantially injured.

from her scalp and fifty stitches inserted to a visible point just below the hairline. She also sustained a severe back sprain.

> It took me a couple of years to stop shaking and not tense up when headlights approach. I am now very nervous in cars and never was before. For two months, I like needed baby-sitters because I couldn't be left alone. . . . I needed help to move around because of my back but. . . . I was like frightened and just afraid of being by myself. When school started in September, I was in pieces and had to take a leave-of-absence. At this point I went to a psychoanalyst and we went over and over the accident. . . . It did some good.

Several accidents involved deep psychological injuries which many of the victims were only able to see retrospectively. Mr. Gomez, a restaurateur, had driven into a telephone pole to avoid colliding with an oncoming car in his lane. Several teeth were dislodged and had to be removed. "I now realize," he told me, "that losing those teeth made me very afraid of losing my youth and my masculinity. It changed my whole personality." In a relatively few cases, the emotional impact is extreme and immediate. This is referred to as traumatic neurosis and is slowly being recognized as a frequent and substantial consequence of accidental physical injury.[12] The emotional strain comes not just from the shock of the accident itself, but from the disorder and feelings of helplessness it creates. Mrs. Lowe, an expensively dressed housewife who fell on steps in Grand Central Station, spent two weeks with ugly body bruises. "During those two weeks I didn't want to see anyone—even my best friends. I looked god awful, and felt like a freak."

Where the victim is already under stress, the accident and recovery period can have a watershed impact. Mrs. Lombard, an articulate woman in her mid-thirties, reviewed the accident "as a catalyst for a lot of things in my life." She had sustained a shattered elbow requiring bone surgery, plastic surgery, and extended traction for the arm. "I went into psychotherapy, I got a divorce . . . a sort of shaking up of my life as I sat in the hospital for a month thinking about it." Central to her divorce was Mrs. Lombard's reaction to her husband's "total incompetence to deal with something like the accident. That's why I turned to my sister and brother-in-law to find a lawyer and a surgeon. I

---

[12] In New York, though not in all jurisdictions, traumatic neurosis is a compensatory damage. *Application of Rotund,* 36 Misc. 2d 332, 234 N.Y.S. 2d 859 (Sup. Ct. 1962). See the following for two different views of this very controversial phenomenon: Frederick Strothman, "Traumatic Neurosis—A Medical-Legal Approach," *Washburn Law Journal* 6 (1967): 350–394; H. A. Shapiro, "Accident Neurosis," *Tort and Medical Handbook,* eds. Albert Averbach and Melvin Belli, vol. 2 (Indianapolis, Ind.: Bobbs-Merrill, 1962), pp. 669–673.

had a lot of time to think about my husband's need to be mothered and my not getting any support back."

Serious accidents frequently disrupt family life. In the case of Mrs. Federman, the demands of her family, as she saw them, precluded her staying in the hospital for a sufficient length of time properly to mend a broken hip. The Federmans live in a cramped and ill-lit apartment in a poorly maintained building. A few weeks before her accident, Mr. Federman had suffered a second paralytic stroke and had become totally disabled. Mrs. Federman was working as a teacher's aid, earning less than $4,000 a year, some of which was earmarked to help her youngest daughter through college. Her husband required constant attention; she could not afford to remain out of work for any length of time. She felt compelled to tell the doctor that the three week hospital rest he recommended was impossible. She obtained a discharge in six days. At the time of the interview, two years later, there was no improvement in her husband's condition, the funds from her settlement had been exhausted by medical bills, and she was still seeing a doctor and taking medicine for chronic hip pains. Mrs. Federman was a trapped woman.

The pressures of work disruption fall most heavily on the self-employed and on the nonunionized laborer. Mr. Abel, a nonunion mechanic injured while driving his employer's delivery truck, was subjected to constant harassment by the employer. He said that,

> My employer thought I was putting on a gag to get money when I complained of bad back pains. He didn't cooperate one bit. He wouldn't give me documents proving my lost wages until my lawyer threatened him with a subpoena. . . . After six months, the workmen's compensation stopped and I had to go back to work for light duty—for which I was paid less than I had been earning before. Two weeks later he wanted me to do heavy lifting again which really killed my back. I refused and he told me to get another job.[13]

Mr. Towle informed me that he was just beginning to break through as a successful artist at the time of his accident. The injury to his back from a fall prevented him from continuing his painting for several months. During this time he lost at least one opportunity for a one-man show and had to turn down two commissions. After one more struggling year, he joined a company as a commercial artist.

---

[13] If the facts were as related, Mr. Abel was entitled to make a further claim for two-thirds of the difference between the weekly wages he earned before the accident and the wages he could earn with the same or a different employer doing lighter labor. *McKinney's Consolidated Laws of New York,* vol. 64 (Workmen's Compensation Law), Article 2, §15.3w (Brooklyn, N.Y.: Edward Thompson Company, 1973).

About one-third (19 of 60) of the claimants had the benefit of extended medical or casualty insurance to draw upon at the time of their injury. This seems like surprisingly few when it is remembered that the respondents are preponderantly middle class. More to be expected, most of them were able to draw upon savings to meet nondeferred expenses. The greater the savings, the better the quality of medical care and the longer the recuperation period that could be afforded. Confirmation of the financial strain of a successful claim recovery is to be found in the fact that not a single one of the clients who lacked medical insurance and had to borrow money obtained a good case result.

If the victim is lucky enough to avoid emotional trauma, if he receives support from his family and employer, if he has the funds to pay for good medical attention, he may still suffer from indignities visited by the personnel of the hospital emergency unit to which he is delivered after the accident.

When an accident victim is injured sufficiently to require an ambulance, he is taken to the hospital emergency room assigned by the City Health Department for that territory in which the accident took place. In many locations, the assigned emergency room is in a poor quality hospital. Based on the stories of six of the interviewees, emergency medical care provides a member of the middle class with a sobering glimpse of what the lower-class medical patient faces as a matter of course.[14] Mr. Meyer, an author, vividly related the following experience:

> I was taken to [X] Hospital. . . . It is incredible what goes on in hospital emergency rooms. . . . I had already heard of the reputation of that hospital and had asked to be taken to Roosevelt Hospital instead . . . unh . . . but in any case I ended up in [X] with a fractured pelvis and in enormous pain. I lay in the emergency room for quite a long time while nothing was done. . . . The policeman who had come with me in the ambulance was off to one side laughing and joking with the two nurses there—completely ignoring me—then, a man in a white outfit came by, tapping me for a moment and then walking on again; a little while later the nurse came and said "You can go." No X-rays, no nothing. I didn't even know that that had been the doctor. When she said, "You can go now," I just lay there and said, "I can't: I can't move." She said, "Well the doctor says you're all right." And I was forced, literally, off the table with a fractured pelvis, and fainted, nearly, and they had to get smelling salts. And I was forced to the door and had it slammed behind me. . . . Subsequently, I have done some research about this and have discovered two cases of worse treatment in the same emergency room of the same hospital.

---

[14] For a sensitive description of the hospital experience of a lower-class patient, see Raymond Duff and August Hollingshead, *Sickness and Society* (New York: Harper & Row, 1968), pp. 124–145.

. . . Apparently, this is fairly routine, especially where they think you might not have the money to pay for treatment. . . . I had Blue Shield medical insurance but nobody bothered to ask me. . . . When I realized that even with a fractured pelvis I would be compelled to leave the hospital, I then asked, "Well, will you please call a number for me". . . . And they said, "Well, if you can get to the phone and walk to the phone you may make a call." But it was inconceivable that I could get to the phone; I could hardly get to the door even with them dragging me. Fortunately I was able to hail a cab which took me home where the driver carried me into my apartment.

In another case, that of Mr. Brackman, an accountant, no doctor was on night duty in a Manhattan hospital; the only medical attendant was a young intern who spoke almost no English. Mrs. Rubio bitterly recalls being taken to the emergency unit of a hospital off the New Jersey Turnpike and made to "strip naked and sit in a room for two hours like that without even a drink of water or chance to get it."

The single worst experience with a hospital was reported by Mr. O'Shea who, at the time of his accident, was a ship's steward. With shore time to spend, Mr. O'Shea took a subway to the racetrack where he had a good day, winning over $200. Flushed with his success, he decided to splurge and take a limousine ride to another racetrack. The limousine collided with a bus and Mr. O'Shea, the only passenger in the front seat, went through the windshield, suffering a concussion, lacerations, broken ribs, internal bleeding, and intensified damage to his already diseased lungs. He was taken by ambulance to the emergency ward of a Queens public hospital where he was made to wait in a hardwood chair for four hours before any doctor examined him or before his wounds were dressed. After receiving some superficial attention at midnight (no X-rays were taken), he was told that no bed was available and he spent the next six hours in the same chair. At 6:00 A.M., still in a dazed condition, he left, unnoticed, without a release. He reached for his wallet and found the $200 missing. He speculates that it was stolen by either a policeman, hospital attendant, or bystander at the accident. He had enough change to take the subway—barely reaching his rooming house before passing out.

These experiences illustrate that in personal injury cases, the accident frequently imposes burdensome physical, emotional, financial, family, and work demands. Attorneys are in a position to assist clients in dealing with these burdens. Rather surprisingly, attorneys receive very little training in how to counsel those clients who have broader needs arising from their legal problems and who desire such counsel. There is hardly even consideration in law school courses or legal education materials of the extent to which it is appropriate for lawyers to provide such broader and arguably "nonlegal" counseling.[15] Of the attorneys who represented clients in the sample and who answered the questionnaire sent to them, approximately 70 percent (32 of 45) said that they generally felt an obligation, where the client sought it, to provide advice about these personal, "nonlegal" aspects of the client's problems.[16] Many attorneys, then, who practice personal injury law say they actually do address the personal, often subjective, needs of their clients as an explicit part of their overall representation. The nature and extent of this counseling is undetermined.

The reader might reasonably think that while serious injuries tend to increase the stress experienced by the claimant, since these injuries tend to involve greater monetary damages, the claimant's chances improve for a satisfactory claim settlement, thus indirectly reducing the stress he experiences. In fact, many of the seriously injured interviewees report that they were encouraged by friends and relatives to anticipate the prospect of a more than compensatory "windfall" settlement. The fact of the matter is the reverse of what common sense suggests. The more serious the accident (the greater the injury, the greater the costs of recuperation), the lesser are the victim's chances of receiving a fair recovery. Thus, the frustrations of the claims process itself tend to be greatest for claimants who have suffered most from their accidents. In the Michigan survey referred to at the beginning of the chapter, for example, "No one with a loss exceeding $25,000 was found to have received a tort settlement even approaching his economic loss."[17] Only one client in our sample, a negligence specialist (who was the least seriously injured), received a windfall. Actually his $2,500 windfall was most likely less an excessive valuation of the claim's worth by the insurer than a conscious payment to promote his good will in future claims negotiations—an anticipated *quid pro quo*. By the time the sample of claimants were interviewed, they were wiser and looked back ruefully at the absurdity of the windfall they had been encouraged to anticipate. "It's a little annoying," says Mr. Getz, for example,

---

[15] Three law school professors who do include consideration of this issue in their courses are Harrop Freeman of Cornell Law School, Louis Brown of the University of Southern California Law School, and Dean Thomas Shaffer of Notre Dame Law School.

[16] This is consistent with the 80 percent response of Manhattan corporate attorneys participating as volunteers in a poverty law program who said that they at least "sometimes" gave this broader counsel. See Douglas Rosenthal, Robert Kagan, and Debra Quatrone, *Volunteer Attorneys and Legal Services for the Poor: New York's CLO Program* (New York: Russell Sage Foundation, 1971), pp. 122–124.

[17] Conard et al., *Automobile Accident Costs and Payments*, p. 6.

that before the blood has stopped running, everyone tells you that you are going to be rich—like hospital attendants and cops and visitors too. It's depress-
ing; they think you've caught the golden ring.

The occasional windfall recovery usually receives sensational press cov-
erage which distorts both its rarity and the full extent of the injuries compensated. Illustrative is an article in the *New York Post* headlined, "Hurt Bowler
Loses Form, Wins 150G." The article makes much of the plaintiff's contention that the injuries ruined his bowling form and implies that the $150,000 re-
covery was compensation for the loss of his bowling skills. However, the
extent of the damage—leg injuries resulting in the permanent shortening of
one leg—might have justified the award on other grounds such as permanent
pain, lifetime partial disability, and reduced earning capacity.[18]

The measure of case value developed in this study was the arithmetic
mean of the five evaluations of each case by the expert panel. In the sample,
clients with claims worth more than $7,500 according to the expert panel
evaluation, had slightly less than a 50 percent chance (11 of 24) of covering
their out-of-pocket expenses. Clients with claims ranging between $2,000 and
$7,500 had a three-in-four chance (25 of 33) of recouping expenses.[19]

The range of case values in the 57-case sample varies from a low of
$2,200 to a high of $37,000. The median case value in the sample is $6,600.
When a rank order correlation between case worth and case recovery is computed, the relationship turns out to be strong and negative. The more a claim
is worth the less favorable the recovery is likely to be. Thus, case worth stands
along with client participation as an independent explanation of why some
clients get better case results. The smaller the claim, the better the chances of
a fair return.[20]

The explanation of this well-documented phenomenon has yet to be finally made. Three factors seem most plausible; two we have already noted, in
passing. First, many clients (and their attorneys) underestimate the true costs
of their expenses in fully recuperating. Settlement demands formulated prematurely frequently do not reflect the true cost of the accident. Second, some
clients are unwilling or unable to wait out the course of recuperative treatment
or the making of an effective claim. They accept an early settlement bearing

---

[18] *New York Post,* November 18, 1969, p. 23.

[19] The negative relationship between case worth and covering specials is significant at the 0.05 level using Fisher's Exact Test. This test is explained in Hubert Blalock,
Social Statistics (New York: McGraw-Hill, 1960), p. 221.

[20] Kendall's Tau $= -0.23$. This is significant at the 0.01 level for a one-tail test of
significance. Kendall's Tau for the correlation between client activity and case result $=$
$+0.21$.

little relationship to the case value. The third factor is the operation of the principal institutions of the claims process which affect the lawyer's ability to get his client a fair recovery. These institutions are (1) the defendant's insurance company, (2) the judges before whom personal injury litigants appear, (3) the trial calendars of the courts, (4) the substantive law of negligence, and (5) the trial jury. Generally speaking, the more money an accident victim seeks, the more likely it is that an insurer will refrain from early payment and contest the claim—to bargain it down. When an insurer chooses to contest a claim these institutions are more likely to act as factors diminishing rather than enhancing the client's recovery. Contesting a claim is expensive for the insurer as well as the client. Where claims are small, early settlement, even for inflated amounts, is often more profitable.[21] Where claims are large, insurers can take advantage of the partiality of many trial judges, the delay of courts, the defendant's advantages under the substantive doctrine of negligence law, and the uncertainties of jury deliberation to bargain the claim down. Thus the seriously injured claimant tends to face a battle to gain his recovery. So far we have seen that the choices in making a claim are relatively open ones for which there are no clear-cut and generalizable best answers and that the subjective needs of individual clients play an important part in evaluating and making those choices. Now we shall find that many of these choices are made with a high degree of uncertainty and considerable risk.

THE UNCERTAIN IMPACT OF THE CLAIMS PROCESS INSTITUTIONS

To understand why the claims process is risky and not predictable for the personal injury claimant and his attorney, it is necessary to consider the role played by five institutions, integral to the claims process, whose impacts are largely beyond lawyer and client control. Such consideration will not only illumine the complexities of the claims process, but will also show why client activity and lawyer competence have only a limited influence on case outcome.

The Defendant's Insurer

The liability insurance industry in America is, for the accident victim, the primary antagonist. In New York, virtually all claims arising out of serious ac-

---

[21] While Conard et al., *Automobile Accident Costs and Payments,* found that seriously injured accident victims tend not to cover their expenses, Hunting and Neuwirth report that victims with minor injuries and smaller claims tend to recover more than their out-of-pocket expenses. *Who Sues in New York City?,* p. 15.

cidents are made against insurers or against the assets of self-insured companies rather than against the assets of individuals. Nonetheless, the law requires that the person insured must stand as the putative defendant. The existence of insurance is kept from the jury to discourage overly generous plaintiff's verdicts paid from the insurer's "deep pocket." This concealment is an anachronism. Most New Yorkers probably know that insurers defend liability suits.

There are two main types of liability insurers: insurance corporations which sell publicly traded stock, and mutual insurance societies in which the policy owners themselves, rather than outside shareholders, own the company assets. Municipal authorities tend to be self-insurers and so too are a few private companies, notably cab companies which are permitted under New York law to purchase one $10,000 liability bond per cab, in lieu of an insurance policy. A fifth important insurer is the New York Motor Vehicle Accident Indemnification Corporation (MVAIC) to which all licensed insurers contribute a portion of earnings prorated to their share of the New York State insurance market. The 60 sample claimants received payment from these sources in the following proportions:

1. Stock insurance company, 32 claims (53.0 percent)
2. Mutual insurance company, 15 claims (25.0 percent)
3. Private self-insurer, 8 claims (13.3 percent)
4. Municipal authority, 5 claims (8.3 percent)
5. MVAIC, 0 claims

Available statistics indicate that except for the lack of representation of MVAIC claims (of which approximately 6,500 were settled statewide in 1968, the year of the sample),[22] this is a representative sample of policies. Twice as many stock insurance as mutual insurance premiums were paid by American households in 1968.[23]

The three plaintiffs' lawyers who evaluated the worth of the claims, also made an evaluation of the settlement policies of the 39 insurers paying the claims. There were three classifications (plus the disclaimer of any knowledge of a company policy): "(1) will make a reasonable early settlement (within one year after the accident); (2) will make a reasonable late settlement

---

[22] Report of secretary and manager, John J. Corbley, May 19, 1972, Motor Vehicle Accident Indemnification Corporation, 116 John Street, New York City, Schedules E-H.

[23] In 1968, $4,984,000,000 worth of automobile bodily injury liability premiums were earned: $3,291,000,000 by stock insurers (67 percent) and $1,693,000,000 by mutuals (33 percent). Figures were taken from *Best's Aggregates and Averages,* 30th ed. (Morristown, N.J.: A. M. Best Co., 1969), pp. 140, 211.

Table 3.2: Evaluation of Insurers' Settlement Policies

Rating	Number of Insurers	Percentage
1. Reasonable early	8	22.9
2. Reasonable late	15	42.9
3. Never reasonable	12	34.2
	35	
Policy unknown	4	
	39	

(shortly before trial); (3) will never make a reasonable settlement offer." The consensus among the experts here was greater than their consensus on case values. The results are listed in Table 3.2.

None of the mutuals was judged to have a reasonable early settlement policy. Of the 12 unreasonable insurers, 5 were mutuals; 4 were national stock companies. The City of New York and the New York Transit Authority were judged about the most impossible insurers with which to negotiate a fair settlement.[24]

It would be interesting to know precisely what factors go into a company's definition of its settlement policy. From informant interviews two generalizations can be made: First, many insurers will stall before settling until a case is called to trial. In the intervening years, insurers can earn generous interest rates investing their claims reserve fund—especially at the high interest rates of the last several years. Under present law, the client is not entitled to receive interest on his claim until the day he obtains judgment or the day he signs a settlement release. Second, many of those insurers who resist settlement most doggedly tend to have smaller cash reserves, a smaller staff, and a smaller margin of profit. They tend either to sell their policies to the general public at a discount from the general market price for liability policies, or they sell to high-risk insurers such as tenement landlords and cab owners whom more profitable insurers would not underwrite, in either case benefiting policy-holders at the expense of their victims, who get less compensation from them

---

[24] It is thought by some that jurors return smaller judgments against municipal authorities because they fear that large recoveries would boost taxes. Believing this, the thinking goes, City and Transit Authority lawyers apparently have little compunction about making very low settlement offers. The Port of New York Authority, on the other hand, is run more like a private corporation and will, according to the plaintiff attorney panelists, make reasonable settlement offers—although not quickly.

Table 3.3: Comparative Loss Ratios between Two Liberal and Two Tough Insurers for 1968[a]

Insurers	Loss Ratio
Liberal	
Aetna	85.6%
Zurich-American	79.0%
Tough	
Allstate	72.0%
Empire Mutual	69.4%

[a] Figures taken from *Best's Aggregates and Averages,* pp. 126, 129, 202. In contradiction, however, it is interesting that two other tough mutuals, Cosmopolitan and Consolidated, have respective loss ratios of 93 percent and 78.5 percent which are high. Furthermore, when the loss ratios of stock insurers are compared in the aggregate with the loss ratios of mutuals, the putatively more liberal stock companies actually had a lower loss ratio in 1968—75.9 percent compared with 78.5 percent for the mutuals. See *1968 Loss and Expense Ratios,* New York Insurance Department, 123 William Street, New York City, table II, p. 110 (based on addition of columns 3 and 6).

than from liberal insurers. This explanation is predicated on the assumption that companies with tough settlement policies pay out less to satisfy claims than liberal insurers. This assumption is supported by comparing the loss ratios (percentage of premiums paid out to claimants) of the two insurers with the worst reputations among the Manhattan lawyers interviewed (Allstate and Empire Mutual) and two of the companies with good reputations (Aetna and Zurich American). The liberal insurers indeed had higher loss ratios (Table 3.3).

By chance, one of the personal injury victims in the client sample was employed as a defense attorney by one of the smaller New York insurance companies. Mr. Atwood, in his early thirties, had used another attorney to settle his own claim for a whiplash injury. We talked less about his claim than about the unpleasant aspects of his law practice. Mr. Atwood's view of the claims process as defense counsel is a bitter one.

> Frankly, we are in business to wear out plaintiffs. In the process we take our 6 percent interest for as long as we can. Companies are smart to do this. This is big business; it's dirty business. We're not a charity out to protect the plaintiff's welfare. Take the case I was trying today. The other lawyer [for the plaintiff] earns twice what I do and drives around in a Cadillac. But he doesn't know what he's doing. His client's got a good claim for a fractured skull. *I want this bastard to win* [italics mine] . . . and he'll blow it. Today I laid the foundation for contributory negligence, which is very doubtful, and the

other lawyer made no attempt to knock it down. The plaintiff is a sweet, gentle guy—a Puerto Rican. I met him in the john at recess and I told him that there was nothing personal in my working against him, that I was just doing my job. I think he understood this.

Mr. Atwood is bothered by the cruelty and selfishness he finds in his work and needs to rationalize it. "It's not my fault, I want him to win. It's his lawyer's fault and his own fault for not getting a better lawyer like me." "If the client gets nothing," he said, "it won't be my doing; it will be the jury's responsibility and that stupid contributory negligence rule."

The exact extent of unscrupulous insurer practices in the liability claims field is not known. Dispassionate analysis is hard to find in the climate of open antagonism and ideological "war" between insurer trade associations and the negligence bar.[25] On one side, the American Trial Lawyer's Association, the organization that particularly represents personal injury plaintiffs' lawyers, criticizes insurers for inflated profits, dilatory tactics, harassment of their clients, and failure generally to meet the needs of the public. On the other side, the American Insurance Association, the American Mutual Insurance Alliance, the National Association of Independent Insurers, the Federation of Insurance Counsel (representing insurance lawyers), and the Defense Research Institute (which performs a watchdog function against the negligence bar) criticize the lawyer's contingent fee, ambulance-chasing methods, abuse of the jury system, and padding of medical expenses.[26]

Identifying the real and ideal standards of insurer conduct is beyond the scope of this research. It is fair to say, however, that most insurers would feel it is legitimate to exploit the client's anxieties about his potential losses from the claim. Philip Hermann, for example, a "switch-hitting" attorney who has been a lawyer for both plaintiffs and defendants, implies that the defense counsel who fails to exploit the plaintiff's uncertainties is remiss:

> The plaintiff . . . will always be concerned that the verdict may be less than what was offered or may be zero. Too, he may be concerned with losing time from his job and the effect this may have upon his continued employment or

---

[25] This is suggested in the *Wall Street Journal* lead article of February 13, 1967: "Lawyers, Auto Insurers Open Name-Calling War."

[26] Compare, for example, "The Injury Industry and the Law Explosion," a report of the Defense Research Institute, Inc., 1212 W. Wisconsin Ave., Milwaukee, Wis.; with Howard Oleck, "Reforms Needed in Negligence Practice," *Cleveland-Marshall Law Review* 6 (September 1967): 388–409. One of the more constructive confrontations between insurers and plaintiffs' lawyers is summarized in a report of workshop sessions held at the University of Illinois on the *Crisis in Car Insurance*. It is published under that title, edited by Robert Keeton, Jeffrey O'Connell, and Jon McCord (Urbana: University of Illinois Press, 1968), pp. 258–273.

promotion, the economic loss of out-of-pocket expenses, the cost of the court appearance of a doctor or doctors and other expenses that he must bear, the strain of appearing at trial, and what others may say, particularly if he turns down an offer to receive less at the hands of the jury. Although the plaintiff will only be directly accessible to the insurance adjuster prior to his employment of an attorney, sometimes at pretrials and other meetings these fears can be indirectly employed to heighten his uncertainty.[27]

Based on client reports, harrassment by the claim adjuster is not a serious problem. Only one-third of the clients (20 of 59) were ever directly contacted by an adjuster. Only three of these report bothersome treatment. Mr. Meyer described a comic opera experience with an apparent adjuster who came into his hospital room claiming to be a reporter wanting a newspaper interview. Mr. Meyer is convinced that the man wore a thickly waxed false mustache. He left when Mr. Meyer asked to see his press credentials. Mr. Meyer was more amused than aggravated. For most clients, contact with the insurer is indirect—through what the client's attorney reports. It is often useful for the attorney to represent the insurer as a scapegoat even where he is not especially obstructive.[28] A little over half the sample cases (31 of 59) were settled before the pretrial examination mentioned by Mr. Hermann. In the rest of the cases there is direct contact with the insurance lawyer—and the ordeal of the pretrial EBT.

Six interviewees (five of them women) complained of being bullied by the defense lawyer during the EBT. Miss Schiff told me that at the time of the accident, she had been engaged to the man in whose car she was a passenger.

> At the [EBT] the insurance lawyer was a son-of-a-bitch and came right out and said that my boyfriend should deny that we had been engaged. Their lawyer tried to make me out to be some kind of liar and I felt defenseless. The pretrial hearing lasted, oh God, 10 hours, and I put my leg up with fatigue—and one of the defense lawyers accused me of sitting that way in the car at the time of the accident . . . which was absurd . . . and I was appalled at the . . . uh . . . crudity and lack of gallantry and the deliberate . . . uh . . . what's the word . . . besmirching . . . uhn. . . . I thought it was ugly.

To withstand this baiting, the claimant would seem to need emotional reserves of unflappability which many of us lack even in the best of circumstances. The aggressive counterattack of one's own attorney and his continued support and encouragement can also help. This, Mrs. Federman says, she did not receive at her EBT.

---

[27] Hermann, *Better Settlements through Leverage,* pp. 23–24.
[28] See Chapter 4, "How Lawyers Resolve Conflicting Interests With Clients."

> My lawyer had to leave the [EBT] for another appointment early. He left his younger associate to take his place. The defense lawyer questioned me again and again about the accident and, . . . unh . . . I don't know why, he . . . tripped me into seeming to say that I had walked into a parked car [instead of the truth which] was that I was hit by the car while it was moving. My lawyer was furious at me for opening my big yap.

Apparently the young attorney did not bring out in the record on re-direct questioning that Mrs. Federman's misstatement could not possibly have been the true circumstances. The defendant had already admitted to hitting the plaintiff. Subsequently, Mrs. Federman was induced to make a low settlement by her own attorney's warning that her poor performance at the EBT might lead to a jury awarding her nothing at all. This would have been most unlikely given the perfection of the liability issue and the seriousness of her injuries.

The Judge

There are four occasions on which a judge can directly influence a claim. (1) If the injured party is a minor, New York law requires that a judge review the fairness to the child of any settlement offer acceptable to his guardian (usually a parent), and also the fairness of his lawyer's fee. (2) A claimant can choose to have his case tried exclusively before a judge—so long as the other litigant agrees. Either litigant can demand a jury trial. (3) If a case is neither settled nor dropped by the time it is called on the calendar, a mediating judge can influence an eve-of-trial settlement. (4) If a jury trial is held, by his rulings on questions of law and by his facial and vocal reactions to the litigants and their evidence, he can influence the jury's perspective on the case. Each occasion is one of uncertainty for the client and his attorney. The assignment of cases to judges is largely a matter of chance.

If a personal injury case has not been settled by the time it is called for trial on the court calendar, it is reviewed by one judge before being assigned to another for trial. The reviewing judge schedules a conference with the plaintiff's and the defendant's attorneys and tries to bring about an eleventh-hour settlement. Only if this mediation effort fails, is a trial date scheduled. This judge-mediated negotiation is referred to as the "blockbuster" settlement. This slang term was coined to characterize the function of this mediation to break through calendar congestion. But it also accurately, if unintentionally, conveys a fitting sense of the way many judges approach the mediation. They see their function as a "knocking together of blockheads"—the need to ram a settlement down the throats of the reluctant parties in the interests of judicial dispatch. This "blockbuster" approach is widespread in both the Civil and Supreme Courts, even though it receives periodic criticism from leading judges and members of the bar. Bernard Botein, who was until 1969 presiding Justice of the Appellate Division First Department, said this in a 1966 speech:

> I suspect that knowledgeable lawyers in this country delay settling cases which they dare not try, because they are confident that at every juncture of their cases' progress they will find allies in judges who will press (injudiciously) for settlement.[29]

The judge has powerful leverage over trial attorneys. He can threaten to prejudge their future appearances before him if they do not persuade their clients to accept settlement on the terms he thinks fair. Mr. Getz's story illustrates the use by a judge of this leverage and gives a fascinating glimpse into how the "blockbuster" settlement works:

> The judge strongly wanted a settlement, but we were quite far apart. We were asking for something like $55,000 and they were offering something like $30,000. . . . Eventually my lawyer said, "This judge likes to settle. He thinks he's Solomon. He hates to try a case; he's a great one for split the difference"—that would be $42,500. What do you think?' I liked that in my lawyer. He was willing to talk to me—maybe not in as finite detail as I would have liked, but still, well. He said $42,500 was a pretty good settlement figure, that we might get $60,000 or even more before a jury, but you couldn't be sure. There was one other element he mentioned. We might have to try the case before this judge and it would antagonize him if we had rejected his compromise offer. Then the judge asked to see me to see the visible damage. My lawyers coached me that I was to be very deferential and call him "your honor" every time I addressed him. This was a new thing for me. I thought that was only in a courtroom. But you've got to treat a judge with kid gloves all the time.
>
> He called me in and asked me if I thought it was a fair settlement. I was already coached about what to say: "Well, your honor, do *you* think it's fair?" He said, "I do and the important thing is that your lawyers do and they have a lot of experience with these things!" Then came the really interesting part. He called in the insurance company lawyers and turned to the lawyer and, calling him by his first name he said, "Sam, I have one word for you—no ifs, ands or buts, no questions, no comments—the word is $42,500." . . . It was comic relief. The money man for the insurer swallowed his adam's apple and said "no, absolutely no, never." But his lawyer hauled him off to a corner of the room and after a fast huddle, they came out saying "yes" . . . later, we talked to the insurance lawyer. He said to me, "I think you went through a lot, I always thought so and I wanted to see you get some good money. The reason there was that huddle is that my money man was really being difficult.

---

[29] Address before the New York State Bar Association, at the House of the Association of the Bar of the City of New York, February 4, 1966.

This . . . insurer [a mutual] is the worst company I have to deal with. [Sam is the defense trial attorney for several insurance companies.] I was going to take that settlement for two reasons: (1) that was a fair settlement and (2) I'm going to have to deal with this judge in the future." I learned then that the judge has tremendous power—not like on the Perry Mason show. He forced a settlement down the money man's throat. . . . This seems unfair, like unjust pressure. It might have been my throat.

Mr. Getz was willing to accept the judge's dictate. Mr. Patrick, injured in a gas explosion while on duty as a city fireman, was not. In his case, his lawyer persuaded him that he had no choice but to accede to the judge's wishes. According to Mr. Patrick, the judge asked him what was his income after recuperation and retirement from the fire department. In the four years intervening between the accident and the eve-of-trial conference, Mr. Patrick had become a successful salesman—doubling his previous fireman's income. When Mr. Patrick stated his income for 1967, the judge said, "Why do you want so much money when you are now doing so well? I think you should be very satisfied with $8,000." From this statement it would appear that an element in the judge's determination of fair damages was the principle that a man is entitled to less if his income increases after an accident. This principle conflicts with substantive doctrine; damages are only to be based on special damages, disability, and pain and suffering.[30] As Mr. Patrick put it, "My increased earnings don't make the constant headaches I still get [from the explosion] any less painful. I thought judges were supposed to apply the law as it is, not make up their own rules."

The plaintiff has no way of knowing whether he will be assigned to a friendly or a hostile judge. There is impressive evidence, reported by Zeisel, Kalven, and Buchholz, that judges are less friendly to plaintiffs than are juries.

From a nationwide survey of some 3,000 personal injury jury trials in which the presiding judge reported how he would have decided the case had he sat without a jury . . . [It was found that] the total amount which these judges would have awarded was about 20 percent smaller than the total amount the juries did in fact award.[31]

An analysis of this finding awaits further work by the University of Chicago Jury Project. One complaint made by many plantiffs' attorneys is that insur-

---

[30] In fact, "In most states the law is clear that there may be recovery for injury to earning capacity even though the plaintiff may be earning the same or even more after the injury." Joseph Kelner, *Personal Injury: Successful Litigation Techniques* (New York: Bender, 1965), vol. 3, p. 1081.

[31] Hans Zeisel, Harry Kalven, and Bernard Buchholz, *Delay in the Court* (Boston: Little, Brown, 1959), p. 73, fn. 4.

ance lawyers can more easily cultivate the friendship of judges than all but the most successful plaintiff attorneys. It is a common practice—especially in the Civil Court—for a single judge to be assigned exclusively the 100-odd pending cases of a single insurance company. For one month, the judge and the insurance lawyer are in daily contact. Any individual plaintiffs' lawyer will represent two, or at most, three of the claimants. As one of the interviewed attorneys put it:

> Insurers get preferential treatment from many civil judges the same way district attorneys get preferential treatment from criminal judges.

Familiarity may sometimes breed respect.

It is a cliche to refer to Kafka in the context of a courtroom experience. But as Mrs. Silber recounts her experience in Manhattan Civil Court, one can empathize with her feelings of helplessness and defeat. Granted that this is an emotional—even theatrical—woman. Still, how many of us would have remained calm in her circumstance where the judge literally let the insurance lawyer run the show?

> We came into the courtroom and at the long attorney's table there's a fat man sitting with a big cigar. . . . This man is ordering the court attendants [probably his assistant attorneys] around; he's got his papers strewn all over the table. Subsequently I learned he was the attorney for the insurance company . . . the only defendant in all the cases that day . . . acting as if the courtroom belonged to him. One of the most shocking exhibitions I have ever seen is when the judge came in and one of the clerks called out "no smoking" and called him by name, and he kept the cigar in his mouth. As the clerk called out a case, every case, he refused to settle. Where the claim was, say, for fifteen hundred dollars he'd say, "nothing" or "$25." His whole attitude and that of the young men with him was disgusting. This is not a courtroom this is like a Groucho Marx movie. Now whether the judge didn't know enough or care enough I don't know. I was in such a rage. The judge was paying about as much attention to him or what was going on as to last year's snow. You can hardly expect a judge who listens to this stuff day in and day out to take any of this to heart. . . .
>
> We came back from lunch and I don't know how the settlement got arranged —because I wasn't being told anything. . . . We are called in, finally, to the judge's chambers. There are two young men there—apparently the associates of the cigar smoker, and my lawyer, whom I met for the first time at the court that morning. The judge does not rise when a lady walks into the room. One of the young lawyers looks at me and says, "You're prone to accidents aren't you?" I said, "I don't understand, this is the first accident I know of." He says, "hunh (a snort). You live on West _____ Street and you were in four other accidents." I said, "Stop right there. I never lived at that address. I have lived

at my present address for 30 years." "Well," he said "there's a [Mrs. Silber] who lived at that address." At this point I was so mad I started to have a heart attack. And the judge just lets him go on. . . . I had to take some pills; they had to get me some water. I was just so blooming mad. Well, after awhile I thought to myself, "this just isn't worth getting sick over." So I agreed to settle and it was for a truly ridiculous amount. . . . When I got home, the first thing I did was take a long, hot bath. I felt so unclean. . . .

We can thus see that for a number of the interviewed clients, the defense attorneys, judges, and impersonal courtrooms are a threat to their personal composure as well as to the success of their claim. Only one client singled out a judge for special praise in his demeanor. No insurance attorney received a client's praise. Mr. Sugarman highlighted this negative impact when, in referring to being questioned, he said, "He began to 'integregate' [sic] me." The slip of the tongue says it precisely. The client feels like an accused criminal who must undergo constant interrogation. His *integrity* is under attack.

Court Trial Calendars

The best known and most thoroughly documented influence defeating the claims of accident victims is judicial delay. Delay is primarily a problem for tort (personal or property injury) claimants wanting a jury trial. As a matter of policy, the New York courts are administered to facilitate the handling of most criminal, commercial, and nonjury tort cases. In June 1968, the delay between the time a tort case was put on the jury calendar and the time it was pronounced ready for trial was 34 months in the Supreme Court in Manhattan and 30 months in the Civil Court in Manhattan.[32] The delay figures vary from season to season and from court to court in the other four boroughs and in the neighboring counties. The delay in New York has tended to be greater than in most other American jurisdictions. Its relative impact is reflected in the differences between the present sample and the Michigan sample in the time taken to terminate serious injury claims. It is to be noted (Table 3.4), that more than half of the Michigan cases were dropped or settled within one year, while more than half of the Manhattan cases remain pending after two years. Of the Manhattan cases, 25.4 percent are still pending after four years.

For the accident victim, the costs of delay are great. Not only does it work against his rehabilitation by denying him money at the time the rehabilitative expenses are incurred, increase the pressures to take an unfairly low settlement, and play upon his psychological uncertainties, but it hampers the plaintiff's problems of proof if the case is ever tried. Witnesses die and move

---

[32] New York State Judicial Conference, *1968 Annual Report*, pp. 214–216.

**Table 3.4: Comparative Time for Claim Termination between
This Study's Manhattan Sample and the Michigan Sample**

Time	Manhattan	Michigan[a]
Up to 6 months	5% (3)	31%
6–12 months	13% (8)	27%
1–2 years	24% (14)	20%
2 years or more	58% (34)	22%

[a] Conard et al., *Automobile Accident Costs and Payments,* Figure 6–28, p. 222.

away. Details are forgotten. Injuries cease to be visually dramatic. "The delay is a disgrace," said Mrs. Forman. "My leg was a mess for years. Four years later when I get into court, the jury couldn't see the heel was bulged." Apparently court officials have decided that it is more important in our society to attempt to keep non-tort cases more or less up to date, even though criminal delays of more than six or eight months remain common. If this policy were changed, delay would be shifted and the dispatch of jury tort cases could be greatly increased.[33] Why such delay exists and what to do about it is amply discussed elsewhere.[34] There appear to be no easy solutions, though considerable progress has been made in the Civil Court in Manhattan so that, by mid-1972, it had become possible to obtain a trial within a few months of service of the pleadings.

The Substantive Legal Doctrine of Negligence

A fourth hurdle for the claimant is the substantive legal doctrine of the negligence law. To prosecute successfully a personal injury claim in court, the plaintiff's attorney must prove each of the following basic elements of a negligence cause of action:

---

[33] Zeisel, et al., *Delay in the Court,* p. 29.

[34] The best brief presentation of the problem I know is by Maurice Rosenberg, "Court Congestion: Status, Causes and Proposed Remedies," in *The Courts, the Public, and the Law Explosion,* ed. Harry Jones (Englewood Cliffs, N.J.: Prentice-Hall, 1965), pp. 29–59. In addition to Zeisel et al., *Delay in the Court,* the most complete and up-to-date collection of articles (including Rosenberg's) is contained in Walter E. Meyer Research Institute of Law, *Dollars, Delay, and the Automobile Victim* (Indianapolis, Ind.: Bobbs-Merrill, 1968).

1. A duty by the defendant (usually to exercise reasonable care) toward the plaintiff
2. A breach of that duty ("negligence")
3. The plaintiff's freedom from contributory negligence
4. A causal chain linking the defendant with the accident and linking the accident with the injury
5. That the plaintiff was injured or otherwise damaged by the defendant's negligence

The first three elements determine the perfection of the liability issue.

Under the law of New York, certain factual settings in which accidents occur, totally by chance, weaken the victim's claim. Take, for example, the case of Mrs. Reed: the presence of ice on the broken sidewalk raised questions of whether the City had met its duty to pedestrians to maintain sidewalks generally free from hazards and whether it had met its duty to pedestrians to maintain sidewalks free from ice within the period of time that had elapsed since the last precipitation. To make things more difficult for Mrs. Reed, there were two more issues: First, if the City neglected one duty but not the other, which condition proximately caused Mrs. Reed's fall? If a jury found that it was the ice and not the breaks in the pavement and if they found that the city had not neglected its ice removal duty, Mrs. Reed's claim would fail. Second, was Mrs. Reed contributorially negligent in failing to exercise reasonable care by watching her step? If a jury found against her on any one of these elements, Mrs. Reed would not recover a cent, regardless of her injuries and expenses. The perfection of a claimant's liability can be ranked approximately according to the following scheme: perfect, good, fair, and poor liability. In 60 percent of the cases in this sample the liability is perfect. In 10 percent of the cases the liability is only fair or poor. This confirms that lawyers tend to refuse claims in which there is a substantial risk of no recovery.

The Jury

The unpredictability of juries is the fifth uncertain influence on the claims process. From interviews with trial attorneys, it seems that jury trials are uniformly preferred to nonjury trials; but there is still apprehension that—no matter how strong a case is on paper—a jury may still mysteriously deny recovery to the claimant. Sample clients constantly report that their lawyers warned them about the hazards of giving one's case to a jury. In some instances this probably is a tactic to encourage a pretrial settlement which the lawyer has other reasons for preferring.[35] But I would guess that it also reflects the law-

---

[35] See Chapter 4, p. 109.

yers' own anxieties. All but the most successful fear the all-or-nothing gamble of a trial. From stories told by clients who have served on juries, anxiety is not out of place. Mr. Beanstock, a self-made millionaire, recalls being foreman some years ago of a jury reminiscent of the one in the movie *Twelve Angry Men*. As he recalls that experience, the plaintiff was a totally disabled Polish-American washerwoman. She was asking for $60,000 in damages. Although the defendant's liability was clear, one woman juror thought the plaintiff was overreaching and decided that she didn't deserve anything. According to Mr. Beanstock, "the other members of the jury agreed with her—that the woman should get nothing—so they could get the case over and go home." He claimed that he held them there until they agreed to at least give her $15,000—a compromise verdict which is against the law, but which judges often allow anyway.

One of the client interviewees, Mr. Minton, was warned by his lawyer to accept a settlement after the trial was underway, for fear of jury prejudice. Mr. Minton is a black man married to a younger white woman. It is hard to know if a Manhattan jury would have been offended by an interracial marriage. Mr. Minton wasn't convinced that they would be; but he was not naive. As he put it, "I'm not Rap Brown, but there is a double standard of justice in this country." Reluctantly he took the settlement.

"In the law, nothing is certain but the expense," wrote Samuel Butler. Clients who have been at least part way through the claims process have learned this lesson. The interviewees were asked the following question: "If you were charged with a crime, would you be confident that the court would be just?" Of the 53 who answered the questions, two-thirds (35) said "No." It is clear from the preceding discussion that making a claim for a serious personal injury is a difficult, costly, individual, and uncertain experience.

CONCLUSION

This chapter has identified and tried to make comprehensible three kinds of uncertainty in the claims process. These are (1) the choices presented to the attorney and client in advancing the claim; (2) the victim's problems in adjusting to the accident's impact and the problems presented to the attorney and client in lessening this impact and in handling the claim effectively yet in a way which reflects the client's desires; and (3) the problems presented to the attorney and client in dealing with the uncertainties imposed by the often arbitrary institutions of the claims process largely beyond their control. Some kinds of uncertainty, like tomorrow's weather, are easily tolerated. The uncertainties of the claims process, at least for the seriously injured, tend, however, to be burdensome. It is tempting to react to this costly uncertainty as if it were a defect in the law. Two eminent lawyers have gone so far as to conclude that "The two chief defects in the American law are its uncertainty and its complexity."[36] We so want the law to be clear and simple that we half fool ourselves into believing that for the legal expert it is. This is a keystone of the traditional model: the expert is objective and possesses objective techniques that make things simple and clear. The expert can master the criteria and techniques of professional problems which are too complex and uncertain for the layman.

On the contrary, the uncertainty is of such a nature that the client is in a good position to respond to it constructively. Neither the client nor the lawyer can make certain what is uncertain. However, through a process of mutual adjustment to their respective wants and concerns, they can balance the risks and adopt a strategy that will selectively minimize those kinds of uncertainty that are most threatening. It is because so many of the factors that will influence the claim outcome are unforseeable even to the specialist, that a lay client who knows his own feelings is qualified to participate in the assessment of what is to be gained or lost by alternative choices. If certainty is the goal of professional problem solving, then the problems of personal injury law are too complex even for the experts. If the goal is something less, to cope with uncertainty, to live with it, and make as few mistakes as possible, the law need not be seen as too complex for either the lawyer or the client. The very fact that the client has so much to gain or lose by the responses made to the uncertainty of the claims process makes the complexity of this uncertainty accessible. Practical consequences provide a ready tool for stripping complexity down to essentials. Furthermore, the explanation of the claims process in this chapter demonstrates that in spite of its complexity that process can be made intelligible to laymen—even uninvolved laymen. It would seem, then, that the third tenet of the traditional model governing professional-client relationships, that client problems have a single best technical and predictable solution inaccessible to lay understanding, may properly be questioned—at least with respect to personal injury claims.

---

[36] Albert Blaustein and Charles Porter, *The American Lawyer* (Chicago: University of Chicago Press, 1954), p. 320.

Chapter Four: Conflicts of Interest between Lawyer and Client in Personal Injury Problem-Solving

An attorney plays many roles while performing his work. In the abstract, he is supposed to serve as an "officer of the court" maintaining "the public interest." Concretely, he deals with judges and court clerks in relationships continuing beyond any individual client's case. He builds and maintains contacts with claims adjusters, defense lawyers, and medical witnesses in the role of negotiating intermediary between the claimant and the insurer. He tries to project an attractive image to potential client markets—both to the lay public and to colleagues who may refer cases to him. Concurrently, he tries to avoid difficulties with public and professional agencies which enforce professional norms. Throughout, there are the demands of his private life. Each attorney who takes negligence cases must develop his own distinctive strategy for meeting and balancing his set of roles. This balancing process is a source of considerable pressure because each role is demanding in itself and the several role demands continually conflict, not only with each other but with the lawyer's role as a fully vigorous and disinterested representative of each of his clients. These conflicts decisively influence the way in which the client's claim is handled.

Although sociologists have depicted in numerous monographs the conflicts that arise for men and women in dealing with others in highly structured work settings, and have even developed a theory to describe and explain this "role conflict,"[1] the traditional notion that competent professionals are able to avoid conflicts of interest harmful to their clients continues to prevail. In this chapter we shall see that attorneys making personal injury claims are in

---

[1] Bruce Biddle and Edwin Thomas, eds., *Role Theory: Concepts and Research* (New York: Wiley, 1966).

many cases, in an economic conflict of interest which restricts their motivations and capacities for serving the "best interests" of their clients.

THE LAWYER'S CONFLICT WITH HIS CLIENT

The single source of pressure upon the lawyer most likely to affect adversely the client's interest, and which can most easily be documented, is the strain of prolonged litigation and the economics of case preparation. Simply put, a quick settlement is often in the lawyer's financial interest, while waiting the insurer out is often in the client's financial interest. To understand how this can be, consider the illustrative schedule (Table 4.1) of how a plaintiff attorney's time might plausibly be spent on a single medium-value claim, raising no special problems, where the attorney is experienced and very conscientious in case preparation. Two competing pressures affect the lawyer's motivation to terminate the case: on the one hand, the sooner he settles, the less effort expended pursuing the claim; on the other hand, given the reluctance of most insurers to make generous early settlements the longer he holds out the greater the recovery he can anticipate. If attorneys billed their clients on an hourly basis, the lawyer's motive for early settlement would be canceled. This, however, is almost never done. Instead, the client pays a fee contingent upon the eventual recovery. If there is no recovery, there is no fee; with some recovery, a large percentage of it goes to the attorney as a fee. Since January 1, 1957, the size of a lawyer's profit in Manhattan and the Bronx and within the last few years in Brooklyn, Queens, Staten Island, Suffolk, Nassau, Westchester, and Rockland counties (but not elsewhere in New York State) has been limited to the upper-limit fee schedule set by the Appellate Divisions, First and Second Department. The schedule makes no distinction between permissible fees for cases settled early with little legal work product and cases that go to trial and take a great deal of the lawyer's time.[2]

The contingent fee "is now the almost exclusive method for financing most claims handled by our courts. There is probably no other single aspect of law practice that has generated so much heated controversy."[3]

Most attorneys who handle negligence claims favor the contingent fee for three reasons: (1) it brings them poor clients who might otherwise be unable or unwilling to hire a lawyer to make a claim; (2) it brings good money

---

[2] Appendix B.

[3] A thorough and noncommittal discussion of the controversy is to be found in F. B. MacKinnon, *Contingent Fees for Legal Services* (Chicago: Aldine, 1964). This quotation is from page 209.

from medium-sized claims settled quickly; (3) if they are lucky enough to get a client with the kind of six-figure claim of which lawyers dream, they can gross more than $50,000 at one shot even if they go to trial. A survey of Mis-

Table 4.1: Attorney Time Schedule

Work Task	Time Expended (in hours)	Cumulative
First interview with plaintiff	2	
Telephone conversations with defendant insurer and plaintiff's doctor	2	½ work day
Second interview with plaintiff	2	
Medical examination of plaintiff by insurance doctor with lawyer present	2	
Collecting accident and police reports	3	
Talking with witnesses	4	
Viewing the accident site	3	
Drafting a summons and complaint, bill of particulars, note of issue and general preference motion[a]	9	
Conversation with insurer	1	3½ work days
Preparation of plaintiff for examination before trial	3	
Examination before trial	8	
Preparation for conference with insurer	3	
Conference with insurer	3	
Motion for summary judgment[b]	4	
Brief on motion	8	
Pretrial conference with judge	3	7½ work days
Preparing plaintiff for trial	4	
Waiting for trial in court	24	
Trial and final wait in court	24	14 work days

SOURCE: Adapted from James Brennan *The Cost of the American Judicial System* (West Haven, Conn.: Professional Library Press, 1966), table 2, p. 8. This and the discussion that follows is based on interviews with lawyer informants and on lawyer questionnaire responses.

a The complaint states the basis for the lawsuit; the bill of particulars states the specific facts on which the suit is based; a note of issue is an assertion of readiness to have the case tried; a general preference motion gets the case put on the regular jury trial calendar.

b A motion for summary judgment is a request that the judge find for the plaintiff without the necessity of a trial, on the basis of the pleadings and additional submitted proof. These are prepared in the form of affidavits or exhibits showing that there is no meritorious defense to the cause of action. It should be granted where there are not triable issues of fact (other than the amount of damages, which may be tried separately from the issue of liability), there is no meritorious defense, and the complaint states a valid cause of action. It is, in practice, rarely granted in tort cases—a source of resentment to many plaintiff's lawyers because it could result in the avoidance of much unnecessary delay.

souri clients uncovered a great deal of public resentment toward the excessiveness of many personal injury contingent fees thought to be unrelated to attorney effort expended. Interestingly, however, contingent fees in principle were overwhelmingly endorsed by the Missouri respondents, although at a lower pro-rata share of the claim than is presently charged in that state.[4] The contingent fee seems to some a better guarantee of disinterested service than the hourly or standard bill (which is thought to be easy to pad).

The widespread assumption that the contingent fee makes the lawyer a "partner" of the client in his claim with complete mutuality of interest in the ultimate case disposition is, in dollars and cents, simply not true. To see why, let us add some details to the hypothetical medium-sized claim, not unlike several made by the sampled clients. Let us value the attorney's work time at $40 an hour (a conservative figure since approximately $20 of this figure usually goes for office overhead) and assume that he is both efficient and hard working and puts in eight productive hours per work day. Assume further that the defendant's insurer's claims adjuster has formulated the following settlement policy: (1) to make an initial settlement offer of $2,000 during the first three months after the accident; (2) to raise it to $3,000 just prior to a scheduled examination before trial (about one year after the accident); and (3) to make a final offer of $4,000 during the final pretrial negotiation (about three years after the accident). Assume further that the plaintiff's lawyer is reasonably confident that he can get a jury verdict if the case goes to trial and that, if tried, the verdict would be for about $8,000. Finally, assume (as is frequently the situation) that the attorney charges the client the maximum fee permitted under the Appellate Division rules. Table 4.2 shows the

Table 4.2: Relative Returns to Lawyer and Client at Each Recovery Stage

Time after Accident	Gross Recovery	Lawyer's Fee[a]	Lawyer's Costs[b]	Lawyer's Net	Client's Net
3 months	$2,000	$ 900	$ 160	$ 740	$1,100
1 year	3,000	1,300	1,120	180	1,700
3 years	4,000	1,650	2,400	−750	2,350
trial	8,000	3,050	4,480	−1,430	4,950

[a] For the sliding-scale fee standard see Appendix B, p. 216.
[b] Based on work tasks set forth in Table 4.1.

[4] *Missouri Bar Prentice-Hall Survey* (Jefferson City: The Missouri Bar, 1963), pp. 118–123.

relative returns that the attorney and his client will realize at each of the four termination stages. In the given case, the lawyer's financial interest lies in quick settlement at the discounted early offer of $2,000. The client's financial interest lies in going to trial. A lawyer who literally made his client's interest his own, in more than a few of these cases, would quickly be out of business.

THE LAWYER'S OPTIONS FOR REDUCING CONFLICT WITH HIS CLIENT

Presented with the need to make a living and the desire to make a good living, the lawyer to whom a client brings a personal injury claim has several possible options. Four of these can reduce the interest-conflict between himself and the client, independent of the lawyer-client relationship. These are: weeding out unprofitable claims at the outset; farming out the case to a specialist for a referral fee; using economies of specialization to reduce overhead without sacrificing work product; and illegally bribing the claims adjuster.

Lawyers regularly refuse cases in which there is a serious doubt about the defendant's liability. Where liability is in doubt, going to trial becomes an all-or-nothing gamble. The more potential clients a lawyer has coming to him, the more discriminating he can afford to be. Lawyers at the top of their profession such as the New York negligence attorneys, the Fuchsbergs, Harry Gair, and Harry Lipsig, can afford to turn down all cases in which the liability is not near-perfect and in which the anticipated recovery at trial is less than five figures. Less successful negligence specialists cannot afford to be quite so selective; but they still can afford to reject very imperfect liability cases. In 60 percent (36 of 60) of the claims made by the sample clients, the liability issue was perfect. In only one case was the liability issue poor.

The second option which attracts many general practitioners is to accept the client's case and then farm it out to a negligence specialist.

Referrals are advantageous to both the referring general practitioner and the receiving specialist. The referring attorney receives a fee with almost no effort. The specialist is provided with a ready-made client market without resorting to advertising—which is strictly proscribed. A rule of the *Code of Professional Responsibility,* Disciplinary Rule 2-107, sets three standards for the ethical farming of cases: (1) the client must consent after receiving full disclosure that a division of fees will be made; (2) the division must be made in proportion to the services performed and responsibility assumed by each lawyer; and (3) the total fee must not exceed reasonable limits which, in

Manhattan, means the Appellate Division fee ceiling.[5] This rule is systematically broken by practicing attorneys. In six of the sample cases clients say they were not informed and did not consent to having their cases farmed out to other lawyers. Moreover, in most of the cases where consent was obtained, the referring attorney was paid between one-third and one-fourth of the total fee even though clients report that, so far as they could tell he made almost no contribution to the work product. This practice is acknowledged but not attacked by the disciplinary institutions of the bar. In fact, one informed observer who declined to be quoted said that there is a tacit understanding among disciplinarians that violation of this rule is not to be treated as a serious matter—unless the conduct is so flagrant as to constitute the solicitation of cases rather than the practice of law. Thus, in *In the Matter of Louis Kaye,* an attorney was disbarred for farming 50 cases within 15 months, rendering little or no service and, in each instance, receiving an advance against his share of the fee.[6]

Whether farming out serves the client's interest is more complex. A 1961 study of the economics of personal injury litigation in the First Department discovered that, in more than half of the sampled cases, lawyers' fees do not reach the permissible fee ceiling. However, bringing in an extra attorney does increase the fee toward the ceiling.[7] In Mr. Getz's case, the referring lawyer did assume considerable responsibility for pursuing the claim—much as a solicitor would do in England. The case was farmed out to an outstanding lawyer whom the client might not have found on his own. But in some sample cases, the referring lawyer had apparently held on to the case in the hope of getting an effortless early settlement. When this didn't work, the case was farmed out, belatedly, causing unnecessary delay to the client. Mr. Brackman, a college professor, told me:

> I found out that one of the other parties [in the three-car accident] had gone to trial and gotten a judgment one year before my case was turned over to a specialist. I know this because I appeared as a witness in this trial.

As it turned out, Mr. Brackman was grateful that his case was farmed out, because the specialist seemed to him to be "excellent—intelligent, perceptive,

---

[5] *Code of Professional Responsibility* (hereinafter cited as the *Code*), American Bar Association, 1969, Disciplinary Rule 2–107, p. 9; see also Section 603.5; Appellate Division First Department Rules, p. 217.

[6] *New York Law Journal* 155, no. 14 (January 20, 1966).

[7] Marc Franklin, Robert Chanin, and Irving Mark, "Accidents, Money, and the Law: A Study of the Economics of Personal Injury Litigation," in Walter E. Meyer Research Institute of Law, *Dollars, Delay and the Automobile Victim* (Indianapolis, Ind.: Bobbs-Merrill, 1968), p. 67.

to-the-point, and very businesslike." The referring lawyer [who had sat on the case for 21 months without filing suit] struck Mr. Brackman as a man unable "to speak one full sentence with proper grammar. He was a bit arrogant and acted bored. I disliked him intensely."

The fault is not with the practice of farming out as much as with un-qualified lawyers taking cases in the first instance and not referring clients to specialists. This is, to a great degree, the result of the bar's policy of treating all lawyers, once admitted to the bar, as "legally qualified to practice any field of law."[8] Many general practitioners are not as qualified as specialists to handle most negligence cases. Ethical Consideration 6-1 of the *Code of Professional Responsibility* states:

> [A lawyer] should strive to become and remain proficient in his practice and should accept employment only in matters which he is or intends to become competent to handle.[9]

But as Mr. Meyer realized about his first lawyer's misrepresenting himself as a specialist, "it is a rare man who will admit his own incompetence if that means losing a potential client." According to one commentator, "no cases have been found in which an attorney has been disciplined or held liable for failing to obtain the assistance of a specialist."[10] This is not to say that only specialists are qualified. Many lawyers who earn less than half their income from negligence claims nevertheless get good results for their clients. The decisive factor is probably not so much how much time the lawyer devotes to negligence practice per se as how talented and experienced he is as a trial attorney. Some lawyers make a speciality of litigation—developing skills in preparing cases for trial and in using courtroom procedures and techniques. Specialists in litigation sometimes develop competence in several substantive legal areas, not only in negligence but in criminal, matrimonial, administrative, and corporate litigation as well. When negotiating a negligence case, they make credible the threat of going to trial if the insurer is not forthcoming with a fair settlement. Many general practitioners, on the other hand, have never tried a case and have no intention of ever trying one. The nonattorney insurance adjuster who served on my expert case evaluation panel said that his employer and other insurance companies, as a matter of course, put different reserves on similar

---

[8] Glenn Greenwood and Robert Frederickson, *Specialization in the Medical and Legal Professions* (Mundelein, Ill.: Callaghan, 1964), p. 119.

[9] *Code*, p. 23.

[10] Russell Niles, "Ethical Prerequisites to Certification of Special Proficiency," *American Bar Association Journal* 49 (1963): 87.

claims according to their knowledge of the skills of the respective attorneys making the claim. If the insurer senses that the plaintiff's attorney has no stomach for a trial he will probably hold back from making a fair settlement.[11] This leaves the general practitioner with the choice of trying to persuade the client to take an unreasonably low settlement or, belatedly, farming out the case.

Other things being equal, specialists can take advantage of work economies not available to the generalist, and large firm specialists can take advantage of economies of scale not available to the solo specialist. When asked, "What about your work do you least enjoy?" an overwhelming majority of the sampled attorneys replied, "waiting in court." One said, "nine-tenths of the time I spend in court is wasted, waiting around doing nothing." This wasted time is the by-product of the procedure of court administration known as the calendar call. Calendar call is a way of determining who is present on any given day to seek a ruling of the court or to proceed with a trial. The clerk of the court reads the calendar, the list of pending legal matters scheduled in advance for hearing on that day. A typical court calendar in New York City involves more than 100 separate cases per day. Attorneys are not informed in advance at what time during the day their case will be called. They must therefore be present as soon as court opens, sitting while others' cases are called first. The courts are like the military: hurry up and wait. For the plaintiff's lawyer the risk of missing calendar call is that of having the plaintiff's suit thrown out of court. One of the longest delays occurs when the final pre-trial settlement effort has failed and both sides are prepared to pick a jury and go to trial. At that point, the claim is one of several cases ready for assignment to a judge to try. If there are many cases to be assigned before his, the lawyer may have to be present and have his witnesses on call until his case is called. Trial assignment may take two days or more of waiting. As can be seen in Table 4.1 approximately half of a trial attorney's time in cases which are actually tried may be spent in court.[12] General practitioners are more tied down to their offices than are trial attorneys and negligence specialists. A specialist is more likely to have several cases pending in any one court and can often dispose of matters involving three or four different cases during the same morning. Furthermore, specialists build up friendships with court per-

---

[11] The general practitioner's disadvantages are discussed by Philip Hermann, *Better Settlements through Leverage* (Rochester, N.Y.: Aqueduct Books, 1965), pp. 89–94.

[12] Recently, in an effort to reduce time wasted in court, clerks are permitting attorneys to leave their phone numbers and be on call only a few hours in advance of their appearance.

sonnel who protect them when they miss a calendar call. As one younger attorney in a two-man firm put it:

> An associate tells the judge, "Mr. Nizer can't be here until 2 P.M. your honor" and the judge says "Alright, we'll begin after lunch." With the rest of us, we have to be ready and excuses are often not accepted.

The more successful attorneys are freed from much of the waiting, which is left to younger associates. Large negligence firms are able to hire full-time accident investigators and maintain extensive legal libraries. Even solo specialists over time build up the contacts with judges and insurance adjusters that facilitate favorable consideration.

Nevertheless, it is not always true that a client gets better service from a big specialist firm than from a solo trial attorney. The one instance in which a client's file was reportedly misplaced, resulting in the case being stricken from the court calendar, happened to the client of one of the biggest and best-known negligence firms in the city. Two other clients whose cases were handled by big firms complained of being shunted off to the less experienced junior associates, never getting to see the firm's big men. Mrs. Mott, a housewife injured in a fall while boarding a plane, referred to herself as the "forgotten woman." She told me that she never personally met anyone from the firm. "All negotiations were handled over the telephone." If personal attention and constant reassurance are important to a client, he or she may be better off with an easily approachable attorney with less prestige. Not all clients benefit from a specialist's network of contacts. As one specialist stated,

> Relationships are very important. I can do better than the guy without them. For example, I can sit down with adjusters and get $500 where the case is worth nothing. In return, I may have to give up a few hundred dollars on another case so as to avoid the reputation of being a chiseler.

Where several claims are settled in a package, it is frequently (though not always) the case that what one claimant gains is at the expense of another claimant in the package. Package settlements, according to another lawyer (though unethical, and a violation of Appellate Division First Department Rules) are not uncommon.[13] "Many lawyers screw their clients," he told me "by waiting till they get three or four claims to settle with the same insurer."

There is one situation in which the client has a great deal to gain from unethical (in fact illegal) conduct by his attorney: where his attorney bribes an insurance adjuster to settle, generously, his client's claim at the insurance

---

[13] *Code*, Disciplinary Rule 5–106, p. 21; Section 603.9, Appellate Division First Department Rules.

company's expense. Mr. Atwood, the client who works as a defense attorney, alleges that a couple of years ago virtually all the adjusters in the New York office of one large insurer were fired when company investigators found they were "on the take." Bribes, when made, are usually placed through intermediaries known as "ten-point men." Ten-point men are lawyers to whom a case is farmed out for settlement. The referring attorney usually gives the intermediary "ten points" (10 percent of the settlement arranged) for handling the matter. The ten-point man keeps 5 percent for himself and uses the other 5 percent to pay off the adjuster. The chances are fair that payoffs were made, without the client's knowledge, in a couple of the sample claims, but it cannot be proved. One suspicious case is that of Mrs. Rolfe. She is a medical technician who reported sustaining badly cut knees (but no fracture) in an auto accident. Mrs. Rolfe sought very little information about or control over the conduct of her claim. Her lawyer's closing statement reports that 15 percent of the fee was paid to an attorney of whom she had no knowledge. The lawyer she used made no mention to her of bringing in outside counsel. The expert panel evaluated her case as worth $2,550. Mrs. Rolfe received $3,500 in settlement one year after the accident. These 15 points may or may not have been legitimately paid. Mr. Taub, the client who settled prematurely, thinks he recalls his lawyer telling him that a "fee had to be paid to the adjuster"; but he is not sure. George Osborne, director of the Coordinating Committee on Discipline for the First Department during the late 1960's admits that bribery is very difficult to uncover. Cash passes hands and no records are kept. If investigated, ten-point men can claim their fee was legitimately earned for their exercise of the special negotiating talents which many attorneys lack. The referring attorney can disclaim any knowledge of those "negotiating" techniques used by the intermediary. All he wants to know is that a settlement is made. There is no reason for the client to learn of the bribe and, even if a few clients were to discover what was going on, how many would come forward to give evidence against the lawyer who benefited them? Osborne does not know how widespread these bribes are, but sees them as a real problem. He guesses that only a small minority of the bar is systematically engaged in the payoffs.

.   The Coordinating Committee on Discipline was created in 1958 as an investigatory arm of the Appellate Division First Department. Its staff of attorneys have been particularly attentive to the problem of "ambulance chasing." They received periodic reports from the Judicial Conference which collects and compiles the retainer and closing statements attorneys are required to submit under the Appellate Division rules. Attorneys filing an unusually high number of statements in any given period are routinely checked. The staff also follows up evidence of patterns of systematic wrongdoing uncovered by local district attorneys and by the regular Committee on Grievances of the Bar Association of the City of New York which require on-going investigation beyond the scope of these latter authorities. The activity of the Coordinating Committee and the Committee on Grievances make an important contribution to the unusually high New York City disbarment rate.[14] Many negligence attorneys resent what they see as excessive and degrading supervision. As one respondent commented,

> Many associates and friends feel it is the attorney [rather than the client or public] who needs help and protection and that too many rules and regulations are promulgated which really harass an attorney and decrease and diminish his dignity. Similar restrictive requirements are not found in kindred occupations such as doctors, accountants or engineers [sic].

Many lawyers are anxious about being disciplined by the bar. They feel that the many are being made to suffer undue strain and harassment for the sins of the few. Only two attorneys interviewed felt that money payoffs were common. The rest acknowledged that business relationships may be maintained by lawyers doing occasional small favors—contributing to the reelection campaign of a judge, giving a Christmas gift to an insurance executive—but not by the direct transfer of money.

To summarize what has been said so far: for all but the largest claims, an attorney makes less money by thoroughly preparing a case and not settling it early. We have considered four options open to the lawyer in small and medium cases that can reduce conflict between his own financial interests and those of his clients. He can (1) weed out the unremunerative cases in order to devote himself to claims that pay. He can (2) farm out a case to a specialist and take a referral fee. He can (3) choose to specialize in negligence cases and utilize economies of specialization to reduce his overhead and promote helpful contacts with insurers and court personnel. He can (4) use ten-point men to insure generous early settlements at the insurer's expense. The first three options are commonly exercised. The fourth is rarer, but not unknown. Even when reduced, the dynamics for a conflict of interest between even the competent and ethical lawyer and his client remain.

---

14 Murray T. Bloom, *The Trouble with Lawyers* (New York: Simon & Schuster, 1968), p. 177; on bar disciplinary institutions in general see chap. 8, "Who's Watching," pp. 157–191.

HOW LAWYERS RESOLVE CONFLICTING INTERESTS
WITH CLIENTS

"Much as we don't like to believe that lawyers are concerned with such collateral considerations," confesses Philip Hermann, "the effect that prolonged litigation may have on counsel's pocketbook" and his temptation to accept for the client, a "substantial offer which he recognizes is totally inadequate," is of "substantial importance" in determining the settlement.[15] Faced with an economic crunch, even after weeding out the thin cases and utilizing economies of specialization, the ethical and competent attorney has four realistic options for proceeding with the claim: (1) He can cut corners in preparing the case. (2) He can build his fee by charging disbursements to the client. (3) He can persuade the client that a discounted early settlement is in his best interest. (4) He can bring the existing interest conflict to the client's attention and negotiate a compromise claims strategy. Lawyers employ various combinations of these options in their work, although the fourth is not used frequently. The first three of these options for making the economics of representation feasible put the lawyer in direct conflict with his client's interest —without making the client aware of the fact.

Cutting corners—case preparation falling short of the treatise standards— is inevitable in all but the fattest cases. A successful New York negligence attorney has recently written that "the average personal injury action without any court appearances will require between fifteen and twenty-five hours of the attorney's time in the office."[16] This is less than half the time allocated in Table 4.1, arguably the optimum time an attorney should spend in preparing a more serious claim. Economies of specialization cannot fully explain the difference. Feasible corner-cutting is ignored as a professional problem in texts on the legal profession generally, and in specific treatises supposed to tell an attorney about the nuts and bolts of negligence practice. Attorneys cannot afford to follow the treatise guidelines. The best that can be found is passing, rather embarrassed acknowledgment that the problem exists. It is mentioned, for example, in an *American Bar Association Journal* article in the following way:

---

[15] Hermann, *Better Settlements through Leverage,* p. 19.
[16] Neil Shayne, "Trial Practice Economics," *New York Law Journal* 168, no. 50 (September 12, 1972): 1, col. 1.

Of course it will often happen that the amount involved in a case does not justify the intensive preparation which the case itself indicates. A man must meet this problem as best he can.[17]

From both lawyer and client interviews, six shortcuts departing from thorough preparation (Table 4.1) seem common. First, many lawyers delay bringing suit for more than 18 months in the hopes of settling before time and money are spent drafting, serving, and filing legal papers. Second, many lawyers do not accompany the client while he is examined by the insurance company doctor. Third, the site of the accident often is left uninvestigated, attorneys preferring to rely on the reconstruction of the accident in the witness and police reports. Fourth, many claimants are given only perfunctory preparation prior to the EBT. Fifth, the time spent preparing a presentation file to impress the insurer in a settlement negotiation session is reduced. Sixth, lawyers discourage clients from making many demands upon their time—"don't call me; I'll call you."

From the data of this study, it is only possible to make a general evaluation of the impact upon the ultimate recovery of the first of these shortcuts—delayed suit. Unless the insurer has made it clear that he intends to make an early and fair settlement offer or, unless the nature or extent of injuries and disability still remain in considerable doubt several months after the accident, the plaintiff's lawyer should almost always commence a lawsuit within nine months after the client has given him the case. When suit is delayed beyond that point, and neither exception is relevant, the shortcut is unwarranted. It lessens the plaintiff's leverage for obtaining a fair settlement in a reasonable time. Occasionally, delay in suit and settlement serves an attorney's financial interest. One such instance is reported by plaintiff's lawyer Robert Lewiston:

> Much of the delay in the prosecution of negligence matters is attributable to claimant's counsel. Months will elapse in his sometimes fruitless negotiations with insurance adjusters. The filing of the suit may occur a year or more after the execution of the retainer agreement [establishing the lawyer-client relationship]. I was once asked by a client to inquire into the status of his employee's negligence matter being handled by another attorney. When I called, more than a year after the accident, I was told that the case had not yet been filed. I asked why, and was informed, "I've got fifty on file now, they'll be settled in the next three years, and I don't want to bunch up my income taxes."[18]

---

[17] Emory R. Buckner, "The Lawyer in Court," *American Bar Association Journal* 27 (1941): 5.

[18] Robert Lewiston, *Hit from Both Sides, An Exposé of Our Auto Insurance System* (New York: Essandess, division of Simon & Schuster, 1968), p. 52.

No such generalization can be made about the other five shortcuts. As has been previously discussed, from the client's viewpoint, the relevant standard for distinguishing what is appropriate from what is not, often will be the amount of emotional reassurance the client needs. A client who is anxious about his claim—Mrs. Lombard, Mr. Abel, Mrs. Forman, and Mrs. Federman are examples—will tend to get reassurance if his lawyer is present at the medical examination, if he is told what to expect during the EBT, if he knows that his lawyer is accessible and willing to answer his questions and respond to his fears as they arise. For a client who needs less support or who responds to his anxieties by declining support even when offered, shortcutting emotional support may be appropriate. Sometimes preparation is still desirable as where the client's lack of preparation leads him to damage his own case—which may have happened with Mrs. Federman in her EBT.

As mentioned previously, the second option for an attorney seeking to maximize his profits on a negligence claim is to build his fee by charging his client for the various payments made in the prosecution of the client's claim.

The First Department Rules state that the attorney's fee

> shall be computed on the net sum recovered after deducting from the amount recovered expenses, taxable costs and disbursements for expert testimony and investigative or other services properly chargeable to the enforcement of the claim or prosecution of the action.[19]

Thus, some costs and disbursements of case preparation can be transferred to the client and need not be paid fully out of the lawyer's fee.[20] Among the "properly chargeable costs" are the following: fees for obtaining motor vehicle, police, and hospital reports, the process server's fee, the fee paid to an accident investigator, stenographic costs of the EBT, court filing fees, the fee to pay an expert medical witness (which may be as much as $400), and the fee a doctor may charge for providing the plaintiff's attorney with a medical report. At the time the closing statements were filed, they required only that the attorney list the total cost figure. Many attorneys did not itemize these costs and disbursements. As of October 1, 1969, itemization was required on the closing statement form. Therefore, it used to be (but no longer is), particularly easy for an at-

---

[19] Appendix B, p. 216.

[20] The lawyer still bears a portion of the costs to the extent they reduce the gross amount upon which his contingency is computed. If, for example, the recovery is $2,000 and there are $400 in properly chargeable costs, the lawyer's contingency will be x percent of $1,600 rather than x percent of $2,000.

torney, if he wished, to pad the legal costs of a case—at the client's expense. One of the lawyer respondents in the sample commented,

> Most negligence specialists today are doing pretty well [ethically speaking], except many add too many expenses, taking an extra couple of hundred from the client.

Only one client, Mr. Schwinn, a salesman, complained about being charged for legal costs. He told me that his lawyer asked him for a check for $370 to cover "his legal expenses such as filing fees, etc." Mr. Schwinn paid this without getting a receipt. He showed me a note he had made to himself at the time which he had failed to have the lawyer initial. I checked back to the closing statement filed by Mr. Schwinn's attorney and found that he had entered a "0" in the blank for legal costs. Even assuming that this was not an inadvertence on the attorney's part, and assuming further that the omission was brought to the attention of the Judicial Conference staff, a single instance of such misconduct would not, under present policy (as explained by a staff official), lead to the lawyer's censure. At most it might initiate a Coordinating Committee investigation of his past filings to uncover more serious infractions; but even this is doubtful. Even though they could legally charge allowable costs, many attorneys feel that the contingent fee is sufficient and decline to do so.

The third option for the attorney to maximize his returns involves manipulating the client. Erving Goffman has been a prime mover in getting social scientists to look at the often subtle and easily missed mechanisms of control that one person uses to manage his relationship with another. One skill that distinguishes between successful and less successful lawyers is their mastery of the "art of impression management," an art Goffman has explored in much of his work.[21] A lawyer with impression management skills is able to use his authoritative position as expert and helper to manage the professional relationship with his client virtually as he sees fit. Several different lawyer management styles have been noted in past research. There is a dominating aggressive pattern of lawyer behavior toward clients and a more permissive, conciliatory style. Some lawyers direct more of their attention to research and analysis, preferring to deal with the client's problem as a technical matter. Others are drawn more to dealing with the client's view of his problem and prefer to adopt a counseling rather than a technical orientation. Still others are primarily interested in making

---

[21] The classic discussion is Erving Goffman, *The Presentation of Self in Everyday Life* (Garden City, N.Y.: Doubleday, 1959), especially chaps. 1, 6, 7.

money and make no bones about this to the client.[22] What has not been sufficiently stressed in past research is that the good lawyers have mastered a repertory of these styles and can shift from one to another as they choose. One lawyer
interviewee, who has done graduate work in sociology, said that this is the important insight he was afraid would not receive sufficient attention in the present
analysis. He put the matter succinctly:

> A main difference between a good attorney and a poor attorney is the number
> of roles and the sensitivity in determining which lawyer role to play in which
> situation, that a lawyer has at his command.

A good lawyer manages not only his client, but also the insurance adjuster, the
judge, and the jury. His clients admire him, adjusters and judges respect him,
and juries believe him. Qualities that impress some of these people in some
situations are not the same ones that work in other settings.

When faced with an economic interest that competes with the client's,
most attorneys employ the device of preparing the client to accept less than he
anticipates and persuading him that it is in his best interest to do so—"cooling
the client out."[23] Cooling the client out is not per se good or bad. Most lawyers
justify the practice because, they claim, most clients expect to become rich out
of their claims. Where this unrealistic expectation is indeed held, the client
must be disabused to forestall inevitable disappointment. However, interviews
indicate that some clients have lost the "pot of gold" mentality by the time they
reach the lawyer. For many of them, being cooled out by their attorney is less
justifiable as a reality principle. Instead, it makes sense only as a way to make
the case disposition economically feasible for the attorney. If the lawyer can
convince the client that holding out for a trial or pretrial last-ditch settlement
offer is dangerous, he can manage the client into an early discounted settlement. This may well be the main reason why a majority of clients receive a
smaller recovery than the panel evaluation of their case worth.

In a few instances, cooling out the client is a breach of legal ethics. One
specific limitation on a lawyer's impression management is the principle that a
case may not be settled without the client's informed consent.[24] A lawyer is

---

[22] See, for example, Robert Redmount, "Attorney Personalities and Some Psychological Aspects of Legal Consultation," *University of Pennsylvania Law Review* 109
(1961): 972–988; Hubert O'Gorman, *Lawyers and Matrimonial Cases* (New York: Free
Press, 1963), pp. 124–128.

[23] Erving Goffman has elaborated this concept in his paper, "On Cooling the Mark
Out: Some Aspects of Adaptation to Failure," reprinted in *Interpersonal Dynamics: Es-
says and Readings on Human Interaction,* eds., Warren Bennis et al. (Homewood, Ill.:
Dorsey Press, 1964), pp. 417–430.

[24] *Code,* Ethical Consideration, 7–7, p. 25.

also obligated to disclose, immediately, every settlement offer made by the insurer.[25] Nevertheless, a few attorneys have conceded that they regularly make unethical misrepresentations to discourage a client's inclination to feel that his lawyer didn't get enough money for him. One admitted,

> Theoretically, it's unethical not to report accurately negotiations with an insurer to the client. But you can't, and no lawyer does. You tell him about it in such a way that he is prepared to be satisfied. Say the other side offers $5,000. You tell the client that they offered $3,000. He'll say, "That's no good." You agree and say, casually, that you will try to get $4,500 out of them which would be fine. He's still not so happy, but reluctantly agrees. Two days later you call him back with the "good news" that you got him more than he expected, $5,000. Now the client is prepared to be happy. You know what is a good settlement and what he should take. If it is necessary to lie and cheat him to get him to accept what's good for him you do it.

A vaguer form of "cooling out" by misrepresentation is probably the one reported by Mrs. Rubio:

> At the beginning, the lawyer told us we had an excellent case. But at the end, when he wanted us to settle and not go to trial, he told us that our case was difficult and that we could lose everything.

Juries have been known to do incredible things, denying any recovery even where, as in the Rubio case, the liability issue is perfect. At trial Mrs. Rubio could conceivably have lost everything. The words the lawyer used are not incorrect; but the way they were expressed was misleading, as if the chances of getting a better settlement offer from the insurer on the eve of trial were poor (while in fact they were good). Nevertheless, by traditional professional standards, the Rubio lawyer was properly expressing his expert judgment of the client's best interest. If his judgment was mistaken, that would not constitute culpable error. An attorney, like a doctor, is not liable in the exercise of discretion as to the better way to proceed, or as to a simple error of judgment where the bases for that judgment are uncertain.[26] The inexorability of the economic conflict of interest between lawyer and client in so many cases, raises a serious question about the appropriateness of the traditional ideal that an

---

[25] *Code,* Disciplinary Rule 1–102 (A)(4.), p. 3: "A lawyer shall not engage in conduct involving dishonesty, fraud, deceit, or misrepresentation." But see *Dorf* v. *Relles,* 355 F.2d 488 (7th Cir. 1966), where the failure to interpose expert testimony as to community standards of due care led to dismissal of a malpractice action, even though the attorney failed to discuss with the client a settlement offer made during trial.

[26] *Hodges* v. *Carter,* 239 N.C. 517, 80 S.E. 2d 144 (1954), and cases cited in John Wade, "The Attorney's Liability for Negligence," *Vanderbilt Law Review* 12 (1959): 755–777.

ethical and competent lawyer can and will make the client's interest his own. Goffman puts the matter as follows:

> Performers often foster the impression that they have ideal motives . . . and ideal qualifications for the role and that it was not necessary for them to suffer any indignities, insults, and humiliations, or make any tacitly understood "deals" in order to acquire the role. . . . Reinforcing these ideal impressions there is a kind of "rhetoric of training" whereby . . . licensing bodies require practitioners to absorb a mystical range and period of training, in part to maintain a monopoly, but in part to foster the impression that the licensed practitioner is someone who has been reconstituted by his learning experience and is now set apart from other men.[27]

The realities of negligence practice for the lawyer as well as the client confront him with constant uncertainties, indignities, and needs to compromise. The nature of the legal problems with which the attorney grapples are uncertain and costly. Error is not always avoidable. Yet the traditional model dictates, and most lawyers and clients accept the dictum, that the lawyer should appear to be a rock of informed judgment, knowing with technical precision the client's true interest and being free from human pressures to compromise that interest. To play the part within the design of the traditional model, to make a living yet keep clients content, the lawyer must engage in impression management generally, and especially in client cool out. As Victor Thompson notes,

> The greater the discrepancy between the self-image projected, on the one hand, and reality, on the other, the greater the load placed upon sheer play acting.[28]

The fourth option for resolving the conflict between the lawyer's and client's interest is to bring the specific conflict issues up for discussion and negotiation between the two parties. As was illustrated in Chapter 2, one of the actions distinguishing some participating from nonparticipating clients is that they tend not to wait for the lawyer to raise these issues. Instead, they themselves spot one or more of them—the extent of the fee, the amount of emotional support to be given, the relative merits of delay—and bring them into the open for joint discussion.

Obviously lawyers find it easier to perform their roles by trying to maintain as much control as possible over all aspects of the way a claim is con-

---

[27] Goffman, *The Presentation of Self in Everyday Life,* p. 46.

[28] Victor Thompson, *Modern Organization: A General Theory,* quoted in *Political Leadership in American Government,* ed. James D. Barber (Boston: Little, Brown, 1964), p. 349.

ducted.[29] The less flexible persist in this behavior even when it antagonizes the client. Mrs. Lowe told her lawyer that his brusqueness and noncommunicability were offensive. Yet she reports he continued responding to her in this ill-mannered way. The few very skilled lawyers, such as Mrs. Lombard's, tactically relinquish some control by disclosure and compromise with respect to a few issues without, however, relinquishing their considerable overall control of case strategy. Lawyers acknowledge the obligation of explaining details of a case to the client—in the abstract. Of the lawyers responding to a question about whether or not they recognize any such obligation, 62 percent (28 of 45) responded, "yes, without qualification." However, when given a list of specific open issues that might possibly be disclosed to the client and discussed with him, a majority favored disclosure only with respect to two: the need to hire an expert witness and the final settlement terms. Less than 20 percent favored discussing with the client when to begin suit, how much to sue for, in which court to sue, whether or not to seek a jury trial, or at what level to set the initial settlement demand.

The American Bar Association's *Code of Professional Responsibility* contains no disciplinary rule mandating that attorneys obtain the informed consent of their clients with respect to decisions made in pursuing claims. The American Bar Association has, however, approved an "ethical consideration" which appears to promote rather broad disclosure. It is worth quoting in full:

> A lawyer should exert his best efforts to insure that decisions of his client are made only after the client has been informed of relevant considerations. *A lawyer ought to initiate this decision-making process if the client does not do so.* Advice of a lawyer to his client need not be confined to purely legal considerations. *A lawyer should advise his client of the possible effect of each legal alternative.* A lawyer should bring to bear upon this decision-making process the fullness of his experience as well as his objective viewpoint. In assisting his client to reach a proper decision, it is often desirable for a lawyer to point out those factors which may lead to a decision that is morally just as well as legally permissible. He may emphasize the possibility of harsh consequences that might result from the assertion of legally permissible positions. *In the final analysis, however, the lawyer should always remember that the*

---

[29] The extent to which lawyers see themselves in control of the lawyer-client relationship is further evidenced by the response of 125 Florida lawyers questioned by sociologist John Reed: 52 percent said that their client was "asked to consent to individual moves or action taken in his behalf"; 30 percent said that "the lawyer was in charge of the problem solution"; and only 18 percent said that "the client sets the limits within which the lawyer decides." None thought the client decided how to solve the problem. "The Lawyer-Client: A Managed Relationship?" *Academy of Management Journal* 12 (March 1969): 76.

decision whether to forego legally available objectives or methods because of non-legal factors is ultimately for the client and not for himself. In the event that the client in a non-adjudicatory matter insists upon a course of conduct that is contrary to the judgment and advice of the lawyer but not prohibited by the Disciplinary Rules, the lawyer may withdraw from the employment." [Italics mine][30]

This paragraph is a remarkably clear and concise statement of operations for an attorney following the participatory model. If implemented, it would virtually insure that most clients would be active participants in claims-making. However, as has just been indicated, more than one-third of a sample of negligence attorneys do not recognize any broad obligation to inform the client about his case, let alone involve him as a decision-making partner, and more than 80 percent of the attorney sample reject any obligation to disclose and discuss arguably material and specific legal alternatives involved in the claim.

One may reasonably wonder why such a disparity between norm and practice exists. Three factors should be noted. First, this ethical consideration is relatively new. It was only adopted in 1969 as part of the *Code of Professional Responsibility,* a considerable departure from the prior *Canons of Ethics* which contain no comparable provision.[31] Many attorneys are unfamiliar with the new provisions of the *Code.* Second, the *Code* states that "ethical considerations" do not have the binding character of disciplinary rules. "Ethical considerations" are aspirational in character and represent the objective toward which every member of the profession should strive. They constitute a body of principles upon which the lawyer can rely for guidance in many specific situations."[32] Lawyers may feel, erroneously, that they have discretionary choice with respect to these ethical considerations.[33] I would contend, rather, that they are no less bound to apply principles embodied in these ethical considerations by the fact that these principles have not been reduced to mandatory rules. Principles of legal ethics are as much a part of the law of professional responsibility as are disciplinary rules. Nonetheless, it must be admitted that many attorneys (and some jurisprudents) believe they have

---

[30] *Code,* Ethical Consideration, 7–8, p. 25.

[31] The now superceded *Canon of Ethics* (Brooklyn, N.Y.: Edward Thompson Company, 1963), was approved by the American Bar Association in 1908 and was thereafter adopted by each state Bar Association. The Canons were adopted by the New York State Bar Association in 1909.

[32] *Code,* "Preliminary Statement," p. 1.

[33] For a critique of this notion of discretion with which the author substantially agrees, see Ronald Dworkin, "The Model of Rules," *University of Chicago Law Review* 35 (1967): 14.

discretion to accept or reject these ethical considerations. Third, Ethical Consideration 7–7 immediately preceding in the *Code* text, may be read as substantially restricting the decisions requiring informed consent:

> In certain areas of legal representation not affecting the merits of the case or substantially prejudicing the rights of a client, a lawyer is entitled to make decisions on his own. But otherwise, the authority to make decisions is exclusively that of the client and, if made within the framework of the law, such decisions are binding on his lawyer. As typical examples in civil cases, it is for the client to decide whether he will accept a settlement offer or whether he will waive his right to plead an affirmative defense.[34]

Attorneys so inclined, may read these two ethical considerations taken together as only requiring informed consent in claims making with respect to decisions about settlements and the possible waiving of basic rights to the claim itself. The present survey shows that virtually all clients engage in this much participation in claims making. But the survey also shows that this limited participation is of limited effect.

Notwithstanding these three mitigating factors, one may still wonder why there is the disparity between norm and practice in a profession which, according to the traditional model, is to police itself. One may also wonder how the traditional model is to be reconciled with ethical norms seemingly better suited to a participatory model. These two questions will be further pursued in the next chapter.

CONCLUSION

Pressures, especially economic ones, often work against the lawyer's providing disinterested service to his client in making a personal injury claim. In many cases the lawyer's financial interest lies in an early discounted settlement while the client's interest lies in waiting out the insurer. The traditional ideal of professional service assists the lawyer in managing the claim so as to make it appear that no conflict of interest with the client exists. Lawyers do not disclose potential sources of conflict and the traditional model inhibits those active client requests for information that could expose issues of conflict, by making such requests appear to be mistrustful client behavior. Although the norms of professional responsibility invite client participation, most lawyers believe that a lawyer-client relationship in which client collaboration is to be encouraged by extensive disclosure of critical issues would be inappropriate.

---

[34] *Code,* Ethical Consideration 7–7, p. 25.

The traditional model justifies minimal participation in professional problem solving not only in terms of the professional's ability to serve the best interest of the client but also in terms of the accessibility to competent professionals. If clients can easily find professionals who are relatively free from disadvantageous economic pressures and who do not need to manage the claims process in a deceptive way but are instead willing and able to bring points of conflict into the open for joint consideration, then potential conflicts of interest are not a serious problem.

Chapter Five: Client Access to Effective Legal Service in Personal Injury Problem-Solving

To what extent do clients have a problem finding effective legal representation? To the extent that the legal profession sets and maintains high and thoroughly enforced standards of legal service, clients need not be concerned with problems of choice in finding a lawyer; virtually any lawyer in good standing can be relied upon to give competent service. If greater client selectivity is appropriate, to what extent do and should clients have access to appropriate criteria of lawyer selection? In Chapter 1 it was suggested that each model of professional-client relationships had distinctive answers to these questions. In this chapter we shall appraise these answers with respect to the "organized bar" and personal injury practice.

HIGH STANDARDS OF PROFESSIONAL PERFORMANCE HAVE NEITHER BEEN SET NOR MAINTAINED BY THE LEGAL PROFESSION AND THE COURTS

The term "organized bar" gives the impression that the legal profession is a cohesive community with bar associations that strictly and consistently police professional conduct. In reality, the American legal profession is, as characterized by an American Bar Foundation pamphlet, loosely organized, with a complex and socially varied membership and a "tendency toward leniency" in the enforcement of professional disciplinary sanctions.[1] General standards for the profession are set by the American Bar Association (ABA). This national association, which is the profession's most important spokesman, is responsible for drafting the *Code of Professional Responsibility* and for interpreting it through advisory opinions rendered by a Standing Committee on Professional Ethics. Each state, and in New York, each Appellate Division, has primary

---

[1] "The Legal Profession in the United States" (Chicago: American Bar Foundation, 1965), p. 18.

authority to enforce professional standards and the discretion to incorporate selectively those ABA principles and policies it sees fit to apply. The standards applied and enforced vary from one jurisdiction to another and even from one Appellate Division to another within New York State.[2]

It is probably not unfair to say that at the national, state, and local levels, the "organized bar" has been rather casual about the problem of professional self-policing. The comprehensive review of lawyer performance commissioned by the ABA shortly after World War II came to the conclusion that criticism of the legal profession is largely unfounded and that while there was room for improvement, the primary fault of the profession was not inadequate performance but poor "public relations."[3] Consistent with the traditional approach to professional performance, the bar has defined the problem as one best dealt with by screening out the untrained and the unfit, treating proficient performance as synonymous with a lawyer being a person of "integrity and good character." The law schools are encouraged to teach legal ethics. Bar associations are encouraged to develop and implement effective certification procedures for admitting new lawyers, and practicing attorneys are encouraged to cooperate in "purging the profession of the unworthy."[4]

However, these traditional principles are not usually implemented. While many law schools teach ethics courses, they are not designed to relate to the specific and real world pressures and dilemmas of practice. Students in most law schools are taught almost nothing about how to deal with clients.[5] Students

---

[2] The "organized bar" is more fully described by Quintin Johnstone and Dan Hopson, *Lawyers and Their Work* (Indianapolis, Ind.: Bobbs-Merrill, 1967), chap. 2, pp. 15–76.

[3] Albert Blaustein and Charles Porter, *The American Lawyer* (Chicago: University of Chicago Press, 1954), p. 38. This conclusion has been radically revised by a 1970 report to the ABA. American Bar Association Special Committee on Evaluation of Disciplinary Enforcement, *Problems and Recommendations in Disciplinary Enforcement* (Chicago: American Bar Association, 1970).

[4] "Statement of Principles," Special Committee on Disciplinary Procedures, American Bar Association, in *Public Relations for Bar Associations* (Chicago: ABA Standing Committee on Public Relations, 1953), pp. 7–8.

[5] Harrop Freeman, *Legal Interviewing and Counseling* (St. Paul, Minn.: West, 1964), p. 233; Andrew Watson, "The Lawyer as Counselor," *Journal of Family Law* 5 (1965): 11–17.

That physicians receive very little instruction about the ethical issues of dealing with patients is evidenced by the finding of Bernard Barber and his associates that only 13% of 307 physicians they interviewed, reported having had a seminar, lecture or part of a medical school course devoted to the issues involved in the use of patients and other human subjects in biomedical research, and only 43% reported having had any experience which raised any issue of medical research ethics during their schooling. Bernard Barber, John Lally, Julia Makarushka and Daniel Sullivan, *Research On Human Subjects* (New York: Russell Sage Foundation, 1973), p. 101.

end their law school careers more cynical than when they started[6] and consistently report that their law school experience did not prepare them for the realities of law practice.[7] The ABA Survey of the Legal Profession itself concluded that

> No uniformity exists in the quality of bar examinations given in the different examining and admitting jurisdictions. . . . As traditionally and currently set, the typical bar examination is not an accurate test of the training that has been and is being offered by the better law schools of the country.[8]

According to a past president of the Oregon State Bar, "The regulation of professional qualification has remained essentially unchanged since 1900."[9] In some circumstances the good character requirement has been used to exclude qualified lawyer applicants because of their disfavored political views, instead of excluding the corrupt and corruptible.[10] Instead of reporting ethical violations and gross incompetence of colleagues (as mandated by Disciplinary Rule 1–103 of the *Code*) lawyers tend to ignore them. The most severe and comprehensive indictment of the bar's self-policing failures has been drawn up by a Special Committee on Evaluation of Disciplinary Enforcement of the ABA ("Disciplinary Committee") in a 1970 report which has yet to be acted upon:

> After three years of studying lawyer discipline throughout the country, this [Disciplinary] Committee must report the existence of a scandalous situation that requires the immediate attention of the profession. With few exceptions, the prevailing attitude of lawyers toward disciplinary enforcement ranges from apathy to outright hostility. Disciplinary action is practically nonexistent

---

[6] Leonard Eron and Robert Redmount, "The Effect of Legal Education on Attitudes," *Journal of Legal Education* 9 (1957): 431–443; Andrew Watson, "Some Psychological Aspects of Teaching Professional Responsibility," *Journal of Legal Education* 16 (1963): 1–23.

[7] Dan Lortie, "Layman to Lawman: Law School, Careers and Professional Socialization," *Harvard Educational Review* 29 (Fall 1959): 363–367.

[8] Blaustein and Porter, *The American Lawyer,* p. 226. In 1972, for the first time, the "Multistate Bar Examination" was offered to lawyer candidates in 26 states. Those who pass this test and a supplemental test prepared by a separate board of examiners in each state, are admitted to practice. This innovation introduces a measure of uniformity into lawyer qualifications. Information about the Multistate Bar Examination has been obtained from Professor Joe E. Covington, Director of Testing, National Conference of Bar Examiners, c/o University of Missouri Law School, Columbia, Mo.

[9] Richard Nahstoll, "Regulating Professional Qualification," in *Law in a Changing America,* ed. Goeffrey Hazard, Jr. (Englewood Cliffs, N.J.: Prentice-Hall, 1968), p. 125.

[10] *Konigsberg* v. *State Bar of California,* 366 U.S. 36 (1961), in which an applicant who passed the bar examination was denied certification for refusing to answer questions about his alleged prior association with communist causes. On appeal, the denial was upheld by the Supreme Court.

in many jurisdictions; practices and procedures are antiquated; many disciplinary agencies have little power to take effective steps against malefactors.[11]

While the bar has been more active in establishing principles of professional responsibility[12] than in enforcing them, the courts have tended to penalize clients by holding them responsible (and therefore without direct remedy) for the nonperformance or misconduct of their attorneys. The general rule regarding the scope of the attorney's power to bind the client when the attorney is acting pursuant to his retainer is this: the attorney has implied authority to do everything necessary and proper in the regular and ordinary conduct of a case, provided his acts affect the remedy only and not the cause of action itself.[13] The proviso protecting the client's cause of action (his rights to recover under the claim) has been held to protect the client from unauthorized release of his adversary from liability[14] unauthorized submission to dismissal, with prejudice, of his claim,[15] as well as from unauthorized compromises or settlements of his claim.[16] However, in other cases, the proviso has been either ignored, or the concept of "affect the cause of action" has been given a restricted interpretation. Thus, in *Federal Fuel Co.* v. *Macy,* 130 Misc. 192, 223 N.Y.S. 710 (Sup. Ct. 1927), the attorney, by virtue of his general retainer, was held to have implied authority to waive without specific authorization his client's right to a jury trial; in *Cohen* v. *Goldman,* 85 R.I. 434, 132 A. 2d 414 (1957), the attorney was held to have authority to compromise his client's claim even though it was alleged that the attorney had forged the client's signature on the release papers;[17] in *White* v. *Sadler,* 350 Mich. 511, 87 N.W. 2d 192 (1957),

---

[11] Disciplinary Committee, *Problems and Recommendations in Disciplinary Enforcement* (Chicago: American Bar Association, 1970), p. 1.

[12] The *Code,* approved by the ABA House of Delegates in August 1969, and adopted by the New York State Bar Association immediately thereafter, is more complete, more detailed, and more liberal in promoting client access than its predecessor. See especially Canon 2, "A Lawyer Should Assist the Legal Profession in Fulfilling Its Duty to Make Legal Counsel Available."

[13] *W. A. Robinson, Inc.* v. *Burke,* 327 Mass. 670, 100 N.E. 2d 366 (1951).

[14] *McLaughlin* v. *Monaghan,* 290 Pa. 74, 138 A. 79 (1927).

[15] *Lusas* v. *St. Patrick's Roman Catholic Church Corp.,* 125 Conn. 206, 4 A. 2d 333 (1939). Dismissal with prejudice means, in essence, that the accident victim could not re-initiate his claim for compensation at a later date.

[16] *U.S.* v. *Beebe,* 180 U.S. 343, 21 S. Ct. 371, 45 L.Ed. 563 (1900); *Bush* v. *O'Brien,* 164 N.Y. 205, 58 N.E. 106 (1900).

[17] The court in *Cohen* did attempt to soften the blow somewhat by reminding the client that he could always sue the attorney for malpractice. This may have been of less solace than was intended; see the discussion of weaknesses in the malpractice remedy, p. 123.

it was held that the client had no right to reopen a default judgment obtained against him by reason of his attorney's dilatoriness; and, in *Link* v. *Wabash Railroad Co.,* 370 U.S. 626, 82 S. Ct. 1386, 8 L. Ed. 2d 735 (1962), the Supreme Court held that it was not an abuse of discretion for a federal district court judge to invalidate the claim of a client whose attorney had failed to appear at a pretrial proceeding. This was the holding even though the statute of limitations had by that time run out on both the client's cause of action in the original claim and in a possible subsequent claim against his attorney for malpractice. He therefore was precluded from receiving any compensation for the damages he had sustained.

Thus it is seen that the case law tends to hold the client responsible for the action of the attorney by not allowing the client legally to undo what the attorney has legally done. Such a trend of judicial decision would appear not unreasonable if the attorney-client relationship were governed in reality by the *Code's* Ethical Consideration promoting active client participation.[18] However, as seen in Chapter 4, lawyers have, in practice, been vigorous adherents of the traditional model and have been inclined to resist any (albeit limited) tendencies on the client's part to become actively involved in the decision-making process. Resistance to client activity has also been expressed from the bench. As phrased by one judge, "clients should not be forced to act as hawk-like inquisitors of their own counsel, suspicious of every step and quick to switch lawyers. The legal profession knows no worse headache than the client who mistrusts his attorney."[19] According to the traditional model, because clients are (and should be) passive and dependent, they deserve the bar's vigilance in weeding out the unscrupulous and incompetent and in establishing principles of lawyer responsibility giving aggrieved clients specific remedies against specific instances of lawyer nonconduct and misconduct. Even if implementation is not as extensive and effective as it should be, the ideals are legitimate and consistent. One reason, however, why the legal profession has become enmeshed in this embarrassingly contradictory position of treating the attorney as the client's agent for making, and effectuating, critical decisions in the claims process while, at the same time, discouraging and resisting efforts by the client

---

18 *Code,* Ethical Consideration 7–8, p. 25.

19 *Daley* v. *County of Butte,* 227 Cal. App. 2d 380, 391–392, 38 Cal. Rptr. 693, 700–701 (1964). This is quoted in Lester Mazor, "Power and Responsibility in the Attorney-Client Relation," which is the best discussion I have found of conflicting principles in the doctrine of professional responsibility. *Stanford Law Review* 20 (June 1968): 1120–1139; quote is on p. 1126.

to exert control over the attorney's acts, is the fear that granting relief for every attorney error will tie up the courts with endless petitions from "overly litigious or chronically dissatisfied persons who refuse to accede to the sound judgment of their lawyers."[20] The bar—especially the judiciary—is torn between the policies of putting an end to litigation and guaranteeing clients effective legal representation. To resolve this conflict, the courts have tended to abandon the traditional model just to the extent that it would provide a rationale for the client being able to escape the consequences of his attorney's actions. Thus, as the Supreme Court ruled in *Link* v. *Wabash Railroad Company,* errors of judgment or performance by the lawyers are presumed to be approved by the client. The majority in *Link* stated,

> Petitioner voluntarily chose this attorney as his representative in the action, and he cannot now avoid the consequences of the acts or omissions of this freely selected agent. Any other notion would be wholly inconsistent with our system of representative litigation.[21]

In dissent, Justice Black (joined by Chief Justice Warren) reminded the Court that lawyers want and encourage clients to be passive and are therefore being unfair in punishing them for this trusting behavior.

> How could [the client] know or why should he be presumed to know that it was his duty to see that the many steps a lawyer needs to take to bring his case to trial had been taken by his lawyer. . . . So far as this record shows [the client] was simply trusting his lawyer to take care of his case as clients generally do.[22]

One early South Dakota decision goes even further than *Link* in adopting an active client rationale to frustrate any client remedy. In *Olson* v. *Advance Rumely Co.,* 42 S.D. 331, 175 N.W. 192 (1919), it was held that the client seeking to vacate a judgment obtained in his attorney's absence, would have to show affirmatively that he, the client, had not himself been contributorily negligent in so far as he had not made sure that his attorney had appeared when the judgment was entered.

The results of such a case are unjust because they directly conflict with the norms and practices of the attorney-client relationship which the legal profession has encouraged the public to accept. Even if the (undocumented) premise of the courts is correct, namely that giving clients the opportunity to

---

[20] Ibid., p. 1128.
[21] 370 U.S. 626, at 633, 634 8 L.ed.2d 734, 82 S. Ct. 1386 (1962).
[22] Ibid., at 643 (dissenting opinion).

undo what their attorneys have misdone will unduly congest the courts, that is no mitigation of the injustice of acceptance by the legal profession and the courts of the benefits of the traditional model without the assumption of the self-policing burdens it imposes. In only one case that I have found (in addition to the dissent in *Link*), has a court squarely recognized the consistency requirements of the traditional model.[23]

A second justification for holding clients accountable for their lawyers' conduct in lawsuits is the contention that even if the client cannot directly undo what his attorney has done he still has an effective remedy against being victimized by professional irresponsibility, by initiating a second lawsuit—against his own attorney for malpractice. Malpractice suits are brought by aggrieved clients represented by a second lawyer against the lawyer who represented them in the prior lawsuit. If successful in this second suit, the client may recover from his first attorney the compensation to which he was entitled had his prior claim been properly handled.

In hearing malpractice suits, the courts have fashioned three overlapping standards to delineate the performance owed a client by his attorney. A lawyer is responsible

> for any loss to his client which proximately results (1) from a want of that degree of knowledge and skill ordinarily possessed by others of his profession similarly situated, or (2) from the omission to use reasonable care and diligence, or (3) from the failure to exercise in good faith his best judgment in attending to the litigation committed to his care.[24]

The first standard has been incorrectly interpreted by some courts as setting as the norm the average conduct of general practice attorneys in the same community. This interpretation is repudiated in the *Restatement of Torts 2d* (*Restatement*).[25] According to the *Restatement,* the proper degree of knowledge and skill of an attorney is that minimally required for membership in good standing in similar communities. Yet, Comment e to Section 299A of the *Restatement* clearly implies that a lawyer can *escape* liability by showing that his conduct was average or normal in the profession. The evident assumption (questionable in light of this study's findings) underlying the *Restatement* position is that the general run of people act imprudently in prosecuting their daily

---

[23] *Daley* v. *County of Butte.*

[24] *Hodges* v. *Carter,* 239 N.C. 517, 80 S.E. 2d 144, 146 (1954).

[25] *Restatement of Torts 2d* (St. Paul, Minn.: American Law Institute, 1965), 299 A, Comment g, p. 73.

affairs, while attorneys in the prosecution of matters entrusted to their care act, in general, prudently and competently, thus turning the traditional law of negligence on its head. The traditional doctrine is that a person is not freed from liability for negligence on the mere showing that his conduct was average or normal.[26]

The third standard implies, among other things, that if a lawyer is specially trained in a specific area of the law, he may be held to a higher standard of care—the skill and knowledge reasonable for a specialist. Though widely approved, it has yet to be applied in a specific case.[27]

The second standard (mandating the exercise of reasonable care) is most often applied to the omissions of attorneys, less often to their misdeeds. Attorneys have been held not to have exercised reasonable care for failure to apply settled principles of law to the legal matter at hand,[28] for failure to pursue procedures necessary for preserving a client's right of appeal,[29] for failure to draft pleadings properly,[30] for failure to appear and defend suits entrusted to their care,[31] for failure to assert all possible claims or defenses on behalf of the clients,[32] for failure to present relevant evidence,[33] for delay in initiating prosecution of a suit,[34] for lack of diligence in prosecuting a suit once initiated,[35] for improperly serving process,[36] for not researching the relevant law of a

---

[26] See William Curran, "Professional Negligence—Some General Comments," *Professional Negligence,* ed. T. G. Roady and W. R. Anderson (Nashville, Tenn.: Vanderbilt University Press, 1960), pp. 1–6.

[27] Albert Blaustein, "Liability of Attorney to Client in New York for Negligence," *Brooklyn Law Review,* 19 (1952): 233 at 254. The *Restatement* position on the issue is that a professional is bound to exercise that degree of skill or knowledge *which he represents himself as having* (Comment d, §299A, *Rest. Torts 2d,* p. 74). Thus, if the Bar Associations continue to enforce the rule against a lawyer's advertising his field of specialization, it is unlikely that any cases turning on the point will arise.

[28] *Trimboli* v. *Kinkel,* 226 N.Y. 147, 123 N.E. 205 (1919) (Cardozo).

[29] *Childs* v. *Comstock,* 69 App. Div. 160, 74 N.Y.S. 643 (1st Dept., 1902); *Pete* v. *Henderson,* 124 Cal. App. 2d 487, 269 P.2d 78 (1954).

[30] *Senftner* v. *Kleinhans,* 80 Misc. 519, 141 N.Y.S. 533 (Sup. Ct., App. Term, 1913).

[31] *Masters* v. *Dunstan,* 256 N.C. 520, 124 S.E. 2d 574 (1962).

[32] *Dulberg* v. *Mock,* 1 N.Y. 2d 54, 150 N.Y.S. 2d 180, 133 N.E. 2d 695 (1956).

[33] *McLellan* v. *Fuller,* 220 Mass. 494, 108 N.E. 180 (1915).

[34] *Reynolds* v. *Picciani,* 29 App. Div. 2d 1012, 289 N.Y.S. 2d 436 (1968); *Siegel* v. *Kranis,* 29 App. Div. 2d 477, 288 N.Y.S. 2d 831 (1968).

[35] *Kamp* v. *Syracuse Transit Corporation,* 284 App. Div. 1028, 134 N.Y.S. 2d 919 (1954).

[36] *Von Wollhoffen* v. *Newcombe,* 10 Hun. 236 (N.Y., 1877).

[37] *Degen* v. *Steinbrink,* 202 App. Div. 477, 195 N.Y.S. 810, (1st Dept., 1922), *aff'd mem.,* 236 N.Y. 669, 142 N.E. 328; *Rekeweg Federal Mutual Ins. Co.,* 27 F.R.D. 431 (N.D. Ind., 1961).

foreign jurisdiction,[37] for misdrafting a will,[38] for improperly preparing papers in support of a judgment,[39] and for misapplication of legal principles in advancing a suit.[40]

An attorney may be liable for failing to follow with reasonable promptness and care the explicit instructions of his client—even in the honest belief that the instructions were not in the client's best interest.[41]

Unfortunately, however, the doctrine of informed consent has been little used in the area of attorney malpractice. The attorney is clearly constrained from acting on his client's behalf without his permission only with respect to two issues: he may not settle, drop, or compromise the claim unilaterally[42] or waive judgment in his client's favor agreeing to a new trial;[43] and he may not farm the case without the client's consent.[44] More than 70 years ago, New York courts were unsettled on whether an attorney could stipulate not to appeal a decision without his client's permission.[45] No more recent case has settled the matter.

These rulings may appear to constitute strong protection for the client's right to competent representation. In fact they fall far short of extensive protection. An important erosion of the due care standard has come with the application of the principle that an attorney is freed from liability where the law is considered uncertain or unsettled.[46] Judges and juries are invited to view a negligent act or judgment as an honest mistake. In a recent California case, for example, an attorney was not held liable for damages resulting from drafting a will which excluded an intended beneficiary from an inheritance. The court so held notwithstanding that the particular error had been the subject of prior authoritative California court decisions interpreting the relevant statute. The court felt that the area of law was sufficiently difficult, anyway, that the honest mistake was not negligence.[47] Ironically though "ignorance of the law will not

---

[38] *Biakanja* v. *Irving*, 49 Cal. 2d 647, 320 P. 2d 16 (1958).

[39] *Armstrong* v. *Adams*, 102 Cal. App. 677, 283 P. 871 (1929).

[40] *Whitney* v. *Abbott*, 191 Mass. 59, 77 N.E. 524 (1906).

[41] *Lally* v. *Kuster*, 177 Cal. 783, 171 P. 961 (1918); *W. L. Douglas Shoe Co.* v. *Rollwage*, 187 Ark. 1084, 63 S.W. 2d 841 (1933).

[42] *Burgraf* v. *Byrnes*, 94 Minn. 418, 103 N.W. 215 (1905).

[43] *Quinn* v. *Lloyd*, 5 Abb. Pr. (n.s.) 281 (N.Y. Super. Ct., 1868).

[44] *Code*, Disciplinary Rule 2-107, p. 9.

[45] *People* v. *New York*, 11 Abb. Pr. 66 (N.Y. Sup. Ct., 1860); court said consent must be obtained. *Contra, Smith* v. *Barnes*, 9 Misc. 368, 29 N.Y. Supp. 692 (1894).

[46] *Patterson* v. *Powell*, 31 Misc. 250, 64 N.Y. Supp. 43, (1900), *aff'd mem.*, 56 App. Div. 624, 68 N.Y. Supp. 1145 (1st Dept., 1900).

[47] *Lucas* v. *Hamm*, 56 Cal. 2d 583, 364 P.2d 685 (1961), *cert. denied*, 368 U.S. 987 (1962).

excuse" the client,[48] it may excuse the lawyer who is trained to the law.

Beyond the erosion of the due care standard, there are serious additional hurdles to be surmounted in conducting a malpractice suit. First of all, there is also a three-year statute of limitations on suits claiming attorney negligence. In all but a few states the three-year period begins to run from the time the negligent act is committed, not from the time that the client discovers it. Even if the lawyer conceals the negligence from his client until the statute has run, New York courts have held that the lawyer is not liable for fraudulent concealment (with its longer six-year statute of limitations).[49] Thus in the *Link* case, the client would have been denied a malpractice remedy. The statute of limitations had elapsed since his attorney failed to meet the initial trial date.

The second hurdle for the client is that in the malpractice action he must show not only that the first attorney was negligent but that the result would have been different *but for* that negligence. As has been noted, the client must win a "suit within a suit."[50] Courts, so inclined, are given the "easy out" of finding that while, yes, the attorney was negligent, his negligence did not "proximately cause" the client's damages since the client might well have lost the first suit anyway.

The third hurdle is that in many communities (though probably not in Manhattan) it is difficult to find attorneys who will represent clients in malpractice suits against colleagues. The fourth hurdle is the inclinations of the judges who hear malpractice cases. In the words of a *Columbia Law Review Comment:*

> Although the overwhelming majority of decisions indicate that the question of negligence is one of fact, judicial reluctance actually to submit the negligence issue in any attorney malpractice case to the jury is manifest. Allocating responsibility between judge and jury in attorney malpractice suits raises questions even more delicate and complex than those presented in ordinary negligence cases, which normally involve mixed questions of law and fact. The

---

[48] This famous principle, enunciated in *Shevlin-Carpenter Co.* v. *Minnesota,* 218 U.S. 68 (1910) is, fortunately, often honored in the breach.

[49] *Goldberg* v. *Bosworth,* 29 Misc. 2d 1057, 215 N.Y.S. 2d 849 (Sup. Ct., 1961). But see a recent case in which the appellate court avoided this result by finding a continuing relationship between lawyer and client that tolled the statute of limitations. The finding of continuous professional responsibility, analogous to the continuous treatment doctrine in medicine, permitted a client suit. *Siegel* v. *Kranis,* 29 AD 2d 477, 288 N.Y. Supp. 2d 831 (2d Dept., 1968). Recently, the California Supreme Court adopted the rarer "run from discovery" rule. *Neel* v. *Magana, Olney, Levy, Cathcart & Gelfand,* 98 Cal. Rptr. 837, 491 P.2d 421 (1971).

[50] Richard G. Coggin, "Attorney Negligence—Suit within a Suit," *West Virginia Law Review* 60 (1958): 225.

nature of the relationship between bench and bar inevitably influences judicial attitudes. . . . Notwithstanding their frequent statements that attorneys occupy a position with respect to those they serve similar, if not identical, to that of members of the medical profession, the courts have treated attorney malpractice suits as sui generis. The majority of decisions reflects a superficial analysis that is almost certainly colored by the fraternal concern of the judiciary for members of the practicing bar. . . . The defense that "errors of judgment" were made has generally been sustained uncritically.[51]

Even if the client overcomes these hurdles and wins the malpractice suit he may well find that the negligent lawyer is not sufficiently covered by malpractice insurance to pay damages. The costs of malpractice insurance are steadily rising as more suits are undertaken.[52] The one most likely to be underprotected—or not protected at all—is the general practice attorney who may be the one most likely to make a mistake in representation. Some local bar associations have established client security funds, with contributions provided by member attorneys, to pay defaulted claims brought against liable attorneys. Unfortunately for the victims of attorney negligence, client security funds, presently, are only used to pay the victims of serious willful misconduct—misappropriation of trust funds, fraud, forgery, larceny, and the like.[53]

There is one other possible "remedy" for aggrieved clients who fail to recover damages. They may receive the moral satisfaction of seeing the attorney "disciplined" by the court or, somewhat more likely, by the local bar association grievance committee. While there have been cases of attorney suspensions for negligence in dealing with the client,[54] such measures usually are reserved for the most flagrant forms of attorney misconduct and the discipline imposed rarely exceeds censure, often handed-down privately without being reported to the public. The attorney is free to continue his practice otherwise unimpaired.[55] It has been found that the effects of a malpractice suit on the practices of a sample of 58 Connecticut physicians were insignificant.[56] The same may well be true for the practices of censured attorneys.

---

[51] "Attorney Malpractice," *Columbia Law Review* 63 (1963): 1292, at 1309, 1313.

[52] "Suing the Lawyer," *The Wall Street Journal,* October 10, 1969, p. 1.

[53] John T. Hardy, "The Disenchanted Client v. The Dishonest Lawyer: Where Does the Legal Profession Stand?" *Notre Dame Lawyer* 42 (February 1967): 382–399.

[54] See, e.g. *Rock* v. *State Bar of California,* 57 Cal. 2d 639, 2 Cal. Rptr. 572, 371 P. 2d 308 (1962); and *In re Somers,* 22 App. Div. 2d 325 (1st Dept., 1965).

[55] See *In re Meltzer,* 30 App. Div. 2d 544, 290 N.Y.S. 2d 1009 (1968); and *Matter of Sheldon,* 7 App. Div. 2d 135 (1st Dept., 1959). Also see generally 96 *A.L.R. 2d* 823 (1964).

[56] Robert Wycoff, "The Effects of a Malpractice Suit upon Physicians in Connecticut," *Tort and Medical Handbook,* eds. Albert Averbach and Melvin Belli (Indianapolis, Ind.: Bobbs-Merrill, 1962), vol. 2, pp. 862–875.

In sum, current legal doctrine is designed to frustrate the personal injury claimants, and the legal client generally, who is seeking effective representation. If he behaves passively and trusts his lawyer, as encouraged under the traditional model, he will be held liable for all but the most serious forms of misconduct by his attorney, thereby risking forfeiture of his claim. If he behaves actively and tries to monitor the actions of his attorney, he risks incurring the displeasure of the lawyer and being branded a troublemaker. The legal profession departs from advocacy of the traditional model of client passivity only so far as to deny the client the very protection the profession claims to provide. Since laymen thus cannot rely upon the legal profession to insure that virtually all practicing lawyers give good service or that poor service will be recompensed, choosing a lawyer becomes a critical matter.

LAYMEN TEND NOT TO "CHOOSE" LAWYERS

According to the traditional model, lay choice of competent lawyers is not seen as an especially important problem. Laymen are thought capable of finding lawyers and of choosing among lawyers based on the criterion of a lawyer's reputation among his colleagues and reputation among knowledgeable community laymen. They are not generally thought to need to know more about the choice of a lawyer. Let us evaluate these judgments according to the evidence of this study.

It has been suggested that laymen who can afford legal service can and do choose lawyers the way they choose doctors, by using a "lay referral system": relatively structured social contacts with lay "influentials" which are used to identify legal problems, find lawyers, and appraise their ability.[57] The concept of a lay referral system implies that the layman has several sources of information, knows a few knowledgeable informants whose judgment he respects, and continually consults with these influentials as a regular part of personal problem solving.

There is no evidence from the sample interviews that claimants do use a lay referral system to deal with legal problems or to find and appraise lawyers. People do not seem to respond to legal problems in the same way in which they respond to medical problems. Unlike doctors, lawyers are rarely used preventively—to anticipate and avoid legal difficulties. A lawyer tends to be sought only to meet a crisis—like a serious personal injury. After their accident, a mere 20 percent (12 of 59) of the clients consulted with an attorney they had used

---

[57] Wilbert E. Moore and Gerald Rosenblum, *The Professions: Roles and Rules* (New York: Russell Sage Foundation, 1970), chap. 5, and sources cited therein.

before, whom they thought of as their "family lawyer." On these relatively rare occasions, people do not "consult" lawyer friends or relatives or even lay influentials seeking background information, do not check with several sources; rather they ask the influentials simply if "they know a good lawyer." There is a lay referral system for legal problems only in the sense that most of the sample clients (75 percent) do select a lawyer to handle their negligence claim primarily on the recommendation of an influential adviser who is thought to be knowledgeable about such things. Hunting and Neuwirth have found that the chances of a person's making a personal injury claim are significantly enhanced by his being in contact with an "authority figure" who can point him to an attorney.[58] Sixty-four percent of the sampled clients (38 of 59) have a lawyer "as a good friend or close relative." In many instances he is their knowledgeable influential and about two-thirds of the time he takes the case himself. Twenty-five percent of the sample (15 of 59) chose a lawyer on simple grounds of convenience: the man down the hall where they worked, the unknown brother of a friend, or somebody an inexperienced neighbor had met at a party. Generally speaking, clients choose the first lawyer they know who comes to mind, the first lawyer recommended to them, or the first lawyer they meet.

Why do so many clients choose lawyers less carefully than they choose doctors? One reason is that many people care more about their health than about their financial condition. Mr. Beanstock goes to three top heart doctors since suffering a mild heart attack a few years ago. He told me,

> Only one knows about the other two. The doctor with the best reputation doesn't have time to study my case. The youngest of the three has the most time to devote and has given me the best attention. . . . A lawyer or a doctor isn't God. By seeing more than one I'm getting insurance.

When I asked him why he didn't shop around for a lawyer in the same way he replied, "A second legal opinion is less important than a second medical opinion. I want health more than money." A second reason why people choose lawyers haphazardly is that in our culture medical problems are a more permissible and safer topic of conversation than legal/financial problems. Somewhat anomalously, bodily malfunction is less intimate, less private because it does not reflect on a man's worth and achievement, as does his financial status. Mrs. Mott, illustratively, didn't consider mentioning her case to friends because "it's a private thing." Perhaps the main reason, though, that middle class

---

[58] Roger Bryant Hunting and Gloria S. Neuwirth, *Who Sues in New York City?* (New York: Columbia University Press, 1962), pp. 65–70.

people tend to choose doctors more carefully than lawyers is that they generally have more experience with doctors and know more about medicine than they have experience with lawyers and know about the law. Miss Schiff observed:

> I know about doctors and dentists because I've been to enough of them . . . but I don't feel that I've been exposed to the law enough to be able to make a really good judgment as to who to see and where to go and how to handle things; nor do I know of any place to go to get advice. . . . That may be my insufficiency, or my lack, or it may be that there has been insufficient publicity.

People are bothered about approaching a lawyer for advice when they are not sure that they have a legal problem. Before Mr. Stacey became friendly with the lawyer who handled his personal injury claim, he told me,

> I had often had legal questions, or what I thought were legal questions but I hadn't known how to go about them. Do you just go into a lawyer's office and say, "Look, I'd like to know something?" I was worried about how a lawyer would react and how much it would cost me to get this advice.

In the year between the time his son's accident case was settled and this interview, Mr. Stacey had consulted with "his" (newfound) lawyer about no less than five legal questions. Prior to the accident he had used a lawyer twice. With some knowledge and experience in using a lawyer preventively, Mr. Stacey now reacts to legal problems much more the way he reacts to medical problems. He is atypical however.

Being better informed about medical problems, laymen can more freely question elements of the traditional professional model such as the idea of an objectively precise medical diagnosis and the idea that all certified doctors are competent. Knowing less about lawyers they are less confident that legal problems are not routine, are less sure about what legal specialties exist and how important it is to consult a specialist. Appraising a doctor is a formidable task for patients, but there is some social support for judging a doctor according to such criteria as how much time he spends with the patient, how accessible he is when a medical problem arises, and whether he is affiliated with a well-reputed hospital.[59] Criteria for lawyer appraisal are less familiar.

When asked the question, "How can someone tell if he has chosen a very competent lawyer?" 24 percent (14 of 59) of the client interviewees said by his reputation, 37 percent (22 of 59) said by his manner once you have met him, and 39 percent (23 of 59) said that there was really no way to tell. Though more than a third of the clients expressed a belief in their common

---

[59] Eliot Freidson, *Patient's Views of Medical Practice* (New York: Russell Sage Foundation, 1961).

sense ability to judge a man's competence by the impression he makes, no client declined to give his case to a lawyer during the initial consultation and only three of the 24 clients dissatisfied with their attorney took the case to another lawyer. It is one thing to recognize a standard and another to implement it. Two criteria were most often employed in practice: the attorney's convenience and his reputation with one thought to be knowledgeable. Neither was particularly productive. Clients who reported having used an attorney known to be wellregarded by the referring influential did not receive significantly better results than clients who found a lawyer without consulting a referrer thought to be knowledgeable.[60] Many putative knowledgeables are not in fact very well informed about either personal legal problem solving or the professional standing of the attorneys they refer people to. People frequently offer advice they are unqualified to give. Then, too, many nonlitigating attorneys, when asked for informal advice about a suit from a friend or relative, try to keep the case for themselves, lured by the often unrealistic prospect of quick settlement and a maximum profit.

Moreover, the recommendation of even a knowledgeable reference with respect to a particular lawyer or law firm may be based on factors irrelevant to the one seeking the reference. This is illustrated in Mrs. Lubin's case. Mrs. Lubin, herself a dentist, said, "I trusted the lawyer because I trusted the man who recommended him." The referrer was a businessman whose company had used a respected negligence firm to defend it against employee and customer personal injury lawsuits. In the company's cases the senior attorney himself took charge of the defenses. Mrs. Lubin's case was apparently turned over to a younger associate. According to the panel evaluation, she received in settlement less than half of what her case was worth.

The one criterion most clients (65 percent of the sample) seem to accept is that negligence specialists perform better than nonspecialists. However, most clients didn't know whether or not their lawyer was a negligence specialist. Sometimes, even knowledge of negligence specialists is not enough. Mr. Thorp, an insurance broker for 30 years, gave his injury claim to a relatively inexperienced lawyer who, Mr. Thorp now thinks, induced him to settle for too little too soon.

> It's my fault that I didn't get a better lawyer. With all I know about the big specialists and with all the contacts in the industry, I should have looked further.

---

[60] Of the referred clients, 60 percent (26 of 43) received a good case result while 50 percent (7 of 14) of the clients not so referred received a good recovery. The difference is not statistically significant. The indicator of case result is discussed in Chapter 2.

In sum, clients have difficulties finding effective legal service, in part because they are unsure about the nature of legal problems, about the criteria relevant for lawyer choice, and about ways to apply the criteria in which they do believe. They tend to rely too heavily on the advice of influentials they think to be knowledgeable who in fact are not a significant source of guidance to effective legal representation. Client use of legal services is less a matter of informed choice than of taking the first lawyer who comes along. If a client cannot rely upon the fact of a lawyer's bar certification or on his reputation among referrers, what are reliable indicators of professional effectiveness? The data of this study provide three useful answers.

RELEVANT INDICIA OF PROFESSIONAL COMPETENCE

Size of Firm

In his study of the New York City Bar, Jerome Carlin found that the size of the firm with which an attorney is affiliated is a prime indicator of his status within the legal profession. Carlin reports that size of firm tends to correlate highly with other indicia of status such as attendance at an elite law school, high personal income, wealthy clients, and type of practice. At the top of the profession stands the senior partner in the large corporate firm. In the lower strata are the solo practitioners.[61] Using firm size as a measure of professional standing, this study provides data to test the proposition that professional status is a reliable indicator of professional competence.

There were 62 attorneys with offices in Manhattan who represented the sample clients and had direct contact with them. Five of these men each represented, independently, two of the sample clients. Seventy-one percent (42 of 59) of the clients dealt with one lawyer or law firm alone. Thirteen clients (22 percent) had their cases farmed out to negligence specialists by the first attorney; five specialists never met the client. Four clients (7 percent) took their cases away from the first lawyer and gave them to a second. Information about 60 of these lawyers was solicited; some data were obtained with respect to 55 (91 percent) of them.[62] In Table 5.1, it is seen that the same pattern of stratification that Carlin finds for the general bar exists within the negligence sub-bar (or at least that portion of it employed by the sample clients).

---

[61] Jerome Carlin, *Lawyers' Ethics* (New York: Russell Sage Foundation, 1966), chap. 2. See also Jack Ladinsky, "Careers of Lawyers, Law Practice and Legal Institutions," *American Sociological Review* 28 (1963): 47–54.

[62] For the criteria and method of gathering the lawyer data, see Appendix A, "The Research Method."

Table 5.1: Negligence Attorneys by Size of Firm

Firm Size	No.	Percentage	Stratum
Solo	7 }	56	Lower
2 men	20 }		
3–4 men	8	17	Medium
5–10 men	8 }	27	Upper
More than 10 men	5 }		

As part of the same pattern, we would also expect to find positive associations between firm size and personal income, and firm size and educational background, within the negligence sub-bar. This is, in fact, the case. Of the "lower stratum" lawyers, 26 percent (7 of 27) report earning more than $30,000 annually compared with 85 percent (11 of 13) of the "upper stratum" lawyers. Of the "lower stratum" lawyers, 18.5 percent attended one of the more highly respected law schools,[63] compared with 38.5 percent (5 of 13) of the "upper stratum."

Applying the Carlin measure of status to our lawyer sample and comparing it with the recoveries received by the clients they represented, it is seen (Table 5.2) that lawyers with high professional status tend to get better case

Table 5.2: The Relation between Firm Size (Lawyer Status) and Case Outcome

Case Result	Five or More Lawyers	Four or Fewer Lawyers	
Good[a]	75% (12)	55% (17)	29
Poor	25% (4)	45% (14)	18
	N = 16	N = 31	47

[a] A good result is actually recovering at least 70 percent of the mean panel evaluation.

outcomes.[64] The chances of a poor outcome are one in four where the client employs attorneys from a larger firm, compared with almost 1 in 2 where the client employs an attorney from a firm having 4 or fewer practitioners.

---

[63] The more highly respected law schools are Harvard, Columbia, Chicago, and N.Y.U. None of the sample attended Yale, Stanford, Berkeley, or Michigan.

[64] The relationship is not significant, using Fisher's Exact Test, at the 0.05 level. However, it is quite possible that the relationship would have been statistically significant had the sample been larger.

Specialization

A second respected indicator of legal competence is whether or not the lawyer specializes in a particular area of law practice. Jerome Carlin, in his New York City study, defined a specialist as a lawyer who earns 50 percent or more of his income from one type of practice. Basing his figures on a large sample involving interviews with more than 800 New York City lawyers, Carlin found that 15 percent of the general New York bar are negligence specialists, 45 percent specialize in commercial law, 17 percent in trusts and estates, 14 percent in real estate law, and 3 percent in matrimonial and/or criminal law.[65] Forty-eight of the attorneys to whom I sent questionnaires replied to the question, "Approximately what percentage of your own work, in terms of income, is personal injury practice?" Applying the 50 percent criterion, 60 percent (31 of 48) of the attorneys were negligence specialists.

In Table 5.3, it is seen that a claim is improved by employing a negligence specialist.[66] The chances of a poor outcome with a negligence specialist are 1 in 3.

Table 5.3: Relation between Lawyer Specialization in Negligence Law and Case Result

Case Result	Negligence Specialist	Nonspecialist	
Good	67%	47%	
	(20)	(8)	28
Poor	33%	53%	
	(10)	(9)	19
	N = 30	N = 17	47

As indicated in Chapter 2, a third set of criteria useful to clients in appraising lawyers are the following: (1) congeniality of personality, (2) responsiveness to questions and requests, (3) consistency of answers, and (4) willingness to inform the client. These criteria can be applied not only to appraise a lawyer once selected but to choose a lawyer after an initial consultation. Knowledge that lawyer status and degree of specialization are useful indicia of effective service is not much help so long as clients cannot get direct information about the status and specialized training and experience of the lawyers they consider consulting. This is the kind of information the public has not been provided by the legal profession.

---

[65] Carlin, *Lawyers' Ethics,* pp. 12–13, table 1.

[66] The relationship is not significant at the 0.05 level using Fisher's Exact Test. Here again, it might well be statistically significant were the sample larger.

THE "ORGANIZED BAR" HAS RESTRICTED CLIENT INFORMATION RELEVANT TO OBTAINING EFFECTIVE LEGAL SERVICE

There is more to making an intelligent choice of a lawyer than simply knowing what are some of the relevant criteria of choice. Nevertheless, it is probably true that the more relevant information about competent lawyers and their availability that laymen have, the easier it is for them to make informed choices and thus gain access to effective service. Instead of helping clients to learn about available legal services, the bar has spent much of its energy restricting clients' access to information and thereby, their opportunities for effective representation.

For one thing the public has been provided with very little information about the indicators of legal competence. In fact, there has been very little legal scholarship that bears on developing this information. Status as an indicator of professional competence is assumed to be valid by the one national rating service for lawyers published in this country. It is the *Martindale-Hubbell Law Directory,* in five volumes, revised annually. This directory is published by a private company and lists almost all practicing attorneys in each town and city in America. It is intended for the use of lawyers in selecting associate counsel or in referring clients in distant jurisdictions. It is not intended for use by clients seeking an attorney.[67] A "Confidential Key" printed on the inside cover of each volume states that:

> No arbitrary rule for determining legal ability can be formulated. Ratings are based upon the standard of ability for the place where the lawyer practices. Age, practical experience, nature and length of practice, and other relevant qualifications are considered. Lawyers are given an a,b,c ranking, or not ranked at all. Absence of rating characters must not in any case be construed as derogatory to anyone, as we do not undertake to publish ratings of all lawyers.[68]

A telephone call to their executive offices failed to provide any elaboration of how the rating system works, what sources of information are utilized or why and when ratings are not undertaken. Personal inquiry among experienced corporate lawyers revealed that ratings are primarily based on anonymous information solicited from prominent corporate colleagues, judges, and bar lead-

---

[67] However, clients are occasionally advised to make use of it anyway. See, e.g., Edward Siegel, *How To Avoid Lawyers* (New York: Information, Inc., 1969), p. 413.

[68] Martindale-Hubbell, Inc., 1 Prospect Street, Summit, N.J., 1969 ed.

ers. Barlow Christensen, research attorney for the American Bar Foundation has written,

> The Martindale-Hubbell system is based essentially upon hearsay, and while anonymity may encourage informants to be frank, it may also invite evaluation on bases other than proficiency. It is said that in some communities an "a" rating in Martindale-Hubbell is more a sign of social acceptance than of superior proficiency, and indeed it is fairly common to find "c" or "b" rated lawyers who are actually more proficient than certain "a" rated lawyers in the same community.[69]

The publishers refuse to be pinned down into specifying what criteria, if any besides reputation, they use to determine professional standing. But their ratings and nonratings imply that professional standing—however impressionistically derived—is crucial. Recently, an antitrust lawsuit was filed against Martindale-Hubbell alleging that the Directory permits established attorneys to suppress potential competitors by basing its ratings on their solicited, and presumptively biased, evaluations of their competitors' competence.[70]

Even if the Martindale-Hubbell (M-H) rating system were accessible to the public and were reliable, it would be of little help in choosing a negligence lawyer. Only 2 of the 62 attorneys in the sample were rated by M-H at all. Excluding, as it does, several attorneys well regarded by their colleagues, it not only reflects the relatively low status of the negligence bar among the primarily commercial lawyers and the judges consulted by M-H, but demonstrates the system's impracticality as a reference source for a client with a medium-sized claim.

The putative justification for restricting client access to such information is the need to combat "commercialization" of the profession. Among the proscribed forms of "commercialization" are direct advertising to the public, client solicitation such as referral fees paid to nonlawyers, unauthorized legal practice by nonlawyers and, until recently, group legal services for lay organizations.

The assumptions behind the policy of attacking commercialization are stated in a 1925 opinion of the ABA Committee on Professional Ethics:

> Furnishing, selling or exploiting of the legal services of members of the Bar is derogatory to the dignity and self-respect of the profession, tends to lower

---

[69] Barlow F. Christensen, *Lawyers for People of Moderate Means* (Chicago: American Bar Foundation, 1970), p. 121.

[70] *Steingold* v. *Martindale-Hubbell, Inc.,* Civil Action No. 72–1460 (N.D. Cal., filed Aug. 11, 1972). The action is discussed in a comment, "The Applicability of the Sherman Act to Legal Practice and Other 'Non-commercial' Activities," *Yale Law Journal* 82 (1973): 313.

the standards of professional character and conduct and *thus lessens the usefulness of the profession to the public,* and that a lawyer is guilty of misconduct when he makes it possible, by thus allowing his services to be exploited or dealt in, for others to commercialize the profession and bring it into disrepute. (Italics mine.)[71]

The bar associations and the courts have placed restrictions on forms of activity which have come to be a regularly accepted part of normal business practice for other professionals. Thus, lawyers are prohibited not only from buying advertisements, but also from stating their areas of special competence in the yellow pages or from stating their specialties or professional honors and accomplishments on their office signs or business cards.[72] Nor have any states but one provided any alternative certification procedure to help clients identify lawyers with special training or specialized practices.[73] The one exception is California, where in early 1973 the state bar association announced standards under which California attorneys will now be able to qualify as specialists in the fields of criminal law, workmen's compensation and taxation. Lawyers have been censured, suspended, and disbarred for paying "investigators" to solicit clients—even where the clients have legitimate legal claims and where it is conceded that the "ambulance-chasing" attorney gives the clients competent representation.[74] Lawyers have been rebuked for offering competitive fee quotations to clients and for systematically charging fees below the minimum fee schedules set by many local bar associations.[75] Furthermore, the courts have

---

[71] *Opinions on Professional Ethics* (Chicago: American Bar Foundation, 1967 ed.), Formal Opinion 8, pp. 243–244

[72] Ibid., Formal Opinions 260 and 286, pp. 581–582 and pp. 631–633. The Appellate Division First Department has enjoined two Manhattan attorneys from displaying office signs, stating in "large gold letters," "Law Offices—Accountants—Insurance—Real Estate." Reported in *The New York Times,* April 19, 1969.

[73] See "Recognition of Specialization in the Legal Profession," in Glen Greenwood and Robert Frederickson, *Specialization in the Medical and Legal Professions* (Mundelein, Ill.: Callaghan, 1964), Chap. IV, pp. 99–120. One medical sociologist has suggested that opposition to specialization in medicine in the 1920s and 1930s was at about the same point it is today in the legal profession: J. Bernhard Stern, "The Specialist and the General Practitioner," ed., E. Gartly Jaco, *Patients, Physicians and Illness* (New York: Free Press, 1958), p. 353. The full text of the California Standards may be obtained from: Director, Legal Specialization, The State Bar of California, 601 McAllister Street, San Francisco, California 94102.

[74] See for example, *In Re Cohn,* 10 Ill. 2d 186, 139 N.E. 2d 301 (1957) and the comment on the case in "A Critical Analysis of Rules against Solicitation by Lawyers," University of Chicago Law Review 25 (1958): 674–685.

[75] See *Opinions on Professional Ethics,* Formal Opinions 292 and 307, pp. 646–647, pp. 673–676. But see *Goldfarb* v. *Virginia State Bar,* 355 F. Supp. 491 (E. D. Va. 1973) which recently ruled that such schedules violate the anti-trust laws.

restricted the practice of members of occupations which overlap the lawyer's
function—bank officials, tax accountants, and title insurers among others.[76]
The effect of these latter rulings is to restrict the supply of specialized consumer services by foreclosing "unauthorized legal practice" even where the
nonlawyer is more expert in his field than many general practice lawyers. Another traditional restriction, the prohibition of lay corporate and associational
intermediaries between lawyers and classes of clients is in the process of revision under recent Supreme Court decisions holding unconstitutional the blanket
prohibition of group legal services. Group legal services have already been
shown to produce economies of scale and specialization and have extended legal representation to clients who otherwise would not have found or used
attorneys.[77]

These anticommercialization measures have two consequences which may
be more harmful than the dangers to which they are addressed. First and most
important, they pose formidable barriers to lay client access to competent attorneys. It is difficult for clients to gain information relevant to the choice of
an expert adviser when the supply of expert information is noncompetitively
restricted. Second, these measures tend to increase status inequalities within
the profession. Lawyers starting out and lower-status attorneys are denied
competitive opportunities for challenging the more successful firms. One solo
specialist said bitterly,

> I can name you a dozen of the top negligence attorneys who have regularly
> retained press agents to get their names in the news. . . . Those guys won't
> take cases which don't have 100 percent liability, and they lose a lot of them
> anyway.

The top negligence lawyers are assured of a constant flow of potential clients
who read about them or who are referred by attorneys who know their repu-

---

[76] *Connecticut State Bar Association* v. *Hartford Bank & Trust Co.,* 145 Conn.
222, 140 A.2d 863 (1958); *Oregon State Bar* v. *John H. Miller & Co.,* 235 Or. 341, 385
P.2d 181 (1963) (in which it is conceded that the tax accountant was knowledgeable);
State Bar of Arizona v. *Arizona Land Title Co.,* 90 Ariz. 76, 366 P.2d 1 (1961). An excellent critique of the unauthorized practice doctrine is contained in Johnstone and Hopson, *Lawyers and Their Work,* pp. 163–197. Restrictions on unauthorized practice are
defended in the publications of the Standing Committee on Unauthorized Practice of
Law of the American Bar Association. See especially the seasonal newsletter, "The Unauthorized Practice News."

[77] Leading cases are *NAACP* v. *Button,* 371 U.S. 415 (1963); *Brotherhood of
Railroad Trainmen* v. *Virginia ex. rel. Virginia State Bar* 377 U.S. 1 (1967), *rehearing
denied* 377 U.S. 1027; *United Mine Workers* v. *Illinois State Bar Association,* 389 U.S.
217 (1967); and *United Transportation Union* v. *State Bar of Michigan,* 401 U.S. 576
(1971).

tation. Less successful specialists have to rely almost completely on contacts they can establish with general practitioners who will route referrals exclusively to them. All negligence lawyers are disadvantaged in comparison with commercial lawyers. Few of their clients are likely to return even when satisfied. Most people do not bring more than one personal injury legal action in a lifetime. It is harder to establish a regular lay clientele—unless one is lucky enough to have satisfied clients who are opinion leaders in various social circles. While this disadvantage results from the nature of the practice, commercial lawyers have an additional and unnecessarily inequitable opportunity to exploit indirect (therefore ethical) channels of advertising and solicitation. As Judge Bristow of the Illinois Supreme Court noted in his dissent in *In Re Cohn,*

> Opulent lawyers and large law firms who do not employ "runners" to attract business do spend large sums of money for memberships in country clubs, entertainment in fashionable surroundings and other similar amenities of social intercourse. That the primary purpose of these expenditures is the attraction of law business and not hospitality is attested by the fact that such lawyers regularly claim and the Internal Revenue Department regularly allows deductions for these expenditures as "business" and not "personal" expenses.[78]

Put another way, the traditional justification for anticommercialization measures is that they insulate the lawyer from just those market pressures that lessen his detachment, thus freeing him to give his client disinterested service.[79]

In Chapter 4, evidence was presented suggesting just the reverse: the pressures of practice are increased for many lawyers—especially the specialists —by restrictions on competitive practices. These restrictions virtually force specialists to make the (theoretically) unethical but (tacitly) permitted practice of giving large referral fees to general practice attorneys who farm cases into which they have put almost no work. The client tends to pay a higher fee and further, to lose access to the decision making in his case.

Since World War II, the Bar Association of the City of New York has sponsored a Lawyer Referral Service ("LRS") to put interested, fee-paying potential clients in touch with competent attorneys. This is one major attempt at resolving the conflict of values between the bar's desire to fight commercialism, yet promote the use of lawyers. The bar association through institutional

---

[78] 10 Ill. 2d 186, 196, 139 N.E. 2d 301, 306 (1957).

[79] The justification is presented, though not necessarily endorsed, by Talcott Parsons in his article, "A Sociologist Looks at the Legal Profession," in his *Essays in Sociological Theory,* rev. ed. (New York: Free Press, 1954), pp. 370–385.

advertising informs the public of the service's availability.[80] A panel of lawyers in private practice is selected to receive the referrals. The panel lawyers are screened by a bar association committee and agree to accept all cases referred to them, insofar as possible, and to charge the client a reasonable fee. Potential clients are briefly interviewed in the LRS office by a staff attorney. If they appear to have a legal problem, the clients are referred to one of the private practitioners on the panel.[81]

Though widely endorsed, LRS has been criticized both by lawyers who see it as unfair competition and by those who feel it is, as presently constituted, an insufficient answer to the need for adequate legal services for the middle class.[82] Judged by the lack of impact of the LRS on our client sample, its effectiveness could be questioned. Only 4 of the 59 interviewees had ever heard of the service. Of these, two were lawyers themselves. The two lay clients who had heard of the LRS said they had sought its help. One of these clients reported being turned away when he informed the staff attorney that he had been living in New York for eight years. He claims he was told the service is only available for new residents of the community who have not yet had the chance to become acquainted with available lawyers. This may well be so, for the LRS *Handbook* states:

> The referral service is not designed to help clients who have already engaged lawyers or who number lawyers among their acquaintance. Since such persons normally have little difficulty in obtaining legal advice without assistance from the bar association, referrals in these instances are generally refused.[83]

This "newcomers-only" policy overestimates the knowledgeability and resourcefulness of most urban people. It is based on a view of community life more appropriate to a small town in the last century in which

> people could know, from firsthand acquaintance with their whole community, where to go for help; everybody could know something of everybody else's

---

[80] This type of institutional advertising has been held to be ethical. *Jacksonville Bar Association* v. *Wilson*, 102 S.2d 292 (Florida, 1958).

[81] The goals and procedures for establishing and administering LRS offices are set forth in the *Handbook of the Standing Committee on Lawyer Referral Service*, 6th ed. (Chicago: American Bar Association, 1968). The Manhattan office is located in the Bar Building at 36 W. 44th Street. Its director is Richard Haydock, one of the pioneers of the national program to establish the service.

[82] Elliot Cheatham, *A Lawyer When Needed* (New York: Columbia University Press, 1963), believes that LRS "has probably been even more effective than the statistics of the referral offices can reveal" (p. 69). Criticism from hostile lawyers is presented and answered by Charles O. Porter, "Answers to Objections to the Lawyer Reference Service," *Oregon Law Review* 31 (1959): 15–27.

[83] *Handbook of the Standing Committee on Lawyer Referral Service*, 5th ed. (1965) p. 13.

business, and this knowledge could curb the layman's natural suspicion of professional mysteries.[84]

Having used a lawyer in another community or a lawyer in New York who was found to be unsatisfactory, or even knowing a commercial lawyer one trusts has little bearing on choosing a proper lawyer to handle one's personal injury claim.

The second client who sought the help of LRS, Mr. Winter, was served even though he had resided in New York for four years. He found the first attorney to whom he was referred "uncooperative" and returned for a second reference, which he received. Neither lawyer considered himself to be a negligence specialist. Mr. Winter received $13,000 in settlement on a claim valued at $20,000 by the evaluation panel. LRS has been criticized for not adequately checking the competence of the lawyers on its panel. Generally speaking, LRS panel lawyers are not the most successful men in the profession, but rather those lawyers who have some difficulty obtaining clients by other routes.[85] Apparently, too, the service has not been well advertised. Institutional legal advertising generally has been characterized by a leading legal historian as "unimaginative, limited and too sporadic to have lasting effect."[86] Ironically, the one program which the bar appears to have made effective is cracking down on ambulance chasing. As stated earlier, not a single one of the client interviewees reports having had his case chased. With not even this unethical source of accessibility, Manhattan clients have a greater problem learning about lawyers than residents of communities where the bar is less vigilant.

In sum, clients have a problem obtaining effective representation (1) because the legal profession and the courts do not maintain uniformly high standards and do not provide adequate remedies to clients victimized by incompetent service, (2) because clients are uninformed about choosing lawyers, and (3) because clients receive minimal assistance from the bar in obtaining information relevant to effective choice.

---

[84] J. Willard Hurst, *The Growth of American Law* (Boston: Little, Brown, 1960), p. 326.

[85] Christensen, *Lawyers for People of Moderate Means,* pp. 183-204; Murray Schwartz, "Changing Patterns of Legal Services," in *Law in a Changing America,* ed. Geoffrey Hazard (Englewood Cliffs, N.J.: Prentice-Hall, 1968), p. 122.

[86] Hurst, N.J.: *The Growth of American Law,* p. 326.

Chapter Six: Principles and Policies Governing Professional-Client Relationships

THE REALITY OF THE TRADITIONAL MODEL

In Chapter 1 a traditional model for the conduct of professional-client relationships, widely accepted by professionals, by laymen, and by social commentators on the professions, was delineated. This model is both normative and descriptive: it is both a statement of the ideal standards by which such relationships ought to be governed and a statement of the way these relationships usually are conducted in reality. The traditional model was stated in terms of six propositions. The central proposition is that clients who trustingly and passively delegate responsibility for the decisions involving their problems get better results in dealing with their problems than clients who actively seek information about their problems and participate in and share responsibility for dealing with them. Five additional interrelated propositions provide much of the justification for this central idea that clients are better off by delegating responsibility and control to professionals. These propositions are that: (1) ineffective professional service is rare; (2) professional problems have a best technical solution inaccessible to lay understanding; (3) professionals are capable of giving disinterested service which avoids any conflict of interest with the client; (4) high standards of professional performance are set and maintained by the professions themselves and by the courts; and (5) effective professional services provided by the professions are readily accessible to the paying public.

The four preceding chapters have assembled and analyzed data drawn from interviews with 60 New York City clients of lawyers who represented them in personal injury claims; from questionnaires submitted to their attorneys; from texts about personal injury practice; from interviews with informed participants in the personal injury claims process; and from codes, statutes, and case law as they apply to attorneys generally and to attorneys who handle negligence claims in particular. These data offer a direct challenge to the realism of each proposition of the traditional model. In Chapter 2 evidence was presented showing that clients who actively participate in the conduct of their claims get significantly better results than those passively delegating decision making responsibility. The main explanations offered are that clients can play a constructive role in appraising and assisting the performance of their attorneys and that continuing client appraisal of lawyer performance is warranted by the frequency with which attorneys perform ineffectively in making personal injury claims. It was shown, in Chapter 3, that there is no single, routine best solution to clients' legal problems in claims-making because there is so much uncertainty in the claims process and because important facets of the problems and of the criteria for dealing with them are dependent on the unique circumstances and subjective feelings of each client. Furthermore, evidence was presented that these problems are capable of lay understanding not only in that clients tend to be in the best position to identify the criteria for decision most relevant to their own needs but also in that the uncertainty of the claims process can be explained in terms of open choices and the risks of alternative actions at each stage of making a claim and in terms of key institutions of the process which operate largely beyond the control of either client or attorney— insurers, the courts, the doctrine of negligence, judges, and juries. In Chapter 4, a fundamental economic conflict of interest between the negligence attorney and his client was identified. This interest conflict necessarily leads to actions on the attorney's part which often do not reflect the best interests of the client. Evidence was presented in Chapter 5 demonstrating that the professions and the courts have failed to set or maintain high standards of performance by negligence attorneys or to insure that the public is provided with informed choices in seeking effective professional personal injury claims service. The case law of professional responsibility fails to protect clients against incompetent attorneys by unfairly treating the client as if he were the informed and responsible decision maker in the claim while, at the same time, the legal profession denies the client access to the very information which might provide a basis for the assumption of some client responsibility. In sum, clients are forced to delegate decision making responsibility to attorneys who then refuse to accept this responsibility when performance breaks down.

THE GENERALIZABILITY OF LESSONS DRAWN FROM NEW YORK CITY PERSONAL INJURY LAW PRACTICE

Over and above disputing the research method, the validity of which is discussed in Appendix A, what is to be made of these findings? Three plausible responses about their generalizability may be anticipated. One response is to try to distinguish the New York City situation from professional environments elsewhere in America. Some observers will be tempted to believe that New York City lawyers are less effectively disciplined and are less competent than lawyers elsewhere. This belief remains to be tested by further studies, but it is questionable for three reasons. First, professional self-policing in the bar is probably more effective in New York City than elsewhere in the country. The Defense Research Institute, the insurers' interest group whose purpose is to criticize the policies and counter the public positions adopted by the American Trial Lawyers Association, has given New York credit for "having the most consistent (negligence practice) regulation of any of the fifty states."[1] Jointly, the Coordinating Committee on Discipline, the Judicial Conference, and the Committee on Grievances of the Association of the Bar of the City of New York, have the largest and most active staff in the nation to monitor and enforce professional performance. Second, in several respects, the performance of negligence attorneys may well be of a higher calibre in New York City than elsewhere. For one thing, the New York Bar is more specialized than the bars of smaller communities.[2] More negligence work is handled by litigation and negligence specialists. Specialists tend, as was suggested in the last chapter, to be more proficient. Because New York City has the highest accident rate, because New York juries have a reputation for favoring plaintiffs, and because many of the largest insurers have main offices within the City, New York has attracted many of the top negligence specialists in the country. While there may be three or four negligence specialists with top reputations in a medium-sized city, there are dozens in New York. Their activity in the New York Trial Lawyers Association and the Practicing Law Institute seminars in continuing legal education and their example in the courtroom probably has a beneficial impact on the competence of many New York negligence attorneys below the top. New York negligence lawyers, as reflected in the reports of sampled clients, are rarely guilty of the more serious forms of professional misconduct. Not a single client reported having his case "chased" by an attorney. Nor did any client report evidence of attorney misconduct of a nature that presently induces bar association discipline. Some lawyers apparently violated norms of due care by such "nonconduct" as unreasonable delay in commencing a legal action, by not promptly and accurately reporting to their clients insurer settle-

---

[1] "Contingent Fee; Insurance Company Group Asks Canon 13 Revision To Limit 'Abuses,' " *New York Law Journal* (June 23, 1966): 1.

[2] See, for example, Joel Handler, *The Lawyer and His Community* (Madison: University of Wisconsin Press, 1967), p. 40.

ment offers, or, in six cases, by failing to inform the client that his case had been farmed out to another attorney. However, as we have seen, failure to meet these "nonfeasance" norms generally is tolerated by judges and bar associations. They are probably breached frequently in all strata of the profession and in all problem areas of the law. Third, we have tried to show that failure of the professional ideal is not a question of incompetence or lack of integrity, but the result of situational and role pressures experienced by all negligence attorneys. Data from other studies amply show that these pressures are part of the personal injury claims process everywhere.[3]

A second response to my findings about the traditional model is to distinguish between the negligence bar and other branches of the legal profession. If the negligence bar were a nonprofessional exception to otherwise professional legal performance, the traditional model would remain valid. I doubt that the view of negligence practice presented here departs dramatically from the realities of law practice in probating estates, domestic relations, personal taxation, realty conveyancing, landlord-tenant problems, or consumer complaints. In these areas too, aggressive and powerful adversaries, often arbitrary and peremptory courts, and one-sided laws pressure against the easy resolution of disputes. Decisions are complex and open, interest conflicts between lawyers and clients are pervasive, clients are generally discouraged from actively participating in the decisions of their cases, professional performance is uneven, and lawyer generalists are often at a disadvantage in providing effective service. Fees tend to be based on a percentage of the amount of money at issue, usually unrelated to the quality of service provided; professional standards are vague and unenforced, except with respect to extreme violations; and clients do not know how to go about choosing effective legal representation. Where the legal problems are anticipatory, as in the drafting of a will, mistakes may not be discovered for years, until it is too late.[4] One area of the law about which we have some empirical knowledge is criminal law. In the crimi-

---

[3] Alfred Conard et al., *Automobile Accident Costs and Payments* (Ann Arbor: University of Michigan Press, 1964); Hans Zeisel, Harry Kalven, and Bernard Buchholz, *Delay in the Court* (Boston: Little, Brown, 1959); Walter E. Meyer Research Institute of Law, *Dollars, Delay, and the Automobile Victim* (Indianapolis, Ind.: Bobbs-Merrill, 1968); Jerome Carlin, *Lawyers on Their Own* (New Brunswick, N.J.: Rutgers University Press, 1962).

[4] As in *Lucas* v. *Hamm,* 56 Cal.2d 583 (1961), 364 P.2d 685 *cert. denied,* 368 U.S. 987 (1962). For a discussion of estate planning which accords with my view of the nature of personal injury problems see John Appleman, "Estate Analysis: The Role of the Family Attorney," *American Bar Association Journal* 36 (1950): 982–985.

nal law the norms of procedural due process and the constitutional right to effective representation are most explicit and supposedly most carefully scrutinized by appellate courts.[5] In fact, there is less professional service provided to criminal defendants than is provided negligence plaintiffs. The norms of client protection are systematically violated by the police in the interest of "law and order,"[6] by the courts in the interest of administrative efficiency,[7] and by criminal lawyers in the interest of making a living.[8] It is admittedly difficult to make informed and precise comparisons with performance in other fields of personal legal problem solving. Actual as opposed to idealized conditions need to be investigated systematically.

Even if it does not apply to lower-class or middle-class law practice, many would say, the traditional professional model probably does fit the practice of corporate law by elite lawyers of the profession. Evidence is reported by Carlin and by Erwin Smigel to support this distinction—at least with respect to the frequency of violations of ethical norms.[9] There is no direct evidence to support or dispute the judgment that most corporate lawyers give most of their clients effective service. Smigel has identified some "strains and dilemmas" that pressure elite lawyers[10] and the temptations to act more like businessmen than like professionals.

Whether or not corporate lawyers tend to follow the norms of the traditional model, the behavior of corporate clients is often that of considerable participation. Many corporations adopt a strategy of relatively extreme client activity when contrasted with the behavior of most middle-class clients. They employ their own house counsel to monitor and appraise independently the details of legal advice provided by the retained corporate law firm. Sometimes two or more law firms are retained to give different viewpoints on the same problem or to check each other's advice. Fees are subject to negotiation and

---

[5] Kenneth Goldman, "Criminal Waiver: The Requirements of Personal Participation, Competence and Legitimate State Interest," *California Law Review* 54 (1966): 1261–1299. For an introductory discussion see Anthony Lewis, *Gideon's Trumpet* (New York: Knopf, 1964).

[6] See Michael Wald et al., "Interrogations in New Haven: The Impact of Miranda," *Yale Law Journal* 76 (July 1967): 1519–1648.

[7] Goldman, "Criminal Waiver"; Lester Mazor, "Power and Responsibility in the Attorney-Client Relation," *Stanford Law Review* 20 (June 1968): 1129–1134.

[8] Abraham Blumberg, *Criminal Justice* (Chicago: Quadrangle Books, 1967).

[9] Jerome Carlin, *Lawyers' Ethics* (New York: Russell Sage Foundation, 1966), chaps. 4–7; Erwin Smigel, *The Wall Street Lawyer* (New York: Free Press, 1964), pp. 262–275.

[10] Smigel, *The Wall Street Lawyer,* pp. 288–307.

companies do not consider it perverse to comparison shop among law firms for the most suitable counsel. Furthermore, sophisticated nonlawyer corporate officials recognize the policy implications of putatively "technical advice" and inform themselves about the legal issues, insisting on taking ultimate decision making responsibility. Admittedly, corporations have manpower and financial resources and sophisticated businessmen have access to relevant information unavailable to middle-class citizens. However, it has been seen in this study that the principle of active and questioning client participation can be used as well for personal problem solving. Most importantly, the fact that many corporate clients adopt a strategy of active participation shows that, at least for them, the corporate legal experience does not support the traditional model but rather raises further evidence for its reevaluation. On the other hand, it is no doubt true that many executives of large and successful companies accept the traditional passive client role.[11] The corporate lawyer-client relationship with respect to issues of responsibility and control is obviously a matter that merits investigation.

A third response to these findings would be to accept that the traditional model is no longer an appropriate ideal for legal practice, but remains valid in other professional areas—especially in the "purer" professions of medicine and scientific research. This too is a matter deserving further study. I am skeptical about the distinction. It was once made to distinguish the law from "lesser" commercial professions. Commercial practice has more in common with the practice of law than many lawyers would like to admit. In Chapter 1 several sources were cited from the fields of medicine and medical sociology with evidence of the inappropriateness of the traditional model as applied to the doctor-patient and researcher-experimental subject relationships. Instances of desultory professional performance comparable to those described in this book were found to be common in two imaginative and elaborate published reports offering empirical evaluations of physicians at work. In 1953, a team of medical researchers observed the work of 88 North Carolina general practice doctors for one month as they treated their regular patients. Each doctor was graded on the techniques of six activities: history taking, physical examination, use of laboratory diagnostic aids, therapy, preventive medicine, and record-keeping. When the results were compiled, only 25 percent (22 of 88) of the physicians were rated highly; 31 percent (27 of 88) were rated only satisfactory and fully 44 percent (39 of 88) were rated unsatisfactory. Only seven doctors received the highest rating because,

---

[11] So Wilbert E. Moore has observed: *The Conduct of the Corporation* (New York: Random House, 1966 Vintage ed.), especially pp. 180–189, 243–250.

only they knew exactly what they were doing and did it thoroughly and systematically. Even more important . . . they seemed to enjoy the intellectual challenge of medicine. [At the other extreme], sixteen doctors did a sketchy, hap-hazard job . . . some of them had evidently never had the basic training needed for the practice of good medicine. Others knew better, but didn't seem to care enough.[12]

In the second empirical evaluation of physicians' performance involving a sample of patients who had medical insurance claims paid by Blue Cross (in May 1962) to hospitals in New York City, a panel of 13 clinician specialists reviewed copies of the patients' hospital records. The panel concluded that

only 57 percent of the care given in the total of all admissions reviewed represented "optimal" medical care; 43 percent of the care was believed to have been performed in a "less than optimal" fashion when viewed in light of the standards of present day medical practice.[13]

Relatively recent concern with the rights of medical patients and experimental subjects is leading to a reexamination of many assumptions of the traditional model.[14] While the patient's right to be informed has been better accepted in medicine than in law, very little of its potential has been so far

---

[12] The study is summarized by Lois Hoffman, "How Do Good Doctors Get That Way," in *Patients, Physicians and Illness,* ed. E. Gartly Jaco (New York: Free Press, 1958), p. 367. The full report is authored by Osler Peterson and associates and is published under the title "An Analytical Study of North Carolina General Practice, 1953–1954," *Journal of Medical Education* 31, Part II (December 1956); 1–165. In interesting contrast to my data, the North Carolina evaluators found status criteria of competence to be unreliable. When the clinical skills of the doctors (as rated by trained research observers) were compared with their medical school academic records, the prestige of the school attended, their practical experience and age, no relationships were found. A brilliant student from an elite school was neither more nor less likely to be proficient in practice.

[13] "There was variation by specialty in the proportion of medical care considered as 'optimal'—obstetrics/gynecology, 80 percent; general surgery, 57 percent; pediatrics, 43 percent; and general medicine, only 31 percent. The other specialty areas all had a higher than 80 percent proportion of care considered 'optimal.' The handling of the ophthalmology cases was particularly outstanding; the orthopedic cases were also felt to have received a very satisfactory level of medical care." M. A. Morehead, Director, Medical Audit Unit of the Teamster Center Program, *A Study of the Quality of Hospital Care Secured by a Sample of Teamster Family Members in New York City* (New York: Columbia University School of Public Health and Administrative Medicine, 1964), pp. 7–8.

[14] The best collection of materials dealing with these rights is Jay Katz, *Experimentation with Human Beings* (New York: Russell Sage Foundation, 1972), (hereinafter cited as "Katz").

realized.[15] In fact, barriers to successful medical malpractice actions are even greater than the barriers to legal malpractice suits. The medical testimony of an independent expert is usually essential to establish the standard of reasonable medical care under the circumstances and to show a breach of the standard,[16] whereas, in most jurisdictions, independent expert testimony is not required to prove lawyer negligence.[17] Doctors have responded to the requirement of independent expert testimony with a widespread "conspiracy of silence," a refusal to testify against a colleague. In many communities it is literally impossible to find a single witness to support a malpractice claim.[18] It may be noted that the subjective and idiosyncratic nature of a patient's medical problems have been more generally recognized than the subjective and idiosyncratic nature of a client's legal problems. Some have thought that these personal considerations offer less justification for client collaboration in legal consultations than for patient collaboration in medical consultations because only in the latter is the arena for the diagnosis and cure the patient himself rather than the outside world. This study has tried to show that, on the contrary, the same types of personal considerations occur in legal problem solving where the client, if not the arena for diagnosis and cure, is the principal source of the criteria relevant for choices that take place in the outside world. *A fortiori,* the doubts raised about the traditional view of the nature of professional problems are generalizable to medical problem solving.

While specific comparisons among varying forms of professional-client relationships will undoubtedly reveal significant differences in the nature of

---

[15] The fullest statement and documentation of this viewpoint is Elinor Glass, "Restructuring Informed Consent: Legal Therapy for the Doctor-Patient Relationship," *Yale Law Journal* 79 (1970): 1533–1576. See also Jon Waltz and Thomas Scheuneman, "Informed Consent to Therapy," *Northwestern University Law Review* 64 (1970): 628–650; "Malpractice: Physician's Duty to Inform Patient of Nature and Hazards of Disease or Treatment," *ALR 2d* 29 (1953), pp. 1028–1035.

[16] Sometimes, a skillful plaintiff's attorney can call the defendant doctor as a witness who, if competent to do so, can give the requisite expert testimony about generally accepted community standards of practice. However, considerable skill and luck are required for a doctor to undermine his own defense. See *McDermott* v. *Manhattan Eye and Ear Hospital,* 15 N.Y. 2d 20 (1964).

[17] Allan McCoid, "The Care Required of Medical Practitioners," in *Professional Negligence,* eds. T. G. Roady and W. R. Anderson (Nashville, Tenn.: Vanderbilt University Press, 1960), p. 72. But see *Dorf* v. *Relles,* 355 F. 2d 488 (7th Cir. 1966), where expert testimony was held to be a necessity in a lawyer malpractice suit.

[18] Melvin Belli, "An Accident Therapy Still Applied: The Silent Medical Treatment," *Villanova Law Review* 1 (May 1956): 250 ff; R. M. Marcus, "Conspiracy of Silence," *Cleveland-Marshall Law Review* 3 (September 1965): especially 528–533.

those relationships and the problems each poses for providing effective service, the data of this study seems to present to the traditional model a challenge which cannot be lightly dismissed with respect to any form of professional-client relationship.

THE TRADITIONAL MODEL AS NORM

Some will accept the validity and the generalizability of the evidence presented in this book and yet be unwilling to abandon the traditional model as the ideal pattern of behavior for the professional and client. This is a position justifiable according to at least two concepts of human nature—one conservative and one reformist. The conservative position would be founded on skepticism about the potential for improvement of institutions so dependent upon the frailties of human nature. If men are to rise above their limitations, so the argument goes, it is only by giving them a higher ideal of nobility and selflessness to which to aspire, an ideal which can lift, at best, a few above the pull of human temptations. This higher ideal is admirably provided by the traditional model. The desirability of, as well as the potential for, extensive professional reform is questioned by many of this disposition. They tend to have a view of the development of social institutions such as professional-client relationships which sees existing institutions as a reflection of the desires and needs of those who live and work within these institutions and which mistrusts the ultimate constructiveness of basic institutional reform. "The relationship of authority-dependency between professional and client has developed as it has because that is the way people want it to be." If clients choose a relationship of dependency and if this dependency entails certain risks because of the limitations of professionals and because of the uncertain nature of professional problems then, in the words of Dostoyevski's Grand Inquisitor, it is because "man has no more agonizing anxiety than to find someone to whom he can hand over with all speed the gift of freedom with which the unhappy creature is born."[19]

The reformist defense of the traditional ideal sees it as a potential source of tremendous good. Can it be doubted that many distinguished doctors, lawyers, scientists, teachers, and others have been inspired to careers of extraordinary generosity, probity, and responsibility by the traditional professional ideal? At no time in the past, one may argue, have professionals performed so well, has professional service been more accessible or professional conduct so

---

[19] Fëdor Dostoevski, *The Brothers Karamazov*. Baltimore: Penguin Books, p. 298 (1958 ed., translated by D. Magonshock).

well defined and policed; it is not the ideals that have outlived their usefulness as ideals but an improvable failure of will and initiative in implementing these ideals.

The suitability of norms and models can never finally be proved or disproved.[20] One who believes, as I do, in the uncertainty of professional problem solving would be disingenuous if he were to argue that the traditional model is *certainly* incorrect. Rather, I would suggest that the relevance or appropriateness of models advances or recedes according to the values, skills, interests, and experience which dominate the thoughts of men in particular societies and social settings; and would further contend that knowledge does not advance by disproving models but by exploring newer models which seem more in accord with our values, skills, interests, and experience until they too lose their relevance and are supplanted.

I do not accept the appropriateness of the conservative defense of the traditional model because it relies, I believe, on an unduly pessimistic view of human nature, an undue willingness to tolerate what is wrong with existing institutions, and an unduly fearful attitude about the possibilities of constructive social innovation. Nor do I accept the reformist defense which asks too much from educated professionals and too little from educated laymen. Professionals are asked, under the traditional ideal, to make uncertain problems appear certain, to neutralize their passions, to be uncompromising toward the failings of their colleagues, and to surrender the special privileges of a preferred status. Lay clients, however, are assumed to be virtually helpless in coping with complex personal problems, to be nuisances when they try to involve themselves in the experts' province, and to be incapable of accepting effective decision making responsibility. It seems unfair and unrealistic to ask so much more of professionals than is asked of nonprofessionals. A participatory model which looks to the professional and the lay client more nearly as equals capable of joint collaboration takes a more properly balanced view of human nature. To paraphrase Paul Ramsey's paraphrase of Reinhold Niebuhr's defense of democracy, on both positive and negative grounds, "Man's capacity to become joint adverturers (sic) in a common cause makes the participatory relation possible; man's propensity to overreach his joint adverturer even in a good cause makes the participatory relation necessary."[21]

---

[20] An excellent statement of this conception of models, referred to there as "paradigms," is Thomas Kuhn, *The Structure of Scientific Revolutions* (Chicago: University of Chicago Press, 1962).

[21] Paul Ramsey, "The Patient as Person—Explorations in Medical Ethics," excerpted in Katz, p. 589.

The dominant conclusion of this analysis is that a participatory model for the conduct of professional-client relationships is worthy of serious consideration as a more relevant alternative to the traditional model. Let it be clearly understood, however, that the traditional model is not useless. Not only has it proved a powerful and constructive ideal in the past but also it deals realistically with certain difficulties posed in the practical application of the participatory model. We will, shortly, give some consideration to these difficulties.[22] Moreover, the traditional model suggests certain reforms for improving the effectiveness of professional performance which should be pursued. While there is reason to be moderately skeptical about the prospects for professionals soon adopting these reforms and implementing them effectively, reformers should nonetheless push for them. The four traditional reforms listed below are moves in the right direction.

First, professional education courses should include training in the proper conduct of the professional-client relationship. This training should attend to the client's proper role in the relationship, to the "nontechnical" aspects of the client's problems, to the assumptions and techniques of effective counseling, and to the appropriate disclosure to be made to the client and the appropriate consent to be obtained from him.[23]

Second, the accessibility of competent professional service can be increased within traditional guidelines by the certification of professional specialists, by making available to the public information about the specialties of professionals, and by having professional referral services which refer clients to specialists of recognized standing. This reform, generally adopted by the medical profession, has yet to be adopted by the legal profession.

Third, professional standards can be more vigorously maintained by conducting continuing evaluations of the quality of professional service received by clients, replicating and improving upon the relatively primitive criteria of evaluation used in the relatively few evaluative studies of professional service so far conducted.[24] The recommendations of the Disciplinary Committee, most of which are laudable, can be implemented, including increasing the enforcement staffs of professional associations, publicizing disciplinary proceedings

---

[22] See the section, "The Reality of the Participatory Model," in this chapter.

[23] Some of the issues relevant to such instruction are developed in Jay Katz, "The Education of The Physician-Investigator," in *Ethical Aspects of Experimentation with Human Subjects, Daedalus* 98 (Spring 1969): 480.

[24] One of these, of course, is this book. See footnotes 12 and 13 in this chapter. See also Douglas Rosenthal, Robert Kagan, and Debra Quatrone, *Volunteer Attorneys and Legal Services for the Poor* (New York: Russell Sage Foundation, 1970), especially the discussion on pp. 194–198.

and taking measures such as centralizing authority to promote the censure of such nonprofessional conduct as presently is tolerated.[25]

Fourth, clients who are the victims of negligent, incompetent, or dishonest professional service can be given the greater protection of professionals willing to come forward to testify against their transgressing colleagues in malpractice suits, and can be given greater opportunity for financial recompense through the more extensive creation and publicity of client security funds by professional associations and through the mandatory requirement that professionals carry malpractice bonds or insurance for the benefit of their clients.

THE PARTICIPATORY MODEL AS NORM

The participatory model in the preliminary form presented in this study has six elements:

1. Clients should be active participants in the professional-client relationship, informed of the choices and their attendant risks, involved in the problem solving, and sharing responsibility for those choices with the professional.
2. The nature of professional problems and human nature is such that ineffective professional service should be acknowledged as an inevitably common occurrence.
3. The important decisions of problem solving involve open choices which educated laymen can understand and to which their personal experiences and needs make a positive contribution.
4. Conflicts of interest between professionals and clients are inevitable but nonetheless capable of resolution by collaborative negotiation.
5. Standards of professional and client performance are capable of being defined and maintained by the collaborative effort of professionals and laymen.
6. The calibre of professional service can be increased by giving to the public more information about the nature of problems requiring professional help and the limitations of professional service and by encouraging laymen to shop among available professionals for the service they use.

Informed Consent

The central principle of the participatory model is the principle of informed consent. The principle acknowledges that the professional himself is the most direct source of information relevant to client participation. The pro-

---

[25] Disciplinary Committee, *Problems and Recommendations in Disciplinary Enforcement* (Chicago: American Bar Association, 1970).

fessional should be obligated to disclose to the client the relevant open choices involved in responding to his particular problem. This could include the alternatives involved in identifying the problem, the alternatives for dealing with it, the professional's experience in employing these alternatives, and their anticipated difficulties and benefits. No action should be taken with respect to any of these choices until the client, aware of them, has given his consent. Applying the informed consent principle in concrete situations raises several issues. Four of the most important are the following: (1) What part should the doctrine of informed consent play in the law of professional responsibility? (2) What are the relevant open choices with respect to a particular problem of which the client should be made aware? (3) What additional information, presented by the professional in what way, constitutes adequate disclosure? (4) What form of client deliberation and communication constitutes informed consent? To recapitulate what was pointed out earlier, the doctrine of informed consent is already a part, albeit a small part of the laws of professional responsibility, best developed in the areas of surgical medicine, human experimentation in a medical context, and the criminal law. The requirement of informed consent in these areas, and in personal injury claims making has been generally limited to only (1) consent to those decisions which involve considerable risks with respect to the ultimate success of the problem-solving and (2) consent of a kind a skilled professional of good standing would provide in the same community under similar circumstances.

A recent federal case, *Canturbury* v. *Spence,* represents a breakthrough rejecting both limitations. In that case, the appeals court first held that it is proper to leave to the jury the issue of whether it was a breach of the doctor's informed consent requirement not to tell the patient that there was a 1 percent possibility of paralysis arising from a recommended surgical procedure. The court rejected a standard which looked to the materiality of the risk in the doctor's judgment, instead, making the test for determining whether a particular risk must be divulged (in the court's words), "its materiality to the patient's decision: all risks potentially affecting the decision must be unmasked." Second, it held that the prevailing medical practice with respect to professional disclosure should not define the standard since such a community standard might represent less disclosure than the ordinary care standard set by law.[26] These holdings deserve to become leading precedents. In one respect, however, the court did not go far enough. The court held that even if material risks incidental to a course of treatment were not disclosed, there would be no

---

[26] 464 F.2d 772 (DC Cir. 1972), pp. 785 and 787.

breach of the doctrine if, in the jury's view, such disclosure would not have resulted in the patient's deciding against undergoing such treatment.[27] The standard of causation promulgated in *Spence* is "what a prudent person *would have* decided if suitably informed of all perils bearing significance" [italics mine].[28] In addition to undercutting the materiality standard, the trouble with this is that problems treated by professionals are too complex and idiosyncratic to have any one "prudent," "suitable," appropriate response. Reasonable and prudent men can have very different ideas of relevance. For some reasonable people making personal injury claims, for example, full disclosure of the perils of submitting to an EBT would be relevant to the prosecution of a claim, and to others it would not be. A better standard of both materiality and causation would be full disclosure of all of the perils and burdens involved in a course of professional action, so long as, in the jury's judgment, a prudent person *might* have decided differently if full disclosure had been made.

A special problem raised in medicine is whether certain disclosures to certain types of patients may not be therapeutically counterproductive. This problem is examined in some detail elsewhere. Let it just be said here that before the doctor's "therapeutic privilege" not to disclose is exercised, the doctor must be prepared to make a clear and convincing demonstration, based on some objective evidence applicable to the particular patient which is over and above his subjective professional judgment. Failing in such a demonstration, he should be liable for breach of the informed consent doctrine.[29]

Expanding the doctrine of informed consent is especially important so long as the law remains that a client is responsible for the acts or omissions of his lawyer, whether or not he knows about the lawyer's conduct or about his duty to supervise it.[30] This knowledge is imputed to him by the mere act of his choosing a lawyer.

This rule is incompatible with the traditional model of the lawyer-client relationship and with the present limited doctrine of informed consent. It penalizes client passivity, imputing knowledge of a kind that most clients do not in fact have. It is not necessarily incompatible, however, with the participatory model. If clients are warned by professionals at the outset that their passive delegation will not free them from legal responsibility for "errors of judgment or of neglect" made by the professional, knowledge of the responsi-

---

[27] Ibid., p. 790.

[28] Ibid., p. 791.

[29] See Glass, "Restructuring Informed Consent," pp. 1564–1571; Katz, *Experimentation With Human Beings*, pp. 645–717.

[30] *Link* v. *Wabash Railroad Company*, 370 U.S. 626 (1962, 4–3 decision).

bility becomes a reality not requiring the fiction of imputation. Knowledge of this duty invites clients to adopt an active problem-solving role. However, any client who has not received this warning should not be held liable for his professional's negligence. A relatively simple way to avoid the kind of arbitrary dismissal of client legal rights occurring in the *Link* case is to require the opposing counsel (or possibly a court clerk) to serve the client personally with notice of his attorney's delinquency. Only failure to act in the face of such actual notice should deny a client his right to continue the claim.[31] If professionals have a duty to disclose critical choices and to apprise the client of his rights and duties as a client, they deserve the correlative right to defense against a subsequent malpractice action where the client had timely notice or had knowingly waived a right to notice.

If clients are given realistic opportunities to correct their lawyer's mistakes in the original action, the need for malpractice suits will be lessened.

The term "malpractice" is unfortunate. It suggests that the professional who makes infrequent mistakes harmful to his client is incompetent. Were this true there would be no such thing as a competent professional and what would distinguish skilled professionals would be their ability to hide their mistakes, not their freedom from making them. It would be more consistent with the participatory model to refer instead to professional negligence. Whatever stigma now is attached to a professional's participation in a professional negligence suit should be lessened. Furthermore, the three-year statute of limitations for professional negligence suits should begin to run from the date the client discovers the negligence, not from the date the negligence occurs. The paramount objective of the law of professional responsibility should be to protect the victimized client, not the irresponsible professional.

What are the relevant open choices which are in fact and which ought to be required in the field of personal injury law? From the few norms for lawyers presently promulgated, we noted (Chapter 5) three sets of relevant choices which, under the present limited standards of disclosure, require the informed consent of the client before being made. First of all, a lawyer may not farm out the case of a client retaining him as his personal representative without the client's permission. Second, the lawyer must accurately and promptly disclose every settlement offer made by the adversary. Third, the client must agree to the terms of any settlement offered by the defense before it is accepted.

---

[31] Mr. Justice Black suggested this as an amendment to rule 41, "Involuntary dismissals," of the Federal Rules of Procedure. The proposal was not adopted. *Order*, 383 U.S. 1032, 1036 (1966) (Black J., dissenting). See the discussion in Mazor, "Power and Responsibility in the Attorney-Client Relation," p. 1120ff.

Whether or not to farm and to whom to farm cases are open questions which lawyers decided without obtaining client consent in six cases (10 percent) in our sample. All sampled clients said that their lawyer told them about settlement terms, though there is no data about the promptness or accuracy with which settlement offers were reported. No one complained of not having been told that accepting a settlement would preclude him from making any further legal claim for injuries arising out of the same accident.

What presently constitutes legally sufficient informed consent with respect to making personal injury claims is unclear. At the present time, in practice it is probably true that the requisite disclosure need be nothing more than the perfunctory statement that the lawyer intends to farm the action and wants the client's approval. Thus, a lawyer who says, "I plan to turn your case over to X who is a specialist, OK?" is probably providing sufficient disclosure under present standards even if the tone of his voice is declarative rather than questioning. Similarly, a lawyer who says to his client "X offers $2,000; I think it fair. If you want it, sign this release," is probably making an adequate disclosure under present standards.

What reply by the client constitutes informed consent? Many judges probably would find implied consent even if the client said nothing with respect to the farming of his case. Hearing the statement and failing to make a direct and immediate objection would constitute informed consent. Such a minimal standard would probably also be applied to the settlement. If the client signed the release, even without reading its terms, and even without being told that signing would preclude further recovery, he would be deemed to have made an informed consent.

Following the participatory model, such perfunctory application of the principle is inadequate. The analysis of why some clients do better than others suggests at least five additional sets of choices which tend to have salient impact on the results of a claim and the disclosure of which should, therefore, be required under our improved informed consent doctrine. The first of these involves selecting the proper medical treatment to undergo, in both the qualitative and quantitative senses. Most lawyers do not feel the obligation to tell clients in detail what constitutes compensable damages nor to advise clients on forms of therapy to explore. In some cases, the result is that the client's recuperation and the value of his claim is impaired. Lawyers ought to be required to explain the nature of compensable damages and ought to be encouraged to discuss possible therapeutic procedures. It should be made clear in such a discussion that such procedures will not be considered "padding the claim."

A second set of options involves choosing how much time and what forms of effort the lawyer should put into preparing the claim for settlement or trial. Lawyers should be required to offer to put more work into a case than they would customarily, in return for a larger fee percentage. They should give clients the option—at least in perfect liability cases—of paying a fee based on the number of hours of work actually spent working on the case.

A third choice is how soon to initiate the suit. If a lawyer has not brought suit within, say, nine months of the date of the accident, he should be required to justify further delay. The client should have the option of reimbursing the lawyer for the additional expenses of an early start and an early EBT, or of foregoing added expense in the hope of receiving an early fair settlement offer.

These latter two choices are interrelated with the very much open issue of what is to be the proper fee. Lawyers should be required to refer to the Appellate Division First Department fee schedule as the maximum ceiling, which it is, rather than as an appropriate fee guideline, which often it is not. The lawyer should explain the nature of his overhead, the increasing time he must put into the case as it approaches trial, and the prevailing custom of a contingent fee of at least 25 percent, even on claims settled with a minimum of effort. A fifth choice that affects the client is whether or not to seek a jury trial. The client should have the choice of an expedited bench trial in which he may receive a lower judgment or a delayed jury trial promising possibly greater rewards.

As indicated in Chapter 3, there are several other open choices such as choice of venue, the choice of whether or not to use an expert witness and, if so, whom, which of several possible witnesses to examine and the choices of the court in which to bring suit and of the amount of damages to seek. These choices too should be disclosed by the lawyer, discussed with the client, and approved by the client where relevant to the claim. Informed consent with respect to these issues would give some practical effect to the participatory principle and would be fully consistent with the present ethical standard that "A lawyer should advise his client of the possible effect of each legal alternative," a standard that should not stand in disuse.[32]

Clients should be informed about the importance to the claim of the issue of liability and, particularly, about the necessity of the client's being found to have been free from contributory negligence. They should be informed about the delay of the claims process, the problems of negotiating a fair settlement with insurers, and the possibilities of unpleasant litigation

---

[32] *Code,* Ethical Consideration, 7–8, p. 25.

experiences. A lawyer should inform the client that the client has a right to reject recommended actions and even a right to give the matter further thought and seek outside advice. Thus, the client should be told that the lawyer desiring to farm out a case will receive part of the final legal fee and that for this portion he is obligated to have assisted in making the claim. In recommending a settlement an attorney should advise the client to read carefully the terms of the release and invite him to ask questions about anything he doesn't understand. It should be explicitly stated, orally, that the settlement completely terminates the claim even though the written release sets this forth. A matter of great importance merits repetition. If this kind of disclosure is made by an attorney with respect to the relevant open issues presented by every negligence case, and with respect to farming out the case where the lawyer desires it, an oral affirmative response, "X action is all right with me" should probably be sufficient to constitute informed consent. The absence of a negative response should not be taken as consent.

What about the client who says he doesn't want to be bothered about his case, who commands the lawyer to make all the decisions unilaterally, and who promises to abide by whatever the lawyer does? Under the participatory model, the lawyer still has an ethical obligation to try to tell the client something about what can go wrong and something about how much the client's desires will be affected by some of these open choices. If, having said this, the client insists on being passive, the client should probably be deemed to have waived his right to be informed about all specific choices except farming out and settlement. These latter choices deserve special protection. Bringing in a second lawyer at an intermediate stage of the claim is a substantial alteration of the original contract of legal representation. The client should not be presumed to authorize his lawyer to pass his case on when he vaguely tells the lawyer to "handle it any way you think best." The settlement itself is so much the crucial outcome of a claim that the lawyer should have to make a specific disclosure of an offer each time one is made. If the client gets annoyed each time the lawyer says, "They've upped their offer to $X but it is still not enough as far as I'm concerned," the lawyer should explain that the law of professional responsibility requires this disclosure of him. This is not to recommend that clients be forced to be active participants, but only that they be given reasonable opportunity to know that their participation may be helpful and thus be given reasonable protection against subsequent disappointment of the "nobody told me" variety. With the principle of informed consent, clients remain free to choose noninvolvement—after receiving some encouragement to be active. Lawyers, however, are not free to discourage clients from being active participants.

The lawyer should begin to discuss the client's problem at the first interview with the presumption that the client is capable of informed participation. If the client's behavior indicates that he is unable to understand what is involved in dealing with his problem, the lawyer should invite the client to come back with a lay adviser. This adviser—a relative or friend—could serve as an intermediary, interpreting the lawyer's remarks to the client and articulating the client's reactions to the lawyer. In particular cases, it will be difficult to decide whether client passivity is more a matter of motivation or of intellectual capacity. In the former case, of course, a lay adviser is not appropriate.

SOURCES OF ADDITIONAL INFORMATION

Informed consent by the client to decisions made in professional problem solving, though central, is not the only principle contained in the participatory model. Laymen should be given opportunities to obtain information outside the professional-client relationship that will supplement the information provided by the professional and that will permit a meaningful choice of a professional at the outset.

One constructive way for a client to obtain such additional information is by seeking a second professional opinion. Canon 7 of the now superseded lawyers *Canons of Professional Ethics* did not discourage lawyers from cooperating with clients seeking a second independent legal opinion about their problem or wishing to bring a second lawyer into their case. Canon 7 stated in part:

> When lawyers jointly associated in a cause cannot agree as to any matter vital to the interest of the client, the conflict of opinion should be frankly stated to him for his final determination. His decision should be accepted unless the nature of the difference makes it impracticable for the lawyer whose judgment has been overruled to cooperate effectively. In this case it is his duty to ask the client to relieve him.[33]

This recommendation reflects an awareness that a client may learn more from comparing the advice of two experts than from relying on the single expert to disclose what he alone thinks relevant. However, in the new American Bar Association *Code of Professional Responsibility,* adopted subsequently (August 1969) by the New York State Bar Association, this encouragement to client participation is excluded. In its place the *Code* states:

> If a lawyer knows a client has previously obtained counsel, he should not accept employment in the matter unless the other counsel approves or withdraws, or the client terminates the prior employment.[34]

---

[33] (Albany: New York Bar Association, 1963 ed.), p. 14. The superseded Canons were adopted in New York in January 1909.

[34] *Code,* Ethical Consideration 2–30, p. 7.

The choice of independent counsel is now taken out of the client's hands. Instead it is placed in the hands of the first lawyer. This regrettable change probably reflects the anxiety of many lawyers that a second opinion will lead to the loss of the client to the second man. It should be dropped and Canon 7 should be restored as the appropriate norm.

To make a second opinion truly independent, the client should be in possession of copies of all records prepared or assembled by the first professional. It is not the present custom of many attorneys to give clients copies of the pleadings, of letters drafted and sent to insurers, or of office memoranda. summarizing the evidence of the case. A rule requiring copies to be provided promptly would enable the client, if he chose, to go to a second lawyer without the first lawyer's knowledge and seek an informed review of his work. The second lawyer would, in many cases, be in a position to pass some pertinent judgment about the first lawyer's performance on the basis of these documents without having to approach the first lawyer for clarification. The process could be similar to the way a second physician can read the X-rays taken under the first physician's supervision, if the patient has possession of the X-rays.

A second valuable source of supplemental information for the client is a preliminary diagnostic interview with a professional before the same or another professional is finally selected to prosecute the claim. Lawyers who do negligence work are not accustomed to giving clients diagnostic consultations paid for on a time basis, the way doctors are. Yet it might have been valuable if the victims of the relatively serious accidents represented in this sample had spent one or two hours in preliminary discussion with an attorney exploring the problems of making a claim, what to expect, and the possible special problems raised by the facts of their case, without necessarily entrusting the claim to the attorney consulted. Periodically, some lawyers refer to the usefulness of clients getting annual legal "checkups" but frequently make no provisions for charging an appropriate fee for such a brief consultation.[35] Many lawyers will be surprised by the finding that 75 percent of the sample clients (40 of 53) say they are willing to pay at least $30 an hour for a preliminary consultation about a legal problem such as their accident claim. This largely untapped opportunity for additional income might compensate the attorney for the fear of losing a good prospect to another lawyer.

It is significant that not a single client in the sample decided to "shop" further after meeting the first lawyer he approached. This was even true of the

---

[35] See, e.g., Sidney Pfeifer, "The Personal Legal Check-Up," *New York State Bar Journal* 35 (October 1963): 385–389.

more active clients accustomed to "shopping" for doctors and other professionals. Why? Two reasons are most important. First, the client is under stress and feels that he does not have time to spend shopping around. In fact he does have time. Second, he is unfamiliar with dealing with lawyers and doesn't know that second consultations are possible. Miss Schiff, for example, told me,

> If I had time to interview several lawyers like doctors, I would use my own best instincts to judge and try to see what kind of person they are, who works for them, how they listen, how they talk, what advice they give, any of my judgment that I could bring to bear and then I would compare them. But the bad thing about negligence is that there's no time to compare . . . (pause) . . . but of course there really is, because you can switch; but I didn't learn that until much later.

There is an obvious need to give laymen some information about the claims process and about coping with legal problems more generally. The same is probably true about the nature and techniques of other forms of professional problem solving.

The participatory model implies that citizens should have an opportunity to learn more than they presently know about problems likely to be important to them during the course of their lives—possibly even learning about these problems before they reach adulthood. For many years the public schools have taught courses in civics on the assumption that it is desirable in a democratic society to have politically sophisticated citizens. If the participatory model is appropriate, adolescents might also be given the opportunity to take problem-oriented courses in being sophisticated consumers of professional services, sophisticated personal problem solvers, capable of confronting difficult problems and working with trained professionals to cope with them. Problems for consideration in such a course might include some of the following: dealing with serious physical illness, possibly requiring surgery; dealing with a serious emotional problem; dealing with the death of a close relative; bringing a lawsuit for damages arising out of a serious accident; finding a job; planning one's estate; being charged with the commission of a crime; investing money; or buying a home. There are large issues for profitable consideration if one looks closely and imaginatively at prosaic matters.[36]

---

[36] For a discussion of the teaching of law to nonlawyers see Alex Elson, "General Education in Law For Non-Lawyers" in *Law in a Changing America,* ed. Geoffrey Hazard (Englewood Cliffs, N.J.: Prentice-Hall, 1968), pp. 183–192. An interesting collection of legal education materials has been compiled by Mary Ader, *Community Legal Education Materials* (Chicago: National Clearing House For Legal Services, Northwestern University School of Law, November 1971).

There is a dearth of useful literature assisting laymen to make informed choices of professional consultants and to collaborate with their consultants once hired. Two very useful sources of information for potential clients are a manual by Roger Golde, *Can You Be Sure of Your Experts?*, and a pamphlet by Herbert Denenberg, "A Shopper's Guide to Surgery." In addition to including specific chapters about dealing with doctors, lawyers, and investment advisers, Golde makes useful suggestions about dealing with experts generally.[37] Golde properly (based on the evidence reported in Chapter 5 that attorneys referred by putatively knowledgeable acquaintances performed no better than attorneys contacted according to personal knowledge or by chance), minimizes the reliability of a professional's reputation, stressing instead the rapport one establishes with the professional. He encourages clients to shop around before choosing, and urges clients to continue questioning and appraising the professional's performance even after the initial choice is made. The second source, a six-page pamphlet published by the Insurance Commissioner of Pennsylvania,[38] is one in a series of "Shopper's Guides." Others in the series deal with purchasing life insurance and health insurance, and one is a guide to hospitals in the Philadelphia area. The surgery pamphlet is a direct response to recent evidence that much unnecessary surgery is performed in this country—a finding which is hardly surprising when one accepts that the professional's desire for a good income almost always conflicts with the client's desire for inexpensive problem solving. Still another source of information relevant to the choice of capable professionals should be professional schools in the community. Schools should be prepared to provide upon request the names of able specialists whose work has been appraised by the faculty specialists in the relevant problem area.

The participatory model leads to the questioning of the policy of prohibiting all direct forms of professional advertising.[39] Prior to World War II, this policy was used to prevent advertising by banks. It is not easy to see how the layman has been harmed by the now permitted bank advertising which gives information about services and the costs of those services offered by competing lending institutions. At the least, lawyers and other professionals should be permitted to put fields of special competence, honors received, and profes-

---

[37] Roger Golde, *Can You Be Sure of Your Experts?* (New York: Macmillan, 1969).

[38] Herbert Denenberg, "A Shopper's Guide to Surgery: Fourteen Rules on How To Avoid Unnecessary Surgery" (Harrisburg: Pennsylvania Insurance Department, July 18, 1972).

[39] Illustrated by Ethical Consideration 2–9 of the *Code*, p. 5. See the argument made by Robert Gipson, "Advertising, Solicitation and the Profession's Duty To Make Legal Counsel Available," *Yale Law Journal* 81 (1972): 1181 ff.

sional accomplishments on business cards, office displays, in the Yellow Pages of the telephone directory, and in pamphlets for distribution. Why should the provision of professional services be (and in fact are they?) excluded from the anti-competitive sanctions of federal anti-trust law? Why shouldn't restrictions on professional advertising as well as the setting of minimum professional fees be examined in the light of the existing doctrine, which has developed from the Sherman Act, with respect to the unreasonable restraint of trade.[40]

The participatory model implies that a competitive market for professional services—"the discipline of the market"—and an informed clientele are more effective policing institutions than is the profession itself. A consequence of this is that consumers should be given a wide choice of available forms of professional assistance. One alternative source of assistance that can be made more accessible in certain instances is client self-help assisted by self-help publications and by professionals with whom the client undertakes no formal consulting relationship. While surgical self-help is unrealistic, the possibilities of sophisticated personal injury claimants handling their own claims cannot be lightly dismissed. At present, most clients do better in making a claim with a lawyer (for reasons already indicated in Chapter 2). Yet, in theory, with some help from a good book on do-it-yourself claims and with some help from court personnel if it became desirable to initiate a lawsuit, the layman might do almost as well by himself with a small claim as with an attorney, and save himself the contingent legal fee. In fact, with many small claims or moderate claims with fair to poor liability issues, he may have no choice but to make the claim himself, if a claim is to be made at all. Mr. Sawyer, the advertising executive, reflected on this:

> If they came out with a . . . 25-page book on what to do if you have an auto accident injury, I might have been better off and might have thought about handling my own claim. . . . Is there such a book or does the City have somebody you can call for advice like this? Something could be done so simply to make this less complicated and bewildering. I might have the time to do it if I knew the first step. The layman ought to be able to contact court clerks to file papers himself.

There are at least three books which purport to assist the layman in a do-it-yourself negligence claim.[41] The author of one of them (Siegel) is a lawyer,

---

[40] Comment, "The Applicability of the Sherman Act to Legal Practice and Other 'Non-Commercial' Activities," *Yale Law Journal* 82 (1972): 313–337. See also footnote 75, p. 137.

[41] Robert Constantin, *Sue or Settle* (New York: Crown, 1968); Edward Siegel, *How To Avoid Lawyers* (New York: Information, Inc., 1969), chap. 1; Daniel Baldyga, *How To Settle Your Own Insurance Claim* (New York: Macmillan, 1968).

while the other two authors are insurance claims adjusters. None of these books appears to be adequate. Siegel's discussion is too brief (28 pages), and he gives too little attention to the problems of evaluating the claim and preparing the evidence. Baldyga does not hide the ax he grinds against lawyers. Throughout the text, he scatters antilawyer jokes and aphorisms. Unfortunately for the reader, Baldyga is far less critical of claims adjusters and gives the unwarranted advice that in most cases the accident victim can rely upon the fairness of the adjuster's evaluation. Claims adjusters after all are "professionally competent." Baldyga is helpful in providing a checklist of things to do in building the evidence of the claim.[42] Constantin's is probably the best all-around book but it gives incomplete information about gathering evidence and formulating a settlement strategy. All of the authors caution the reader to make his own claim only if it is a small one or if the defendant has little insurance to reach.

None of the clients interviewed for the sample appeared to be familiar with books of this type. In fact, surprisingly, 67 percent of the interviewees (37 of 59) weren't even aware that they could handle their own claim without a lawyer. There is a special part of the Civil Court which exclusively adjudicates claims brought by laymen and, according to Manhattan Civil Court clerk Frank Restel, the clerks are available to help claimants prepare their cases. There do not appear to be studies of how well these lay claims work out.[43]

New forms of professional service become possible when groups of clients and potential clients organize to receive professional services as members of a group or participate in prepaid professional service insurance programs. A panel of laymen, supplemented in some cases by professional advisers or board members, can seek out effective services and concentrate consumer purchasing power as a basis for shared responsibility in problem solving.[44]

If the participatory model is correct, professionals alone cannot be ex-

---

[42] Baldyga, *How To Settle Your Own Insurance Claim,* p. 156.

[43] The parallel institution for claims under $500 is the New York City Small Claims Court. This too has not received sufficient empirical investigation. See Comment, "Small Claims Court: Reform Revisited," *Journal of Law and Social Problems* 9 (1969): 49–84. The office of the Commissioner of Consumer Affairs has published a helpful 27-page booklet which explains the rules for bringing a claim in the Small Claims Court: "How To Sue in Small Claims Court" (New York: Department of Consumer Affairs, 1970). The booklet, however, does not assist the citizen in formulating his claim.

[44] See Barlow F. Christensen, *Lawyers for People of Moderate Means* (Chicago: American Bar Foundation, 1970), pp. 225–291.

pected to implement reforms that will increase client participation in the professional-client relationship. The traditional idea that professionals can and should have exclusive jurisdiction over the norms and practices of professional conduct should be recast to make room for shared jurisdiction with lay representatives. Though once resisted by the bar,[45] the clear intention of the Economic Opportunity Act of 1964 was to give laymen in poverty neighborhoods "maximum feasible participation" in establishing and operating federally funded community action programs[46] of which legal services became one by virtue of the 1967 amendments to the *Economic Opportunity Act*.[47] Today the principle of lay participation in these programs is established. With but one apparent exception, this participatory principle has not been extended to supervision of legal performance in private nonpoverty settings. The one exception is an innovation just adopted by the Supreme Court of Michigan. The court has created, as of March 1970, a new State Bar Grievance Board with seven members—two of whom are to be laymen appointed by the court.[48] These laymen are to participate in setting and enforcing Michigan disciplinary policies and procedures. This will be an interesting experiment to observe. If laymen are capable of understanding professional issues and if lay interests do often conflict with professional interests, mutual participation is not only appropriate in individual professional-client relationships but also at the level of broader professional policy making.

The participatory model also has a bearing on the role of professionals as lobbyists for the interests of their professions and as "interested" participants in consulting relationships. Under the traditional model, it is difficult to square lobbying activities such as were practiced for many years by the American Medical Association against government financed health insurance for the aged or the public generally, and against government programs to increase the supply of doctors (which activities have restricted the accessibility of professional services, especially to citizens of modest means) with the notion that professionals should serve the public interest only. Once professionals are recognized as having parochial interests which may not accord with and may even directly conflict with the interests of large segments of their actual or potential clientele, there is less reason for branding the pursuit of self-interest

---

[45] See, e.g., *In the Matter of Community Action for Legal Services Inc.,* 26 App. Div. 2d 354 (1st Dept., N.Y., 1966). But see *Washington-Greene Legal Aid Society Application,* 45 D. & C. 2d 563 (C.P. of Wash. County 1968).

[46] P.L. 88–452, September 20, 1964, 78 *Stat* 516, Title II, Part A §202(a)(3).

[47] 42 U.S.C. §2809.

[48] "A Grievance Committee at Work: The Michigan Story," *Juris Doctor* 3 (October 1973): 22.

as unjustifiably unprofessional conduct. If professionals are denied a monopoly over professional policy making, they should be entitled to lobby for those policies of greatest concern to themselves. If clients are to have rights to make demands and articulate concerns in consulting relationships, professionals should be entitled to the same rights. The participatory model posits a norm of collaboration, with shared responsibility and control and not client domination of professional decision.

THE PURPOSES OF THE PARTICIPATORY MODEL

There is more that can be said to justify the normative claims of the participatory model and its use as a paradigm for new patterns of governance of professional-client relationships than merely that it appears more realistically to account for the process of personal injury problem solving. Six constructive functions may be performed by the participatory model.

The participatory model promotes the dignity of citizens as clients. The desire of human beings to be their own master has been described by Sir Isaiah Berlin:

> I wish my life and decisions to depend on myself, not on external forces of whatever kind. I wish to be the instrument of my own not of other men's, acts of will. I wish to be a subject, not an object; to be moved by reasons, by conscious purposes, which are my own, not by causes which affect me, as it were, from outside. I wish to be somebody, not nobody; a doer—deciding, not being decided for, self-directed and not acted upon by external nature or by other men as if I were a thing, or an animal, or a slave incapable of playing a human role, that is, of conceiving goals and policies of my own and realizing them. This is at least part of what I mean when I say that I am rational, and that it is my reason that distinguishes me as a human being from the rest of the world. I wish, above all, to be conscious of myself as a thinking, willing, active being, bearing responsibility for my choices and able to explain them by references to my own ideas and purposes.[49]

Client participation in problem solving makes the client a doer, responsible for his choices. The traditional model, on the other hand, encourages passivity, dependence, and an absence of responsibility for choices.

The participatory model increases the chances for client satisfaction in at least two respects. Client participation not only yields satisfactions which come with achieving a measure of control over one's life but participation also reduces excessive anxieties which are the product of uninformed fears and unexpected stress. Dealing with difficult personal problems is a task re-

---

[49] Sir Isaiah Berlin, "Two Concepts of Liberty," in his *Four Essays on Liberty* (New York: Oxford University Press, 1969), p. 131.

quiring an individual's intellectual and emotional preparation. A client is faced with a previously unexperienced situation, the perils of which can be magnified out of true proportion unless controlled by a realistic assessment of what may be encountered and the likelihood of experiencing various anticipated dangers. Active collaboration with the professional invites the client to obtain the information necessary to anticipate and cope with the real strains of the problem. Evidence continues to accumulate that client satisfactions are increased by meaningful access to full information about their problems.[50]

The main innovative finding of the research reported in this book is that active participation can actually promote effective problem solving. The traditional model is incapable of explaining this finding. Evidence drawn from the personal injury claims process indicates that clients can supplement the specialized knowledge of professionals, fill gaps, catch mistakes, and provide criteria relevant for decision. Conversely, the collaborative task of having to explain and discuss the problem with the client can help the professional avoid mistakes and focus on the relevant aspects of the problem. While this book does not prove that client participation promotes rational decision, it establishes a prima facie case requiring clear and convincing contrary evidence before it can be rejected.

The participatory model serves to protect the integrity of professionals by liberating them from many of the strains and inconsistencies of their traditional ideal. The participatory model reduces the burdens imposed upon the professional by the paternal role. It increases the potential for clients to receive effective service. It removes inconsistencies in the law of professional responsibility, providing the informed consent which can be the only justification for treating, as a matter of law, the professional as the client's agent. It brings professional-client relationships into closer congruence with deeply rooted economic values in our society—the economic norms which prize freedom of contract between supplier and consumer, and free enterprise in a competitive market rather than contracts of adhesion and mercantilist market restrictions. It also brings professional-client relationships into congruence with this society's abiding commitment to democratic values which values are necessarily challenged by the existence within our society of paternalistic institutions.

---

[50] One of the most intriguing of these studies involves the dangerous diagnostic procedure of angiography—testing for arterial blockages. Ralph Alfidi, "Informed Consent—A Study of Patient Reaction," 1971, reprinted in Katz, pp. 584–588. See also Irving Janis, *Psychological Stress* (New York: Wiley, 1958), pp. 352–394; and Lois Pratt, Arthur Seligmann, and George Reader, "Physicians' Views of the Level of Medical Information among Patients," in *Patients, Physicians and Illness,* p. 222.

The participatory model has the potential to increase public respect for the professions and for the institutions of law, healing, science, education and commerce. The model promotes public sophistication about service institutions which increases a true appreciation of their indispensability and invites the more extensive use of these professional services.

Finally, and perhaps most surprisingly to those who see the participatory model as a threat to professionals, it can actually increase the satisfactions of professional practice by freeing professionals both from impossible standards which are bound to be undershot, thereby inevitably disappointing large segments of the public and from the excessive burdens of full responsibility for the solving of the personal problems of individuals. The participatory model invites the professional to assume a broader counseling role than he frequently now assumes and to share in the personal satisfactions and experiences of his clients. It invites personal contact in a society becoming increasingly impersonal. The participatory model liberates the professional from the impossible ideal that he be neutral, disinterested, and passionless. It permits him to articulate and lobby for professional standards and institutions which meet his needs without having necessarily to defend himself against the charges of being selfish, venal, and corrupt. For this freedom, the professional of course pays a price. His preferences are less automatically realized than in a low-visibility vacuum of monopoly professional control. They must win out in the public marketplace of ideas, where they will be challenged by the often competing interests of clients. But this is only fair because clients too must pay a price for the advantages to be gained from participation.

THE REALITY OF THE PARTICIPATORY MODEL

So far, this chapter has presented an unabashedly one-sided argument that client participation in professional decision merits serious consideration as a viable alternative to the traditional ideal of professional control. Several concrete suggestions have been offered for implementing the norms of client participation; benefits to be gained from the promotion of client participation have been proposed. Now, let us consider the burdens client participation entails.

First, confronting complex and uncertain problems with heavy risks is threatening to all of us, professionals and laymen alike. Many clients may find this threat to be too heavy a price to pay for the benefits of participation. The case of one client in the sample, Mr. Sugarman, illustrates that the risks inherent in prosecuting a personal injury claim may make even the legally sophisticated reluctant to participate actively. Mr. Sugarman settled for a net recovery of $2,100 on a claim valued by the expert panel at $12,000. This only payed half of his $4,000 out-of-pocket expenses—a fact which distressed him greatly. A personable and articulate stock specialist in his mid-thirties, Mr. Sugarman comes from a prosperous family, was trained to be a lawyer, and actually spent six months in practice as an insurer's defense attorney. Yet, he was a passive client. Instead of involving himself in his claim he turned everything over to his father—a corporate attorney. "My father insisted that I take a lawyer of his choosing," he said. He may have made a conscious decision that it wasn't worth putting any effort into the case, but probably not. It is likely that deeper personality factors were at work here.

Two advertising executives, Mr. Sawyer and Mr. Towle, referred independently and explicitly to their older lawyers as "father figures." One of the most active clients in the sample, Mr. Stacey, reflected on his feelings toward his lawyer with the following statement:

> The whole negligence process is a fraud. My son was negligent in running out into the street. We had told him a thousand times not to do it. I think also he was unconsciously looking for attention to compete with our newly born baby. The whole process is a game people play and I felt a little guilty about our part in it. But there was sufficient money involved to overcome my guilt feelings. If I had not had a lawyer here I would probably have settled for about $2,000 to cover my out-of-pocket expenses. But the lawyer is a reassuring presence who takes away your guilt feelings. He says, "Hey, this is the way the game is played; you take as much as you can get; it's what they expect; it's the way it's done." He takes upon his own shoulders the burden of your guilt —he's the professional. I hadn't thought of this before but it occurs to me now as what's involved.

Most clients want their lawyer to command their respect by showing an authoritative and businesslike manner; but this can be overdone. They also want him to treat them respectfully, as equals, demonstrating patience, emotional concern, and courtesy.[51] Clients are in conflict. They both want and don't want to be dependent. Clients are also in conflict about the values implied in their passive behavior. Most are aware of and feel obliged to accept the traditional ideals of professional service; they should trust the lawyer, not be critical and not hold back cooperation. But at the same time they want to

---

[51] The lawyer qualities that pleased the client sample were the same as those mentioned by two other client surveys: The *Missouri Bar Prentice-Hall Survey* (Jefferson City: The Missouri Bar, 1963), p. 66; Harrop Freeman, *Counseling in the United States* (Dobbs Ferry, N.Y.: Oceana, 1967), p. 207.

be self-reliant and responsible. Too heavy a reliance may imply weakness.[52]

The participatory model assumes that most clients are able to cope with the emotional stress of responsible participation, especially when the risks of nonparticipation are disclosed. They remain free to be passive, responsible only for the consequences of their passivity. It is one thing to say that all clients are tempted to passivity and that some clients need to be passive. It is quite another to say that most clients need to be passive. Furthermore, it is not necessary that clients be active participants in dealing with every one of their personal problems.

A second difficulty in implementing the participatory model is that even with it the professional retains disproportionate resources for manipulating the professional-client relationship to deny the client effective collaboration. This power is enhanced not only by his more extensive knowledge and experience but by the social setting in which the relationship takes place. Face-to-face interaction between two people is frequently stressful.[53] Feeling the other person out and trying to manage the impression one is making is difficult work, in which professionals have more experience than most clients. The first interview almost always takes place in the professional's office. His position of authority as the professional helper is reinforced by the physical setting. He frequently sits behind a desk, the seat of authority in the room. The client has come to see him in a place where he bosses people (e.g. a secretary, a young associate). Other clients are waiting to see him. He gives the impression of being busy. The interview is interrupted by telephone calls or by a colleague's request for advice. "Clearly," the less confident client thinks, "this is an important man. He is doing me a favor by giving me his valuable time. I had better not ask too many questions or I will appear stupid, better not make any demands that could offend him."

But this is only one side of the story. The reaction of many men to someone seeking their paternalism would be to reject the role. Many professionals, however, seem to need and gain pleasure from being paternalistic and dominating.[54] One negligence specialist I interviewed said,

---

[52] These distinctively American cultural values of self-reliance are concisely summarized by Harry Stack Sullivan, *The Psychiatric Interview* (New York: Norton, 1954), pp. 37–38. The strength of the belief that one should solve his own problems also is discussed by Freeman, *Counseling in the United States,* p. 251.

[53] A brief but informative discussion of the meeting of two personalities is contained in Michael Argyle, *The Psychology of Interpersonal Behavior* (London: Penguin Books, 1967), chap. 3, pp. 46–67.

[54] Harrop Freeman finds lawyers to be generally "authoritarian, directive, parental in their counseling image"—especially with lower-class clients. *Legal Interviewing and Counseling* (St. Paul, Minn.: West, 1964), p. 236.

> The truth is, the client is ignorant. He is the last person to know whether or not his lawyer is doing a good job for him. . . . Because the client is ignorant, I don't let my clients think. If you look for guff from your clients you'll get it.

The attitude is, "Put them in their place or they will walk over you." A litigator with 15 years of experience commented to me:

> I tell the client that I will do all the worrying about the case—period! . . . A little education is a dangerous thing. Just let the client know that the problem is in the hands of an extremely competent counsel.[55]

Using curbstone psychology in reference to the legal profession can easily lead to excess.[56] But two rather limited speculations probably are in order. Lawyers, and perhaps most professionals, seem to have two human needs in disproportionately great measure: the desire to control their environment and aggressive (and competitive) feelings.[57] The pressures of the claims process outside the lawyer-client relationship constantly frustrate the desire for mastery. Uncertainty can never be brought under control no matter how hard the lawyer tries. Forty-five negligence lawyers responded to the question, "If you had it to do over, would you still be a lawyer?" Twenty-two percent said they would not, which is slightly but not significantly, more than the 17 percent (133 of 801) who responded, "Definitely No" in Jerome Carlin's general New York City lawyer survey.[58] The overwhelming majority of the lawyers questioned seem satisfied with their work. A basic part of this satisfaction appears to be the fact that, in dealing with the client, the lawyer is dealing from a position of relative strength. He has the knowledge; he is in the position to help. The client needs him and his control. Exercising this control and receiving a good income for doing it is what a majority of the sampled lawyers say they enjoy most about their work. While there are greater opportunities for mastering their environment within the lawyer-client relationship than outside it, as has been shown, the relationship is by no

---

[55] For a revealing juxtaposition of client and lawyer gripes about each other see Richard Allen, "The Unhappy Client," *New York Bar Journal* (April 1962): 127–134.

[56] One of the few attempts made so far, goes too far I think, and is a proper caution to all who would follow this speculative path: Walter Weyrauch, *The Personality of Lawyers* (New Haven, Conn.: Yale University Press, 1964).

[57] These needs have been noted in print before: by Andrew Watson, "The Quest for Professional Competence: Psychological Aspects of Legal Education," *Cincinnati Law Review* 37 (1968): 101; and Johanna Schwab, "Occupational Attitudes of Lawyers," *Sociology of Social Research* 24, p. 56 (1939).

[58] Carlin's figures are supplied by the Bureau of Applied Social Research at Columbia University.

means conflict free. Just as doctors get angry at the patient who presents difficulties or makes demands,[59] just as some clients get angry at their lawyers when paternalism falls short of their expectations, some lawyers get angry at clients who are critical, uncooperative, or deceitful. Their aggressiveness makes them quick to anger and their competitiveness makes them quick to retaliate in the manner they know best, by reasserting control even more forcefully. These feelings and the dominating style they reflect are reinforced by the traditional professional model. The traditional model serves the function of a professional ideology, justifying the control the lawyer wants, affirming his status and competence, and defining as legitimate a role of client passivity and uncritical trust. The traditional model resolves unilaterally the conflicts inherent in the lawyer's role. It is one way lawyers can cope with the strains of practice.[60]

It is an open question as to whether professionals, especially lawyers, can be sold on the desirability of facilitating client participation. I have indicated ways in which professionals can gain from client participation but am not sure that many will not find these gains inadequate. To the extent that clients are resourceful and energetic in asserting an active client role, including systematically shopping for professionals and obtaining second professional opinions, professionals will have less opportunity unilaterally to control the relationship. An effective solution may depend upon recruiting to the professions men who are attracted by the opportunities for performing extensive counseling as a recognized professional function and for collaborative participation with clients in problem solving. Perhaps some members of this student generation will carry their commitment to participatory democracy forward into professional careers.

A further possibility which must be acknowledged is that in abandoning the traditional ideal, some professionals who now take the traditional model seriously and do their best to live up to its standards will abandon the sense of pride in their work, the sense of the profession as a special and honorable vocation which imposes higher standards of competence and integrity than are adhered to in many other employments. Possibly a few professionals would fall by the wayside, becoming careless and unscrupulous, merely because

---

[59] Howard Becker, Blanche Geer, Everett Hughes, and Anselm Strauss, *Boys in White* (Chicago: University of Chicago Press, 1961), p. 319.

[60] I think that the explanation of the dynamics of occupational ideologies set forth in *The American Business Creed* is appropriate to an understanding of the negligence lawyer's ideology in particular, and professional ideologies in general. In the book of that title by Francis Sutton, Seymour Harris, Carl Kaysen, and James Tobin (New York: Schocken Books, 1962).

some of the mythology has been removed. On the contrary, client participation has the potential for raising public esteem for the professions and for rewarding professional competence thereby reinforcing the sense of professional vocation. Conscientious professionals usually take satisfaction in clients following their advice and benefiting thereby. A recent study reported in *Scientific American* offers some support for the proposition that active patient participation in the interaction of medical consultations is positively related to the willingness of patients to carry out their doctor's medical advice thereafter. If the proposition holds generally, client activity can, in this way too, enhance the satisfactions of being a professional.[61]

A third limitation upon the realistic application of the participatory model is the pervasive public acceptance of the traditional model at the present time. The traditional model performs the function of a self-fulfilling prophecy. Because many clients believe it is proper to trust a professional (whose interests, they believe, never conflict with their own) without the necessity for him to earn that trust, because they believe it is mistrustful to ask too many questions and talk to other professionals "behind the back" of their consultant, and because clients believe that professional problems are too complicated to understand and have a single best technical solution, they think it impossible that their participation could be productive, and they think it is wrong for a client to want to participate. Unquestionably, if client participation is to be given a meaningful chance, clients as well as professionals are going to have to reexamine and alter certain deeply rooted attitudes. It is worth reasserting that this book has marshalled evidence not lightly dismissed, which indicates that we should revise our ideas about the appropriateness of behavior that is proper in general social situations, being appropriate for the special situations of professional-client problem solving. The extent to which the social conventions of politeness and deference can be self-destructive is strikingly illustrated in a study which interviewed graduate students who had been interrogated by agents of the Federal Bureau of Investigation in connection with protest demonstrations against the Vietnam War. The interviewers found that many of those interviewed unnecessarily incriminated themselves because they viewed the interrogation as a general social situation and one of the earliest rules a person learns about social behavior is not to be rude but rather to answer questions, courteously, when addressed.[62]

---

[61] Barbara M. Korsch and Vida F. Negrete, "Doctor-Patient Communication," *Scientific American* (August 1972): 69–73.

[62] John Griffiths and Richard Ayres, "A Postscript to the Miranda Project—Interrogation of Draft Protestors," excerpted in Katz, pp. 669–671.

A fourth limitation upon the participatory model's implementation is the inability of some clients to deal with the complexities of technical language and uncertain, multifaceted decisions. It has been mentioned, quite properly, that even the active clients in the sample—with a few notable exceptions—did not approach the ideal of full collaborative decision making responsibility in pursuing their claims. Unquestionably, full client collaboration will require that citizens routinely possess more information about the nature of their personal problems and about the opportunities available for coping with them than most now do. We have hardly begun the effort to educate the public about these matters.

A fifth limitation upon the participatory model's implementation is our relative ignorance about the proper scope and form disclosure leading to informed consent should take. In theory it should be possible to develop effective techniques and standards of relevance for disclosure which neither waste the time of the participants, unduly confuse the client, nor unduly threaten him. Experience in developing such techniques and standards, are needed, it would appear, for all professions, save perhaps psychiatry and psychological counseling.

A sixth limitation upon the implementation of the participatory model is that it may well be expensive. Professionals will probably be required to spend more time with individual clients than they do now. Active clients may insist upon receiving more and better services than passive clients are willing to accept. In the law, active clients may prove to be more litigious, thus resulting in extra burdens for the courts. This too is obviously a matter for further investigation. The *Scientific American* study reports the findings that (1) active patient interaction with doctors need not be time-consuming and (2) doctors who are skilled at disclosure take less time in consultations than doctors who have difficulty explaining diagnoses and other matters in language understandable to laymen.[63] In any event, before one concludes that client participation is too expensive to be encouraged, it should be borne in mind that there are substantial hidden costs of traditional professional practice which deserve to be reflected in any economic cost-benefit accounting. What are the costs in ineffective service of processing more clients more rapidly, of taking shortcuts in serving them, of discouraging them from seeking the best possible solution they can obtain? The stories of several of the clients interviewed in this study suggest that the hidden costs of client nonparticipation may be tremendous.

---

[63] Korsch and Negrete, "Doctor-Patient Communication," p. 71.

A seventh limitation is the limitation of time itself. Active client participation is time consuming as well as expensive. The participatory model will not alter the fact of everyday life that people, consciously or unconsciously, have to establish their own priorities of importance among their personal concerns. Active participation as a client strategy will be used, even by the most committed, selectively. What the model does is add to the repertory of possible responses by a layman to his personal problems, the response of active participation. At the present time, this is not part of the repertory of most laymen, even in crisis situations.

A final limitation inherent in the participatory model is that in reducing the professional's domination of the professional-client relationship, professionals will probably lose some of the ability they now have to restrain clients from taking immoral, illegal, or simply unfortunate actions in coping with their problems. For example, lawyers sometimes presently feel that their clients should fail in their claims if social justice is to be achieved, as in the family law situation where the parent he represents seeks custody of a child, and the parent, in the lawyer's judgment, is unfit to have custody. Presently, lawyers in such situations are sometimes able to work out arrangements satisfactory to their own views of what is right, behind the clients' backs. Such practices often are justified on the grounds that lawyers have a duty to the legal system as "officers of the court." The traditional model is more likely to sanction such lawyer conduct than the participatory model. Under the former, if the lawyer honestly believes that it is in the long-term interests of the client not to get custody of the child, by whatever criteria of interest the lawyer deems appropriate, he is justified in seeking to deny that custody regardless of the client's desires. Under the participatory model, the lawyer may not act contrary to the desires of the client, without assuming liability for negligence or even for an intentional tort. Under the participatory model, the lawyer has three choices: to persuade the parent to surrender custody, vigorously to seek custody of the child for the client in spite of his misgivings, or to withdraw from the case.

The costs of pursuing the participatory model are I believe tolerable, especially when weighed against the advantages to be gained from client participation. We can only learn if, as both professionals and as clients, we make a serious effort to test the participatory model in our daily conduct.

Appendix A: The Research Method

DEFINING THE RESEARCH

I began this research (for a PhD in political science at Yale University) to find out how lawyers and clients actually behave with each other, to compare their actual behavior with existing published reports of what the lawyer-client relationship is and what it should be, to evaluate the effectiveness of differing strategies of lawyer and client conduct, and especially to look for different types and degrees of client participation in the consultation. With these purposes in mind I approached 18 experienced lawyers with the following proposal: I would like to be present during one or more consultations they would conduct with two or three of their clients who would be apprised of the research and whose permission to be observed would be obtained in advance. Clients would be free to decline involvement. Each observed consultation would be followed up with questions asked of the client and the lawyer, separately, to see how each viewed what had transpired. These observations would be kept in strict confidence and the final draft of the manuscript would be submitted to each attorney to assure his own and his client's anonymity.

Politely, every lawyer refused. First, it was felt that my presence during an actual consultation about a pending legal matter might jeopardize the confidential nature of the client's statements to his attorney. The law of New York states that a third person present during a consultation who is neither the agent of the lawyer nor of the client—such as a legal associate or language interpreter—may be compelled to testify in court as to the specific things communicated by the client, despite the client's objection.[1] Thus, if the legal problem under discussion were actually to lead to litigation and if the opposition lawyer were to learn of my presence at a lawyer-client meeting, he might compel me to testify against the interest of my interview subject. So far as I have been able to discover, a social researcher has never been used in this way, nor has any court ruled explicitly on the question of whether allowing

---

[1] *People* v. *Cooper,* 307 N.Y. 253 (1954).

a qualified researcher to observe consultations for a valid research purpose necessarily waives the attorney-client privilege. An argument can be made that under present law it should not; but most lawyers are understandably reluctant to take the chance that the argument will not be upheld in their client's case.

The second reason given for the attorney refusals was that even the request to participate would be an imposition upon their clients: the attorneys were unwilling to risk incurring the displeasure which the mere invitation to participate in such a research inquiry might engender in the client. Interviewers tend to find that, on the contrary, people usually like to be interviewed. Nonetheless, there is a legitimate issue of the value conflict between the researcher's desire for knowledge and possible invasion of the subject's privacy, an issue to which lawyers should be sensitive.[2]

I sensed that two other considerations were involved in the attorneys' refusals. There was "nothing in it" for lawyers to cooperate with me. Why should they expose themselves to what would be at best an inconvenience and at worst a serious disruption? Their real but unenthusiastic interest in the research findings was hardly sufficient motivation. Furthermore, lawyers are not used to having people—even colleagues—look over their shoulder when they talk to clients. The presence of an outside observer would put them on the spot and might lead to disquieting findings about their desk-side manner. All of these objections applied with equal force to the idea of taping actual conversations with no observer present. This variation had been explored by Freeman and abandoned when he met with lawyer resistance.[3]

I next thought of simulated interaction between real lawyers and people posing as clients, but this raised formidable and personally uninteresting tactical problems of experimental design, preparing realistic legal problems and client roles, enlisting participants and coping with the inevitable distortion of an artificial situation in which the crucial variable of a direct and palpable client interest was absent. Simulation requires either a rigorous and explicit theory or detailed knowledge about the subject under investigation to give the experimental situation descriptive validity. I didn't know enough to meet either standard.[4]

After direct observation, the next best source of data are interviews with

---

[2] Oscar Ruebhausen and Orville G. Brim, "Privacy and Behavioral Research," *Columbia Law Review* 65 (November 1965): 1184–1211.

[3] Harrop Freeman, *Counseling in the United States* (Dobbs Ferry, N.Y.: Oceana, 1967), p. 53.

[4] Some of the problems and possibilities of experimental simulation or "prototyping" are raised by Harold Lasswell, *The Future of Political Science* (New York: Atherton, 1963), chap. 5, pp. 95–122.

lawyers and clients about what went on during their interaction involving recently terminated legal problems (concerning which there was no significant chance of future litigation). Even this modification was met with reluctance by the same 18 lawyers, apparently for the two generally unarticulated reasons already indicated. I soon realized that the only way to obtain meaningful information in order to get on with the inquiry would be to go to clients directly, rather than to lawyer intermediaries. After five fruitless months, this was the approach I adopted.

Partly by necessity and partly by intent, I decided to give primary attention to the client's experience of a legal problem by conducting extended personal interviews with 60 clients, but with only 20 lawyers. Some will object to this asymmetry on the grounds that clients have an incomplete and distorted picture of lawyer-client interaction and of the legal process. To this I have three answers. First, any participant in complex events comes away with an incomplete and distorted picture. But we have a great deal more printed information by and about lawyers and their perspective than we do about clients.[5] Second, it is possible to balance an appraisal, even when primary research is asymmetrical.[6] Third, I found a procedure enabling me to make a plausible evaluation of legal problem solving independent of either the lawyer's or the client's personal appraisal. This shall be discussed shortly.

To increase the precision and manageability of the analysis, I decided to concentrate on client experience with lawyers in confronting one relatively homogeneous type of legal problem. Law practice varies over a broad range of services, relationships, and problem areas. Generalizations from one area to another would require careful qualification. Some legal work relates to the problems of partnerships, corporations, or nonhuman entities. Some relates to humans in representative capacities—as trustees, brokers, agents, and elected officials. Most people, however, only encounter lawyers and the law in their private or family capacities. The nature of private legal problems often gives people a greater stake, a more personal involvement in solving

---

[5] One of the main findings of an evaluation of a poverty legal services program which I directed was that clients and attorneys tended to agree strikingly on the quality of legal service offered by the program. See Douglas Rosenthal, Robert Kagan, and Debra Quatrone, *Volunteer Attorneys and Legal Services for the Poor: New York's CLO Program* (New York: Russell Sage Foundation, 1971), chap. III.

[6] Successful examples include Eliot Friedson, *Patients' Views of Medical Practice* (New York: Russell Sage Foundation, 1961), where a balanced view of the doctor-patient relationship was provided in what was essentially a patient survey; also, David Caplovitz, *The Poor Pay More* (New York: Free Press, 1967), where description of the dealings between ghetto merchants and impoverished consumers was primarily based on consumer interviews.

them. Also, many personal legal problems are costly. The client has a lot to lose, materially and emotionally, if the problem is disposed of badly. The question of how a client should deal with his lawyer arises only because the client has a stake in his problem. Without the stake—without a lot to lose— there is little risk for the client in uncritical reliance upon his attorney. There- fore, high value negligence cases were a good candidate.

I decided to concentrate on the personal injury claims process. Not the least of the reasons for this choice is that in New York City court records are kept of the names and addresses of personal injury clients—thus providing me with direct client access. In New York State, the intermediate appeals court —the Appellate Division—is divided into four districts or judicial departments. Each department has the authority to supervise and administer the profes- sional conduct of attorneys practicing within its territory. Moved by its con- cern with incidents of ambulance-chasing and excessive fee charging by some lawyers, the Appellate Division First Department, comprising Manhattan and the Bronx, developed and instituted a then unique procedure for monitoring the conduct of local lawyers. Since January 1, 1957, by rule of the court, a statement of retainer must be filed by any attorney charging a contingent fee who has offices in Manhattan or the Bronx (or by an attorney who brings suit in a Manhattan or Bronx court) in the following five types of action: per- sonal injury, property damage, wrongful death, property condemnation, and change of property grade.[7] The statement must include, among other things, the terms of the legal fee and the name, address, occupation, and relationship of the person who referred the case. Once a case of any of these five kinds has been terminated—even if unsuccessfully without fee or recovery—a closing statement must be filed, informing the court of the disposition, the amount of recovery (if any), the actual fee received, the name of the defendant paying the claim, and the legal costs incurred in making the claim.[8] Both statements must contain the name and address of the client making the claim. These state- ments are filed at the New York City office of the State Judicial Conference which organization administers and prepares descriptive statistics about the state court system. Access to either set of statements gives direct access to legal clients.

To avoid a possible confidentiality problem in an ongoing case, I decided

---

[7] Within the past few years, similar procedures have been established not only in New York's Second Judicial Department, but also, according to John Bonomi, in the State of Massachusetts and the City of Philadelphia. Bonomi is director of the Grievance Committee of the Association of the Bar of the City of New York.

[8] See Appendix B, p. 213.

to try to collect a case sample from closing statements only. These are filed within 30 days after a claim is fully terminated. By court rules, the data contained in these files are open to nonofficial inspection only upon written order of the Presiding Justice of the Appellate Division First Department. On January 2, 1969, Judge Harold Stevens authorized my sampling up to 400 closing statements for this study.[9]

THE CLIENT SAMPLE

My interest in testing the impact of active client participation in personal injury cases led to the setting of four limiting criteria for the statements sampled. First, three of the five classes of reportable claims (those classes where the plaintiff is not a personal injury victim) were eliminated. Property condemnation cases, grading change cases, and wrongful death actions (brought by the surviving relatives who suffer financial loss from the death of a breadwinner) were easily excluded. These actions can usually be identified by noting the reported parties to the claim. Condemnations and grading changes usually involve realty corporations and municipal authorities (and no doctors' bills). Wrongful death actions are brought in the name of the deceased by an executor or administrator of his estate. It is necessary to infer the nature of the claim because the statement nowhere makes it explicit. This is a potential handicap in distinguishing some claims involving personal injury from claims for property damage alone. However, the second criterion that was employed, that the claim be one with a gross recovery of at least $2,000, not only served to weed out superficial personal injuries but sole property damage claims as well. The one exception was a composer who lost $2,000 worth of composition manuscripts when a hot-water pipe in his apartment ruptured during his absence. He was excluded from the sample.

Third, to facilitate recall about the part the client played in the problem solving of his case, only closing statements filed during 1969 were drawn. This put a limit on the remoteness of the commencement date of cases; claims very rarely take more than seven or eight years from the date of accident to try to settle. The longest settlement period for any respondent turned out to be less than nine years.[10]

Initially I assumed that in our society many fewer women than men would qualify as active clients. Since I wanted a meaningful subsample of active clients, I initially decided to define an all male sample. Therefore, as a

---

[9] In October 1969, authorization to draw an additional 100 statements was received.
[10] See Figure A.1.

fourth criterion, I stipulated that there be at least one adult male as a listed plaintiff on the closing statement—suing either for himself, or as the natural guardian of his child. I assumed that in most cases where a wife was also joined as plaintiff, the husband would have taken the more active part in dealing with the attorney. I was to learn that many wives play the principal role in dealing with the lawyer when they suffer the more serious injury. The final sample thus did include women, a total of 16 (27 percent). However, none of the dozen most active clients was a woman. The women's liberation movement may promote active participation of female clients in the future.

Among possible factors explaining differences in the extent of client participation, the extent of a client's formal education seemed crucial. Research has shown that educational level correlates strongly and positively with an individual's activity in social and political life.[11] Educational level is also a good indicator of social status. There is some evidence that the condition of low social status is associated with a culture which handicaps a person in meeting the intellectual and emotional demands of interaction with professionals. Equally important is the further evidence that professionals are handicapped by their higher status from dealing effectively with "uneducated" and "impoverished" clients.[12] For this reason, I wanted to interview educated clients primarily—clients with at least a high school education—who might reasonably be expected to have received sufficient intellectual training to participate in complex interpersonal problem solving. Since the closing statements do not record client educational levels, I divided a street map of Manhattan into high-education and low-education plots according to 1960 census tracts. Interview requests were mailed only to residents of the high-education tracts (in which the median educational level was 12 years or more). With respect to education, the tracts proved quite homogeneous. Fewer than one out of five respondents turned out not to have completed high school.[13]

I was not permitted direct access to the microfilmed file of closing statements. Instead, I was supplied with photocopies of 414 closing statements in two relatively equal drawings and a third replacement drawing of 81, for a total of 495. The first drawing was made from residents of the boroughs of the Bronx, Brooklyn, and Queens, as well as Manhattan. I decided only afterward to concentrate on Manhattan residents for easier interviewing. With

---

[11] Lester Milbrath, *Political Participation* (Chicago: Rand McNally, 1965), pp. 42–43.

[12] August Hollingshead and Frederick Redlich, *Social Class and Mental Illness* (New York: Wiley, 1958), pp. 369–370.

[13] See Table A.3.

the exclusion of 144 non-Manhattan cases and 61 Manhattan cases which represented either repeat counts or non-personal injury cases, I "lost" 205 potential subjects from the total drawing. Of the 290 usable Manhattan closing statements drawn, 159 were for residents of the low-education tracts. Thus the interview sample of educated Manhattanites was 131 persons. The sampling procedure was not truly random. Since a true random sample was uneconomical, I had requested that equal drawings be made for each month of 1968, from the middle one or two days of the month—taking the first 18 consecutive statements which met the criteria. Instead, in the first drawing, 13 statements were taken from the first week of each of the first 11 months, and 78 statements were taken from six days during the second and third weeks of December. I received no explanation for this deviation from the agreed procedure, nor could the sampling be redone, consistently. Since many more cases are settled at year's end—for the lawyer's tax purposes and the insurer's accounting purposes—than at any other time, the imbalance more nearly reflects the actual rate of case dispositions.[14] The second drawing, three months later, was made from Manhattan residents only. This time 16 or 17 monthly drawings were made for each month, from one day during the third week of the month. Frequently, each month's sample represented virtually every closing statement on the date which met the sampling criteria (injury case, male plaintiff, ended in 1968, $2,000 or more recovery, Manhattan resident). Occasionally, there were not even 16 qualifying cases on that date, and the last few had to be drawn from the following day's log. A third replacement drawing was made nine months after the second (in October 1969), to provide enough cases for 60 interviews. Seven cases were drawn from one day during the second week of each month from January to November; four were drawn from the second week of December. Initially I had hoped to conduct between 80 and 100 interviews. However, interviewing proved much more time consuming than anticipated. I stopped at 60 usable interviews. There were two reasons in addition to the time factor. First, I had almost run out of upper-education tract Manhattan closing statements—the Appellate Division only authorized a sampling of 500 statements. Second, 60 clients is a sufficient sample to test statistically the principal hypothesis relating client activity and case result.

Each of the 131 plaintiffs selected from the larger sample of closing statements was sent a multigraphed letter, in two phased mailings, on Yale Political Science Department stationery. The letter explained, briefly, the nature of the

---

[14] See Figure A.2.

project, offered a small honorarium, and requested the recipient to fill out and mail an enclosed stamped reply postcard expressing his interest. A letter supporting the research, from the chairman of the department, also was enclosed. One week after each mailing, all subjects who had returned postcards, and all of those with listed phone numbers who had not, were telephoned and asked to participate. Forty-seven people responded favorably to the initial letter or telephone contact and interviews were arranged and conducted between February and November 1969. Twenty-three initial solicitation letters were returned as undeliverable—the addressee was either unknown or had moved without leaving a forwarding address. These letters were registered and remailed, with a return receipt request stating person to whom delivered and place of delivery. This failed to turn up any of the 23. Several weeks after the initial mailing, a follow-up letter was sent to all uninterviewed persons whose first letters had not been returned, renewing the request for an interview. These were people who had either (1) been telephoned and had not participated or (2) had unlisted phones and had not responded to the first mailing. Fourteen of these responded favorably to the second letter and follow-up phone call and were interviewed. The interview response breaks down into the following four categories:

(a)   61 persons interviewed
(b)   20 persons refusing to be interviewed during telephone follow-up
(c)   27 persons not replying to mailings and not reached by telephone
(d)   23 persons for whom mailings were undeliverable
      ——
      131 Total

The response rate for those actually contacted and for those presumed to have been contacted was 56.5 percent (61 of 108).

The research raises problems, at four levels, of the representativeness, and therefore the generalizability of the sample findings. First of all is the problem of the disparity between the designated sample initially approached and the sample population actually interviewed. The 56+ percent response rate is not high in general survey research, but probably is not low for a detailed legal survey.[15] A major factor working against the interviewer is the intimidating nature of legal institutions, the fears that participation in an interview about personal legal matters may open the door to legal—even penal—consequences, or even a reopening, for ill, of the accident victim's case. The

---

[15] Roger Bryant Hunting and Gloria S. Neuwirth regarded as "extraordinarily high" their 51.4 percent (165 of 321) response rate. *Who Sues in New York City?* (New York: Columbia University Press, 1962), p. 144.

high interview refusal rate also reflects the topic's emotional content. In addition, I suspect that the respondent self-selection process worked to weed out a slightly disproportionate number of less educated, and possibly more passive clients. More than half of the people with whom I talked over the telephone and who were not interviewed, spoke English with an accent or with lower-status speech patterns. Most of those who declined to be interviewed expressed open (or thinly veiled) suspicion about my research intent and how it might hurt them. There was a slight relationship between suspiciousness and passive client participation among the people actually interviewed. One interviewee out of three of the total number interviewed was noticeably guarded in the preinterview phone conversation and during the first minutes of the interview itself. However, only about one relatively active client interviewee out of five appeared guarded. Assuming that the suspicion among the uninterviewed is like the suspicion among the interviewed—only more so—the respondent sample is somewhat "overpopulated" with active clients.

The second level of generalization is to go from the interview population to the Judicial Conference file population taken as a whole. One distortion created by the initial criterion that a male plaintiff be listed on any closing statement is that women, and especially single women, are underrepresented.

The third level of generalization is from the sample population to the universe of highly educated, Manhattan-resident recent personal injury clients with high-stake claims. It may be that some attorneys violate the rules of the court by failing to file retainer or closing statements, or by filing reports which intentionally understate the amount of the gross recovery received from the claim. Presumably, these infractions would be committed by the least reputable and least careful members of the Manhattan and Bronx negligence bar. Therefore, the sample cases may be biased in the direction of reflecting somewhat higher standards of legal service than actually obtain in New York City.

Generalization of the findings to the universe of urban-educated Americans is a jump some will be reluctant to make. In their 1959 study of judicial delay, Zeisel, Kalven, and Buchholz analyzed the variation in personal injury claim rates among different regions of the United States. They found that New York City has the highest rate of claims in the country. While New York City also has the highest accident rate, Zeisel and associates concluded that this alone could not explain the disproportionate number of claims.[16] They hypothesized a personality-cultural factor of "claims-consciousness" as an explanation. New Yorkers, they advanced, are more claims-conscious than

---

[16] Hans Zeisel, Harry Kalven, and Bernard Buchholz, *Delay in the Court* (Boston: Little, Brown, 1959), tables 88 and 89, pp. 232–233.

people in other locations.[17] If Zeisel and his co-workers are correct, New Yorkers may be unrepresentatively active and sophisticated clients (even though the data of this study show that their activity falls far short of an ideal standard). The concept of claims-consciousness thus bears some consideration.

To begin with, claims-consciousness means different things to different people. Defined minimally as a willingness to hire a lawyer and bring a lawsuit, then all clients in the sample are claims-conscious. A more stringent test of a claims-conscious person is to confine the concept to those experienced in litigation—to more than one-time plaintiffs. By this criterion, only about one-quarter (16 of 59) of the interviewees were claims-conscious—having been prior plaintiffs in small claims court or a higher court of record. Another measure of claims-consciousness (as well as accident proneness, possibly) might be prior experience in making a personal injury claim. According to this criterion, too, most claimants (38 of 59) are not litigious. It is probably true that it takes some information about the law, the courts, and the insurance industry to think of making a claim for compensation. New Yorkers may be better educated than people elsewhere about their legal rights and opportunities, but that is not to say that they are experienced with, or sophisticated about, legal rules or using lawyers for personal problem solving. Eighty-five percent (50 of 59) of the sample claimants were unfamiliar with the contributory negligence rule. Fifty-eight percent (34 of 59) of the respondents had never made a will. A majority of the claimants had never served on a jury (35 of 59).

Another possible indication of claims-consciousness might be whether or not a client has ever before used the services of a lawyer for any kind of business or personal problem. Almost three-fourths of the client sample (43 of 59) had hired a lawyer at least once before. A 1961 poll of Missouri residents, solicited by the Missouri Bar Association, provides a basis for comparing the "lawyer consciousness" of my sample with the general population of one midwestern state.[18] Of the Missouri respondents, 64 percent (1,609 of 2,524 questioned) had used a lawyer for some legal matter; 19 percent had been plaintiffs (310 of 1,599), and 25 percent had made a will (640 of 2,522). Missouri residents as a whole have 10 percent less experience with lawyers and have 17 percent fewer wills drafted; 7 percent fewer have been involved in lawsuits.[19] The Missouri poll was stratified to represent proportion-

---

[17] Ibid., p. 239.

[18] *Missouri Bar Prentice-Hall Survey* (Jefferson City: The Missouri Bar, 1963).

[19] Ibid., pp. 19–21.

ately all social classes. The author's sample was biased toward the more (by hypothesis) legally conscious upper stratum. In view of this, the disparities between the two samples do not seem sufficiently great to warrant the conclusion that New Yorkers are particularly claims-conscious. One possible explanation for the disproportionately large number of New York claims is that New York is one of the few states that requires resident motorists to carry at least $10,000 of automobile liability insurance coverage. Also, New York State has established an uninsured motorists' claim fund to provide the minimum coverage for victims of uninsured lawbreakers and uninsured out-of-state negligent drivers. In New York, state policy encourages claims. Zeisel and associates do not discuss this factor.

To help the reader draw his own conclusions about its representativeness, here is further depiction of the client sample according to some qualities that are not discussed in the analysis.

1. *Religion:* 64 percent of the sample (38 of 59) are Jewish; 24 percent (14 of 59) are Protestant, and 12 percent (7 of 59) are Catholic. It is common knowledge that New York City has the highest concentration of Jewish people in the United States. To some, an active problem solving strategy implies aggressiveness, a Jewish stereotypical trait. The data belie the stereotype. Among the most active and passive clients there was, using Fisher's Exact Test, no significant relationship between client religion and client activity (Table A.1). Because of the upper education census tract criterion, there were only four Negroes (Protestants) and three Latins (Catholics) in the sample.

2. *Sex, age, and marital status:* as previously stated, the sampling procedure limited the representation of women clients to 27 percent. Thus no firm conclusions can be drawn about gender as an explanatory factor. The median age of respondents was 53. Fourteen clients were under the age of 40. Ten clients were 65 or older. No relationship was found between client age and client activity. Forty-three interviewees (73 percent) were married at the

Table A.1: Relation between Religion and Client Activity

	Jewish	*Christian*	
Active client	47%	52%	
	(18)	(11)	$N = 29$
Passive client	53%	48%	
	(20)	(10)	$N = 30$
	$N = 38$	$N = 21$	59

Figure A.1: Accidents by Year of Occurrence

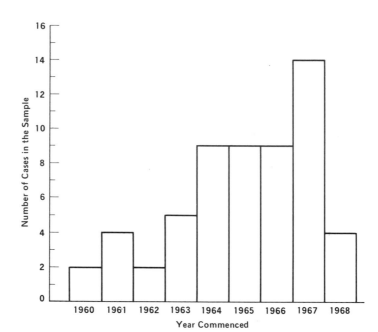

time of the interview. Nine were never married; six were divorced, and one was a widower.

3. *Claim characteristics:*[20] Figure A.1, portrays the distribution of accidents by year of accident. Most occurred within four years of settlement. For 59 of the 60 claims, the closing statement recorded in which court, if any, a suit was filed. In 53 percent (31) of the cases, suit was filed in New York State Supreme Court. In 15 percent (9), suit was filed in the Civil Court of New York City. In two cases, suit was brought in the Federal District Court. In three cases, suit was brought in an out-of-state jurisdiction. In 24 percent of the claims (14), no suit was filed. Figure A.2, shows the distribution of claims by the month, during 1968, in which they were terminated.

Though the sample does not strictly meet the conventions of random selection, the selection does appear to have been sufficiently free of any systematic distortion to permit the assumption of randomness. The research proceeded on this assumption. A definitive test awaits a number of replications.

---

[20] The following data are taken from the closing statements submitted by the attorneys of record.

Figure A.2: Cases by Month of Termination

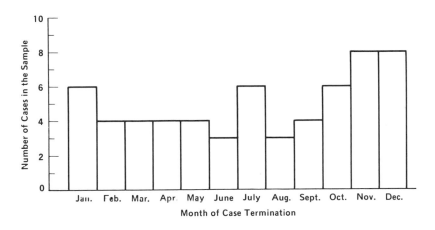

THE CLIENT QUESTIONNAIRE

The client interview questions were divided into nine broad topics of research interest:

1. The accident, the injury, and the injury's financial impact
2. How the injury was established as a legal problem by the client
3. Prior client experience with, and attitudes toward, the legal process
4. Client experience with and attitudes toward the interaction with the lawyer
5. Present feelings about the claims experience and the institutions of the claims process
6. General attitudes toward personal problem solving
7. Attitudes toward various legal reform proposals
8. The degree of political activity of the client
9. Personal descriptive data

The interview began with an open-ended invitation to tell the story of the accident experience in the client's own terms. Only the subject's request for approval of what he was saying or for more explicit direction led to more specific, detailed questions. The questionnaire was designed for flexible administration. Questions were often asked out of sequence to follow a train of information stressed in the opening narration. The first seven topics were discussed orally. The last two were administered and answered in writing. A recurring question pattern was to ask about specific actions or events—what

happened and how the client felt about it—inviting open-ended answers which
were then clarified by further, more detailed follow-up questions. Oral questions usually were asked in the exact words of the instrument but impromptu
modification was common.

The first draft of the questionnaire was pretested with five informants
excluded from the sample. The second, shorter draft was administered to the
first ten sample respondents. The final form trimmed and reworded the second draft only slightly.

The questionnaire was not designed for tight coding. It was desirable to
review early interview returns before setting final coding categories. To give
this flexibility, all interviews (except eight where permission was refused)
were tape recorded. Length of interviews ranged between 50 minutes and 3
hours. Data were coded on coding sheets and relevant client quotations were
transcribed from the tapes. Where no tape had been made, quotations were
taken from my interview notes.

The most important data from the interviews were the client's report of
his accident, injuries, and expenses, and his report of his own role in making
the claim. The most important measure was the index of client activity. It was
hard to construct because so little is known about the influential ways that
clients can and do act in the course of consultation with an attorney. I initially developed a nine-item index of the kinds of client activity which might
plausibly occur in the interaction and which might plausibly be expected to
increase the knowledge and control of the client in the problem solving. Three
of the items were subsequently dropped: "the client asks questions of the
lawyer about his case," "the client initiates follow-up contacts with the lawyer," and "the client discusses his case with friends, for their advice." They
did not seem as reliable as the remaining measures. It is not the mere asking
of questions or the mere initiation of follow-up contacts that affects the claim
handling, but the purpose and persistence behind these questions and initia-
tives. Most people discuss their cases with friends and relatives; but not so
much for information and fresh ideas useful for understanding and appraisal,
as for emotional reassurance. A fourth type of activity, "the client bargains
about the fee" was subsumed for reasons of economy under the broader activity type of "makes demands." As indicated previously in the text, a fifth
type of activity, "marshals information to aid the lawyer" was not used in the
final index. However, it was used in an earlier version of the index and did
not change the significant relationship between client activity and case outcome in that version. I am undecided about whether this form of activity is or

is not potentially influential. It is to be expected that further analysis of client activity will improve our understanding of, and ability to measure, these different behaviors, especially when researchers are finally permitted direct access to lawyer-client interaction.

Doubts may be raised about the reliability of the informant reports of activity and about the validity of the coding of the client activity index. In any final sense, only replication of my findings using some independent source of data (preferably direct observation) can answer these doubts. But, within limits, a few cautionary safeguards have been employed. First, to check the reliability of clients' reports about their accidents, damages and activity, seven of the attorneys were interviewed (with the clients' permission). In only one of the seven cases was the client's report of these matters disputed by the lawyer. There was a conflict between Mr. O'Shea and his lawyer about the time of Mr. O'Shea's request for a special trial preference and about the extent of his lost wages. There was a peripheral dispute between Mr. Winter and his first lawyer on the reason why Mr. Winter gave the case to a second attorney. Otherwise the lawyers corroborated their clients' stories. Second, special effort was made not to tip off any of the subjects to my specific interest in client activity, or my personal predilection for active client behavior. On the whole, the effort appears to have been successful. Before beginning the interview, I invited the respondents to question me further about the nature of my study—after the interview was completed. Those who did expressed curiosity and surprise when I explained the hypothesized relationship between client activity and case result. It struck them as a novel idea. Though I may be deceiving myself, I doubt that there would have been so much surprise if I had been cuing them during the interview.

Having said this, I must admit that the interview interaction was not totally "neutral." However, the questions about client activity are not those most vulnerable to distortion, but rather the probes to draw out the subject's feelings about his experience. This probing is difficult not only because people are reluctant to express intimate feelings which may damage the impression they are trying to make on me—the noncommittal, authoritative interviewer—but because many of the subjects themselves seemed unaware of the nature, and especially of the depth, of some of their feelings. This was the most difficult interview task: to try to identify the feelings that people seemed to be struggling with in talking about specific emotional experiences and to help in their expression, by sympathy and by suggested interpretations of what I sensed they were feeling. To do this without mistaking one's own feelings for those of the respondent takes skill and training. It is a very difficult problem for even trained interviewers—referred to in psychoanalytic theory as the problem of countertransference and in sociology as the problem of achieving the proper degree of "sympathetic neutrality."[21] My success in this is not so great as I would have liked. In listening again to the tapes, I see several points at which my interpretations were premature and several points where I stopped and should have continued probing. The interview tapes have helped me to try to improve my performance in this respect,[22] and they have enabled me to receive the expert criticism of psychoanalyst Jay Katz and sociologist Lindsey Churchill, who have given patient and insightful critiques. One payoff to this preoccupation with drawing out initially unverbalized client feelings, was discovery of the widespread and intense feeling of victimization experienced by respondents—especially by those who reached the adversary proceeding stage of the claims process. Again and again I was told that "being treated like a criminal" or being "yelled at and called a liar" by the cross-examining defense counsel was an even more degrading, humiliating experience than physical recovery from the injury itself.

As to the bias of the coding, care was taken not to review the subject's closing statement prior to his interview—to avoid knowing beforehand whether or not he had received an unusually large recovery. The distinctions among more significant and less significant forms of each type of action were necessarily judgmental. To give the reader an idea, in each instance, of the factual basis for my judgments I have, in Table A.2, listed the activity score for each client with respect to each type of activity and the reason, where applicable, for assigning positive activity scores of 1 or 2.

Influenced by the measure of social status developed by August Hollingshead, I used five class ranks for each of three status indicators: education, occupation, and personal income.[23] Table A.3 shows the criteria defining each rank and the ranking of the clients according to these criteria. The aggregate status rank order will be found in Figure 2.3 on page 40.

---

[21] Louis Dexter, "Role Relationships and Conceptions of Neutrality in Interviewing," *American Journal of Sociology* 62 (1956): 153.

[22] I did not find that using a small, unobtrusive tape recorder increased interviewee resistance. Instead of creating problems, it freed me "from tedious note-taking [which helped me] to concentrate [my] attention on the respondent and [these] more subtle interactional aspects of the interview." As the paraphrase indicates, my experience affirms the enthusiasm of Rue Bucher and associates for taped interviews. "Tape Recorded Interviews in Social Research," *American Sociological Review* 21 (1956): 359, 360.

[23] Hollingshead and Redlich, *Social Class and Mental Illness,* Appendix Two, "The Index of Social Position," pp. 387–397.

Table A.2: Independent Activity Variable for Each Client with Reasons for Positive Scores

Client Number	Prompt and Thorough Medical Attention	Follow-up Demands	Seeks Second Opinion	Impresses Wishes	Marshals Information
1	0	0	2 (took away from first lawyer)	0	2 (took photos)
2	0	0	0	0	1 (obtained witness)
3	2 (top specialists)	2 (phone contacts)	2 (used solicitor lawyer)	2 (pushed for big recovery)	0
4	2 (special treatments)	0	1 (got no substantive advice)	0	0
5	1 (not much needed)	1 (lawyer avoided answering questions)	1 (from head of union)	0	0
6	0	1 (kept phoning)	0	2 (wanted early settlement)	0
7	2 (specialist; maid service)	2 (wanted to deal with senior partner)	0	0	0
8	2 (specialist)	2 (threatened to take case away)	2 (from referring lawyer)	2 (fee bargained; stressed $ value wanted)	1 (overheard admission of defendant's liability)
9	0	0	1 (3 yrs. after accident)	0	0
10	2 (specialist; good hospital)	0	0	0	0
11	1 (no specialist needed)	2 (threatened to take case away)	1 (informal; with several lawyer friends)	2	0

Client Number	Prompt and Thorough Medical Attention	Follow-up Demands	Seeks Second Opinion	Impresses Wishes	Marshals Information
12	0	1 (after years)	0	1 (after years)	0
13	1 (no specialist)	0	0	2 (had radiologist make contact)	0
14	1 (no specialist)	0	1 (from insurance broker)	0	0
15	0	0	0	0	2 (took photos)
16	2	0	0	0	0
17	1 (good doctor; minimized injury)	0	0	0	0
18	2 (specialists)	0	0	0	0
19	2 (specialists)	1 (asked lawyer about fees and progress; brushed off)	0	0	0
20	2 (specialist; extended hospitalization)	0	0	0	0
21	2 (specialists)	0	2 (wife an attorney)	0	0
22	2 (specialist; psycho-therapy)	1 (critical to top partner of treatment of underlings)	1 (lawyer-trained brother-in-law)	2 (expressed fear of EBT)	0
23	2 (specialists; long recuperation)	0	0	0	0
24	1 (adequate treatment; poor hospital)	0	0	0	0

Client Number	Prompt and Thorough Medical Attention	Follow-up Demands	Seeks Second Opinion	Impresses Wishes	Marshals Information
25	1 (not much needed)	2 (threatened to take case away)	0	1 (wanted lawyer to press criminal charges; lawyer refused)	2 (successfully pressed criminal charges)
26	1 (not much needed)	0	0	1 (asked about fee; reduction not given)	1 (insisted on quick property evaluation)
27	0	0	0	0	0
28	1 (not much needed)	0	0	0	0
29	2 (specialists; long recuperation)	2 (constant questions)	0	1 (talked out sense of personal guilt in causing accident)	2 (took photos)
30	0 (out of hospital one day)	0	0	2 (wanted early settlement at all costs)	0
31	2 (hospitalization; for whiplash)	2 (constant questions)	1 (brother a lawyer; not much help)	2 (fee bargained)	0
32	2 (extensive attention)	0	1 (brother a lawyer; not much help)	0	0
33	2 (two sets of x-rays)	2 (many contacts; lawyer came to him)	2 (consulted lawyer friend)	0	0
34	2 (good care provided by nurse)	2 (prompted lawyer)	0	2 (eager for settlement)	0
35	2 (transferred to good hospital)	0	0	2 (didn't want trial)	0

Client Number	Prompt and Thorough Medical Attention	Follow-up Demands	Seeks Second Opinion	Impresses Wishes	Marshals Information
36	0	0	0	0	0
37	2 (protracted treatment)	0	0	0	0
38	0 (poor hospital)	0	0	0	0
39	2 (hypochondriac)	0	0	2 (willing to go to trial)	1 (found note admitting liability)
40	0 (left hospital prematurely)	0	0	0	2 (tracked down a witness)
42	2 (used day worker)	0	0	0	0
43	2 (extensive; including psychotherapy)	1 (asked questions)	2 (took case away from first lawyer)	0	0
44	0	0	0	2 (borrowed money from lawyer)	0
45	1 (excellent care but poor hospital)	0	2 (changed lawyers)	0	0
46	2 (extended care)	0	0	2 (fee bargained)	2 (organized co-plaintiffs)
47	2 (specialized dentistry)	0	0	0	0
48	2 (extended care)	1 (very belatedly)	0	0	0
49	0 (didn't go to specialist)	0	0	0	0
50	2 (day worker)	0	0	0	0
51	1 (no exceptional care)	0	0	1 (didn't push fee bargain)	0
52	1 (not much needed)	0	0	0	2 (pushed property loss assessment vigorously)

Client Number	Prompt and Thorough Medical Attention	Follow-up Demands	Seeks Second Opinion	Impresses Wishes	Marshals Information
53	1 (not much needed)	2 (prodded)	0	0	0
54	1 (not much needed)	0	0	2 (didn't want case pushed)	2 (drafted own summons)
55	1 (not much needed)	0	0	0	0
57	2 (specialists)	2 (many questions)	1 (talked to other law students)	2 (told lawyer not to "claw")	2 (got hospital reports)
58	0	0	0	0	0
59	1	0	0	2	0
60	2 (elaborate health measures)	2 (prodded and questioned)	0	2 (willing to wait out)	0
61	1 (good initially; less good subsequently)	0	0	2 (wanted settlement)	0
Total 59	73	31	23	41	22

Table A.3: Client Ranking According to Education, Occupation, and Income

	Percentage	*Number*
1. Education		
I. College graduate and above	49	29
II. Partial college	17	10
III. High school graduate	15	9
IV. Partial high school	14	8
V. Ninth grade or below	5	3
	100	59
2. Occupation		
I. Major executive, professional or proprietor	19	11
II. Medium exec., lesser prof., or medium proprietor	25	15
III. Administrator, shop owner, or Semiprof.	31	18
IV. Skilled employee	8	5
V. Semi- and unskilled worker	17	10
	100	59
3. Income Per Annum		
I. More than $20,000	29	17
II. $10,001–20,000	34	20
III. $7,001–10,000	17	10
IV. $3,500–7,000	6	4
V. Less than $3,500	14	8
	100	59

I was intrigued by an Almond and Lasswell paper which reports that dominant welfare clients dealing with submissive welfare administrators and vice versa get better results in their welfare claims than do dominant clients dealing with dominant administrators or submissive clients dealing with submissive administrators.[24] I tried to work out an index of dominance-submissiveness (or autonomy-dependency) to identify and test such an explanatory personality trait at least for clients. It was encouraging that several social psychologists had attempted to measure a personality dimension very

[24] Gabriel Almond and Harold Lasswell, "The Participant-Observer: A Study of Administrative Rules in Action," in *The Analysis of Political Behavior: An Empirical Approach,* ed. Harold Lasswell (New York: Oxford University Press, 1948), pp. 261–278.

much like the one I had in mind. This dimension is variously referred to as a trait of dependency, cognitive rigidity, and fear of uncertainty, and is a component of Adorno's famous authoritarian personality trait.[25] Several items in the questionnaire reflect the tarnished product of my attempt. I soon learned that they are too crude, too ambiguous and incomplete, with the result that the responses were too difficult to code. Respondents usually redefined, qualified, and rejected these questions, showing a healthy refusal to play the simpleton. I leave it to those more experienced in designing and testing personality measures to determine whether or not there is a meaningful autonomy-dependency dimension which can explain different patterns of decision behavior.

My inability to develop a psychological variable which relates positively with client activity does not stand alone as a failure. An investigation of personal injury claims making among Michigan automobile victims included an attempt by Robert Pratt to relate interviewee hostility (measured by a subjectively coded five-item questionnaire test) with evidence of active client behavior. Pratt took as evidence of client activity (he referred to it as aggressiveness): (1) client reports of having expressed disagreement with the decisions of their attorneys and (2) client reports of having made demands upon the attorney about how to conduct some aspects of their case. Pratt found no relationship between the personality trait of hostility and this overtly active behavior.[26]

My small sample has only turned up two statistically significant explanations for a good case outcome in addition to the factors reflected in the expert panel evaluations: client activity and claim worth. At several points in the text I have suggested other plausible explanations which might well be significant in a larger client sample or if measured by more sophisticated indicators. That

---

[25] T. W. Adorno et al., *The Authoritarian Personality* (New York: Wiley Science Edition, 1964), p. 248; Harold Webster et al., "A New Instrument for Studying Authoritarianism in Personality," *The Journal of Psychology* 40 (1955): 73–84; Orville Brim, Jr., et al., *Personality and Decision Processes* (Stanford, Calif.: Stanford University Press, 1962), chap. 6; Patricia O'Connor, "Ethnocentrism, 'Intolerance of Ambiguity' and Abstract Reasoning Ability," *Journal of Abnormal and Social Psychology* 47 (1952): 526; Frank Barron, "Some Personality Correlates of Independence of Judgment," *Journal of Personality* 21 (1962): 294; Stanley Eudnor, "Intolerance of Ambiguity as a Personality Variable," *Journal of Personality* 30 (1962): 29; Irving Janis et al., *Personality and Persuasability* (New Haven: Yale University Press, 1959), chap. 3.

[26] Robert Pratt, "Basic 'Hostility' as a Factor in the Behavior and Attitudes of Accident Victims," in Alfred Conard et al., *Automobile Accident Costs and Payments* (Ann Arbor: University of Michigan Press, 1964), pp. 309–321.

I did not devote more attention to alternative explanations of case outcome reflects my primary interest in specifically testing client activity as an important factor. A comprehensive explanation of the outcomes of personal injury cases is a worthwhile assignment I leave to others.

THE EXPERT PANEL EVALUATION

Time and money limited the number of panelists I could select. On the advice of John Osborne of the Coordinating Committee on Discipline, I approached Jacob and Abraham Fuchsberg, the brother team who are among the best-known and most respected negligence specialists in the City. They agreed to serve and introduced me to the other two lawyers, Norman Landau and Cecil Badway, and to the two insurance adjusters, who served on the panel. An acquaintance introduced me to another lawyer, a member of a two-man firm, who impressed me with his thoughtfulness and sincerity. He also agreed to be a panelist. The evaluations took approximately three hours per man. I paid each evaluator an honorarium of $100. Of the seven men who agreed to serve as panelists, two were not included in the final five-man panel used to determine case value. I excluded one of the Fuchsberg brothers to avoid the criticism that the two brothers in joint practice were not sufficiently independent evaluators. I also excluded the lawyer introduced by my acquaintance because his valuations differed substantially from those of the other evaluators. Furthermore, the five-man panel presented a symmetry between the two adversary perspectives: two plaintiff attorneys, a "switch hitter," and two insurance representatives.

There was significant agreement among the panelists in the rank order of the values to be assigned to the sample cases. Using Spearman's rho, Table A.4 shows that each panelist tended to agree with every other panelist about relative case values. There was, however, considerable variation among the panelists in the actual values assigned to each individual case. As might be expected, the claims adjuster for the local mutual insurer systematically valued claims lower than his fellow panelists. Interestingly, however, the adjuster for the national insurance company did not tend to value claims lower than the attorneys who represented plaintiffs. The considerable variation among panelists with respect to each case does not accord with the widespread assumption that experts will tend to reach a consensus on the value of any particular case. Even the two Fuchsberg brothers valued several cases substantially differently.

One of the findings of this study is the variation even among experts in

Table A.4: Intercorrelations among Panelists of Case Value Rank Orders

Panelists	*#1*	*#2*	*#3*	*#4*	*#5*
#1	1	.72	.80	.74	.65
#2		1	.83	.80	.67
#3			1	.78	.71
#4				1	.75
#5					1

assessment of claim values. Why should this be? Take the case of Pablo Pareira in which the variation among panelists is not unusual. Pablo lives in East Harlem and was 16 years old at the time of his accident. Pablo was hit by a car while playing ball in the street. An issue of contributory negligence was raised. Though the insurer was thought by all five of the panelists to have a generally fair settlement policy, two of the panelists felt the insurer would pay a good deal less to a poor Puerto Rican than to a middle-class boy with the same injuries. A factor limiting the extent of recovery was that Pablo had not obtained much medical attention for the torn ligaments he sustained. His expenses were only $500. Giving these factors special weight, one of these panelists evaluated the claim as worth only $1,000; the other put its worth at $2,500. A third panelist, on the other hand, was impressed by the extent of Pablo's disability. Now, three years after the accident, Pablo is unable to run hard and his knee buckles just from being on his feet all day. Pablo, who likes sports, is no longer able to participate in them. This panelist valued the case at $6,500, even with the possible contributory negligence defense. The remaining two panelists apparently weighed both sets of considerations equally, arriving at respective case values of $3,300 and $4,000, virtually splitting the difference. Panelists put different weights on the mutually accepted factors relevant for evaluation.

There are no guidelines to draw upon in determining what variation among panelists in valuing the same case is permissible. For each case I computed the coefficient of variability among the five evaluations.[27] The coefficient of variability equals the standard deviation divided by the mean. It provides a measure of panel variability for each case which can be compared with variability for all cases in the sample. The coefficients of variability are reported in Table A.5. There is an obvious need for refinement in case evaluation which can only come from further evaluative studies.

---

[27] Hubert Blalock, *Social Statistics* (New York: McGraw-Hill, 1960), pp. 73–74. See *supra,* pp. 37–38.

Table A.5: Activity and Recovery Scores for the Sample Clients

Client Number	Activity Score	Actual Recovery[a]	Panel Mean[b]	Panelist Evaluations[c]					Coefficient of Variability
				#1	#2	#3	#4	#5	
1	2	$ 5,800	$ 7,600	$ 6,000	$ 7,500	$ 8,500	$ 8,500	$ 7,500	0.1348
2	0	3,500	21,500	22,500	17,500	40,000	20,000	7,500	0.5490
3	8	42,500	34,000	45,000	40,000	45,000	25,000	15,000	0.3945
4	3	2,000	8,800	8,500	8,500	9,500	8,500	8,500	0.0508
5	3	4,250	3,200	1,800	4,000	4,000	3,500	2,500	0.3102
6	3	3,500	4,300	7,500	5,000	3,500	3,500	2,000	0.4836
7	4	2,000	2,200	2,300	2,000	750	4,500	1,500	0.6370
8	8	5,000	6,600	6,500	5,000	7,500	12,500	1,500	0.6070
9	1	3,000	6,900	11,000	5,800	6,000	8,500	3,000	0.4409
10	2	5,000	11,600	7,500	12,500	20,000	15,000	3,000	0.5680
11	6	3,500	2,800	1,500	4,300	2,000	4,500	1,500	0.5480
12	2	12,000	21,000	17,500	17,500	35,000	20,000	15,000	0.3820
13	3	3,500	2,600	2,000	2,750	2,500	4,500	1,000	0.5010
14	2	6,300	6,700	12,500	5,500	4,000	8,500	2,800	0.5854
15	0	3,250	4,200	2,500	3,000	7,500	4,500	3,300	0.4824
16	2	2,000	3,400	4,500	3,000	3,500	5,000	1,000	0.4580
17	1	2,900	4,800	4,700	4,500	6,000	5,500	3,000	0.2418
18	2	7,500	11,900	17,500	8,500	20,000	10,000	3,500	0.5679
19	3	2,250	10,100	15,000	13,500	8,000	10,000	4,000	0.4349
20	2	5,250	12,600	6,000	30,000	17,500	7,500	2,000	0.8950
21	4	9,000	7,400	3,500	7,500	10,000	8,500	7,500	0.3254
22	6	35,000	37,000	35,000	45,000	40,000	50,000	15,000	0.3651
23	2	14,250	15,800	17,500	11,500	25,000	10,000	15,000	0.3748
24	1	13,500	10,800	15,000	7,500	15,000	7,500	8,800	0.3630
25	4	2,250	3,400	2,100	3,250	3,000	4,500	2,500	0.2979
26	2	2,000	3,500	3,500	3,800	3,500	4,000	2,000	0.2349
27	0	2,000	3,500	3,000	3,750	3,500	3,500	3,500	0.0793
28	1	3,000	3,400	2,800	3,750	5,000	4,500	1,000	0.4639
29	5	7,000	5,000	2,500	5,500	6,000	7,500	3,500	0.4000
30	2	3,150	12,000	3,000	9,500	10,000	22,500	15,000	0.6045
31	7	8,000	9,800	12,500	10,000	12,500	10,000	4,000	0.3545
32	3	5,600	20,000	30,000	25,000	30,000	10,000	5,000	0.5863

Client Number	Activity Score	Actual Recovery[a]	Panel Mean[b]	Panelist Evaluations[c]					Coefficient of Variability
				#1	#2	#3	#4	#5	
33	6	$ 4,000	$ 7,200	$ 8,500	$ 4,800	$ 7,500	$ 7,500	$ 7,500	0.1939
34	6	2,150	2,900	2,500	3,600	2,500	4,500	1,500	0.3952
35	4	2,900	12,000	22,500	5,500	12,500	12,000	7,500	0.5480
36	0	4,530	9,300	6,500	10,000	15,000	10,000	5,000	0.4157
37	2	5,000	24,200	30,000	16,000	25,000	35,000	15,000	0.3599
38	0	8,000	4,800	6,000	6,000	7,500	3,000	1,500	0.5134
39	4	5,200	2,600	1,000	3,750	2,500	3,000	2,500	0.3946
40	0	6,500	10,900	7,000	12,500	15,000	15,000	5,000	0.4258
41	no personal injury								
42	2	3,250	4,500	3,300	4,400	7,500	5,000	2,500	0.3777
43	5	22,500	29,500	15,000	50,000	35,000	30,000	17,500	0.4809
44	2	2,300	3,000	2,000	3,500	5,000	3,000	1,500	0.4564
45	3	13,500	20,000	15,000	15,000	30,000	20,000	20,000	0.3062
46	4	23,200	21,000	20,000	27,500	17,500	20,000	20,000	0.1805
47	2	4,500	8,500	4,000	11,500	10,000	13,500	3,500	0.5310
48	3	17,000	18,000	11,000	20,000	30,000	25,000	4,000	0.5839
49	0	3,000	4,800	8,500	3,500	6,500	2,500	3,000	0.5398
50	2	4,000	3,600	6,000	3,500	6,000	3,000	2,000	0.4099
51	2	2,900	4,100	3,500	6,500	5,000	3,500	2,000	0.4171
52	1	2,200	3,200	3,300	3,500	3,500	3,500	2,000	0.2070
53	3	25,000	10,000	3,000	12,000	25,000	2,500	7,500	0.9226
54	3	2,000	4,600	6,500	3,500	7,500	4,000	1,500	0.5219
55	1	3,400	2,500	1,800	3,700	2,500	2,800	1,500	0.3527
56[d]	–	3,800	1,300	1,500	800	1,500	2,000	750	0.4042
57	7	6,950	5,800	7,500	7,500	7,500	5,000	1,500	0.4545
58	0	2,250	3,500	6,500	3,300	2,500	4,000	1,000	0.5875
59	3	3,250	4,000	4,500	3,500	5,000	4,250	2,500	0.2467
60	6	20,000	22,500	22,500	22,500	22,500	25,000	20,000	0.0785
61	3	5,500	6,000	10,000	4,750	7,500	5,000	2,500	0.4831

[a] Rounded to nearest $50.00
[b] Rounded to nearest $100.00
[c] The two insurance adjusters are panelist #4 and #5.
[d] Lawyer handling own claim.

The fact sheets presented to the panel as the basis for case evaluation listed the following information for each client:

1. Age at time of accident
2. Occupation at time of accident
3. Injury diagnosis
4. Hospitalization period (if any)
5. Disability period
6. Permanent disability or disfigurement (if any)
7. Total specials
    a. medical expenses
    b. lost wages
    c. property losses
8. Nature of accident
9. Perfection of liability
10. Defendant insurer
11. Any additional factors that, in my judgment, might affect the value of the claim

The first seven pieces of information were directly provided by the client. The eighth was based on a conventional classification of the client's accident, based on his account of it.[28] Assessing the perfection of liability (item 9) is not as subjective as might be imagined. The legal concept of negligence puts great weight on the nature of the accident. The case law holds that, excepting unusual circumstances, the one driving into another's rear is negligent. So is the one responsible for falling objects, or for knocking down a pedestrian. The mere fact of an auto accident indicates that somebody is responsible. Thus, an injured passenger tends to have a perfected liability against someone. Freedom from contributory negligence may be a little harder to prove when the victim is an injured pedestrian, harder still when he is the driver in a head-on collision, and reasonably difficult when he is injured in a fall. In the latter situation, the plaintiff must show that the lighting was bad or that there were hidden traps, to escape the suspicion that he was careless about looking where he was walking. The tenth item, the name of the insurer, is not known to many claimants. It is found, however, on the closing statements. Among the factors mentioned in item 11 are whether the client was told of a limit on the defendant's insurance or assets, any special proof problems, and whether the injuries were visually dramatic. In some instances, some panelists asked further questions about the cases, which I answered to the extent such information was known to me. Therefore, there was some variation in information provided to different panelists which may, in part, explain variations in panelist valuations.

---

[28] The classification is set forth in Table 3.1.

The finding that in almost 40 percent of the cases (23 of 59), clients recovered less than two-thirds of the average panel evaluation will be taken by some as evidence that the panel was misinformed about the true situations in the cases. To check on possible client misinformation, I received permission from each of seven clients (including five of the least successful ones) to talk about his case with his attorney. In six of the seven cases the lawyer added no new considerations and corrected none of the existing ones. In the seventh case the lawyer reduced by $4,000 Mr. O'Shea's claim for lost wages. The reduction of special damages would still not, in my judgment, have changed the evaluation that this was a poor recovery.

THE LAWYER QUESTIONNAIRE

A questionnaire was mailed to 60 attorneys who had worked directly with the sampled clients. Its primary purpose was to find out whether or not the attorney was a specialist, the size of his firm, and his attitudes about extensive disclosure of information to clients. The questionnaire also elicited the specific frustrations and satisfactions of negligence practice. These comments were used to supplement material from the 20 lawyer interviews.

From the closing statements I noted the names and addresses of the lawyers of record. I also asked the interviewed client to tell me the name of the attorney or attorneys with whom he had most of his dealings. I did not send questionnaires to attorneys who had little or no contact with the client. A lawyer's questionnaire was designed and pretested (with two nonsample attorneys) and mailed to the men who had represented the client interviewees. The questionnaire response rate was 80 percent (48 of 60). For seven additional attorneys the number of years in practice and the law school attended were located in Martindale-Hubbell.[29] Table A.6 shows that 61 percent of the responding attorneys have been in practice for more than 16 years. Thus, some information was obtained for 55 of the 60 attorneys.

Since, in the lawyer questionnaire, I was not asking for information about any specific case, I did not consider myself to be obligated to seek the client's permission to question his attorney. Similarly, since I was only seeking general information, I did not consider myself obligated to tell the sampled attorneys that I had interviewed one of their former clients. I did feel and did honor such

---

[29] Of the 60 attorneys, 55 are listed in Martindale-Hubbell. However, only 2 of the 60 are given a competency ranking. *Martindale-Hubbell Law Directory* (Summit, N.J., 1969 ed., 5 vols.

obligations when talking to the seven attorneys about their seven specific client cases.

Table A.6: Attorneys' Years of Practice

Period (in years)	Percentage	Number
2–5	2	1
6–10	15	8
11–15	22	12
16–20	20	11
21+	41	23
Total	100	55

Appendix B: Rules Regarding Personal Injury Claims of Supreme Court Appellate Division First Department

PART 603

ATTORNEYS

• • •

603.4 Claims or actions for personal injuries, property damage, wrongful death, loss of services resulting from personal injuries and claims in connection with condemnation or change of grade proceedings. (a) *Statements as to retainers; blank retainers.* (1) Every attorney who, in connection with any action or claim for damages for personal injuries or for property damages or for death or loss of services resulting from personal injuries, or in connection with any claim in condemnation or change of grade proceedings, accepts a retainer or enters into an agreement, express or implied, for compensation for services rendered or to be rendered in such action, claim or proceeding, whereby his compensation is to be dependent or contingent in whole or in part upon the successful prosecution or settlement thereof, shall, within 30 days from the date of any such retainer or agreement of compensation, sign personally and file with the Judicial Conference of the State of New York a written statement of such retainer or agreement of compensation, containing the information hereinafter set forth. Such statement may be filed personally by the attorney or his representative at the main office of the Judicial Conference in the City of New York, and upon such filing he shall receive a date stamped receipt containing the code number assigned to the original so filed. Such statement may also be filed by ordinary mail only addressed to:

> The Judicial Conference—Statements
> Post Office Box No. 2016
> New York 8, N. Y.

Statements filed by mail must be accompanied by a self-addressed stamped postal card containing the words "Retainer Statement", the date of the retainer and the name of the client. The Judicial Conference will date stamp the postal card, make notation thereon of the code number assigned to the retainer statement

SOURCE: *McKinney's New York Court Rules* (St. Paul, Minn.: West, 1969), pp. 42 ff.

209

and return such card to the attorney as a receipt for the filing of such statement. It shall be the duty of the attorney to make due inquiry if such receipt is not returned to him within 10 days after his mailing of the retainer statement to the Judicial Conference.

(2) A statement of retainer must be filed in connection with each action, claim or proceeding for which the attorney has been retained. Such statement shall be on one side of paper 8½ inches by 14 inches and be in the following form and contain the following information:

Retainer Statement   For office use:

TO THE JUDICIAL CONFERENCE OF THE
    STATE OF NEW YORK

1. Date of agreement as to retainer ....
2. Terms of compensation ....
3. Name and home address of client ....
4. If engaged by an attorney, name and office address of retaining attorney .....
   ....
   ....
5. If claim for personal injuries, wrongful death or property damage, date and place of occurrence ....
   ....
6. If a condemnation or change of grade proceeding:
   (a) Title and description ....
   ....
   (b) Date proceeding was commenced ....
   (c) Number or other designation of the parcels affected ....
   ....
   ....
7. Name, address, occupation and relationship of person referring the client ....
   ....
   ....
   ....

Dated: ...., N.Y., ... day of ...., 19..
                     Yours, etc.

....
         Signature of Attorney

Print
or
Type

....
            Attorney

....
       Office and P.O. Address

.... Dist. .... Dept. .... County

(3)   An attorney retained by another attorney, on a contingent fee basis, as trial or appeal counsel or to assist in the preparation, investigation, adjustment or settlement of any such action, claim or proceeding shall, within 15 days from the date of such retainer, sign personally and file with the Judicial Conference a written statement of such retainer in the manner and form as above set forth, which statement shall also contain particulars as to the fee arrangement, the type of services to be rendered in the matter, the code number assigned to the statement of retainer filed by the retaining attorney and the date when said statement of retainer was filed.

(4)   No attorney shall accept or act under any written retainer or agreement of compensation in which the name of the attorney was left blank at the time of its execution by the client.

(b)   *Closing statement; statement where no recovery.*   (1)   A closing statement shall be filed in connection with every claim, action or proceeding in which a retainer statement is required, as follows: Every attorney, upon receiving, retaining or sharing any sum in connection with a claim, action or proceeding subject to this section shall, within 15 days after such receipt, retention or sharing, sign personally and file with the Judicial Conference and serve upon the client a closing statement as hereinafter provided. Where there has been a disposition of any claim, action or proceeding, or a retainer agreement is terminated, without recovery, a closing statement showing such fact shall be signed personally by the attorney and filed with the Judicial Conference within 30 days after such disposition or termination. Such statement may be filed personally by the attorney or his representative at the main office of the Judicial Conference in the City of New York and upon such filing he shall receive a date stamped receipt. Such statement may also be filed by ordinary mail only addressed to:

> The Judicial Conference—Statements
> Post Office Box No. 2016
> New York 8, N. Y.

Statements filed by mail must be accompanied by a self-addressed stamped postal card containing the words "Closing Statement", the date the matter was completed, and the name of the client. The Judicial Conference will date stamp the postal card, make notation thereon of the code number assigned to the closing statement and return such card to the attorney as a receipt for the filing of such statement. It shall be the duty of the attorney to make due inquiry if such receipt is not returned to him within 10 days after his mailing of the closing statement to the Judicial Conference.

(2)   Each closing statement shall be on one side of paper 8½ inches by 14 inches and be in the following form and contain the following information:

Closing Statement   For office use:

1. Code number appearing on Attorney's receipt for filing of retainer statement. (If
   statement filed with Clerk of Appellate
   Division prior to July 1, 1960, give date of
   such filing.)

   ....
                 Code Number

2. Name and present address of client ....

3. Plaintiff(s)   4. Defendant(s)
   ....
   ....

5. If action commenced state date ...., 19..., ...
   Court, ... County. Was note of issue or notice of trial filed?
   .... If "Yes", was action disposed of in open court? .... If
   not disposed of in open court, state date stipulation of discontinuance was filed
   with CALENDAR CLERK of the court in which the action was pending ....
   ...., 19....

6. Check items applicable: Settled (   ); Claim abandoned by client (   ); Judgment (   ).
   Date of payment by carrier or defendant .... day of ...., 19....
   Date of payment to client ...... day of ...., 19....

7. Gross amount of recovery (if judgment entered, include any interest, costs
   and disbursements allowed) $................

8. Name and address of insurance carrier or person paying judgment or claim
   and carrier's file number, if any ....

9. Net amounts: to client $........; compensation to undersigned $........;
   names, addresses and amounts paid to attorneys participating in the contingent
   compensation ....

10. Compensation fixed by: retainer agreement (   ); under schedule (   ); or by
    court (   ).

11. If compensation fixed by court: Name of Judge ....,
    Court ...., Index No. ...., Date of order ....

12. Itemized statement of payments made for hospital, medical care or treatment,
    liens, assignments, claims and expenses on behalf of the client which have
    been charged against the client's share of the recovery, together with the
    name, amount and reason for each payment ....

13. Itemized statement of the amounts of expenses and disbursements paid or
    agreed to be paid to others for expert testimony, investigative or other services
    properly chargeable to the recovery of damages together with the name, address
    and reason for each payment ....

14. Date on which a copy of this closing statement has been forwarded to the client . . . . , 19. . . .

Dated: . . . . , N.Y., ... , day of . . . . , 19. .

Yours, etc.

. . . .
Signature of Attorney

Print
or
Type

. . . .
Attorney

. . . .
Office and P.O. Address

. . . . Dist. . . . . Dept. . . . . County

Closing Statement*   For office use:

TO THE JUDICIAL CONFERENCE OF THE
STATE OF NEW YORK

1. Code number appearing on Attorney's receipt for filing of retainer statement. (If statement filed with Clerk of Appellate Division prior to July 1, 1960, give date of such filing.)

. . . .
Code Number

2. Name and present address of client . . . .
3. Plaintiff(s)   4. Defendant(s)

. . . .
. . . .

5. If action commenced state date . . . . , 19. . ., ... Court, ... County. Was note of issue or notice of trial filed? . . . . If "Yes", was action disposed of in open court? . . . . If not disposed of in open court, state date stipulation of discontinuance was filed with CALENDAR CLERK of the court in which the action was pending . . . . , 19. . . .
6. Check items applicable: Settled ( ); Claim abandoned by client ( ); Judgment ( ).

Date of payment by carrier or defendant . . . . day of . . . . , 19. . . .

Date of payment to client . . . . . . day of . . . . , 19. . . .
7. Gross amount of recovery (if judgment entered, include any interest, costs and disbursements allowed) $ . . . .
8. Name and address of insurance carrier or person paying judgment or claim and carrier's file number, if any . . . .

9. Net amounts: to client $........; compensation to undersigned $........, names, addresses and amounts paid to attorneys participating in the contingent compensation ....

10. Compensation fixed by: retainer agreement ( ); under schedule ( ); or by court ( ).

11. If compensation fixed by court: Name of Judge ...., Court ...., Index No. ...., Date of order ....

12. Itemized statement of payments made for hospital, medical care or treatment, liens, assignments, claims and expenses on behalf of the client which have been charged against the client's share of the recovery, together with the name, amount and reason for each payment ....

13. Itemized statement of the amounts of expenses and disbursements paid or agreed to be paid to others for expert testimony, investigative or other services properly chargeable to the recovery of damages together with the name, address and reason for each payment ....

14. Date on which a copy of this closing statement has been forwarded to the client ....,19....

Dated: ...., N.Y., ..., day of ...., 19..

Yours, etc.

....

Signature of Attorney

Print

or { ....

Type

Attorney

....

Office and P.O. Address

.... Dist. .... Dept. .... County

* This form effective October 1, 1969.

(If space provided is insufficient, riders on sheets 8½ inches by 14 inches and signed personally by the attorney may be attached.)

(3) A joint closing statement may be served and filed in the event that more than one attorney receives, retains or shares in the contingent compensation in any claim, action or proceeding, in which event the statement shall be signed by each such attorney.

(c) *Confidential nature of statements.* (1) All statements of retainer or closing statements filed shall be deemed to be confidential and the information therein contained shall not be divulged or made available for inspection or examination except upon written order of the presiding justice of the Appellate Division.

(2) The Judicial Conference of the State of New York shall microphotograph all statements filed pursuant to this rule on film of durable material by use of a device which shall accurately reproduce on such film the original statements

in all details thereof, and shall thereafter destroy the originals so reproduced. Such microphotographs shall be deemed to be an original record for all purposes, and an enlargement or facsimile thereof may be introduced in evidence in all courts and administrative agencies and in any action, hearing or proceeding in place and stead of the original statement so reproduced, with the same force and effect as though the original document were presented.

(d) *Deposit of collections; notice.* (1) Whenever an attorney, who has accepted a retainer or entered into an agreement as above referred to, shall collect any sum of money upon any such action, claim or proceeding, either by way of settlement or after a trial or hearing, he shall forthwith deposit the same in a bank or trust company in the City of New York in a special account separate from his own personal account, and shall not commingle the same with his own funds. Within 15 days after the receipt of any such sum he shall cause to be delivered personally to such client or sent by registered or certified mail, addressed to such client at the client's last known address, a copy of the closing statement required by this section. At the same time the attorney shall pay or remit to the client the amount shown by such statement to be due the client, and he may then withdraw for himself the amount so claimed to be due him for compensation and disbursements. For the purpose of calculating the 15 day period, the attorney shall be deemed to have collected or received or been paid a sum of money on the date that he receives the draft endorsed by the client, or if the client's endorsement is not required, on the date the attorney receives the sum. The acceptance by a client of such amount shall be without prejudice to the latter's right in an appropriate action or proceeding, to petition the court to have the question of the attorney's compensation or reimbursement for expenses investigated and determined by it.

(2) Whenever any sum of money is payable upon any such claim, action or proceeding, either by way of settlement or after trial or hearing, and the attorney is unable to find his client, the attorney shall apply to the court in which such action or proceeding was pending, or if no action had been commenced, then to the Supreme Court in the county wherein the attorney has his office, for an order directing payment to be made to the attorney of the amount determined by the court to be due said attorney for his fee and reimbursable disbursements and to the clerk of the court of the balance due to the client, for the account of the client, subject to the charge of any lien found by the court to be payable therefrom.

(e) *Contingent fees in claims and actions for personal injury and wrongful death.* (1) In any claim or action for personal injury or wrongful death, whether determined by judgment or settlement, in which the compensation of claimant's or plaintiff's attorney is contingent, that is, dependent in whole or in part upon the amount of the recovery, the receipt, retention or sharing by such attorney, pursuant to agreement or otherwise, of compensation which is equal to or less than the fees scheduled below is deemed to be fair and reasonable. The receipt, retention or sharing of compensation which is in excess of such scheduled fees shall constitute the exaction of unreasonable and unconscionable compensation in violation of canons 12 and 13 of the canons of professional ethics of the New York State Bar Association, unless authorized by a written order of the court as hereinafter provided.

(2) The following is the schedule of reasonable fees referred to above: either,

Schedule A

(i)   50 per cent on the first $1,000 of the sum recovered,

(ii) 40 per cent on the next $2,000 of the sum recovered,

(iii) 35 per cent on the next $22,000 of the sum recovered,

(iv) 25 per cent on any amount over $25,000 of the sum recovered; or

Schedule B

(i) A percentage not exceeding 33⅓ per cent of the sum recovered, if the initial contractual arrangement between the client and the attorney so provides, in which event the procedure hereinafter provided for making application for additional compensation because of extraordinary circumstances shall not apply.

(3) Such percentage shall be computed on the net sum recovered after deducting from the amount recovered expenses and disbursements for expert testimony and investigative or other services properly chargeable to the enforcement of the claim or prosecution of the action. In computing the fee, the costs as taxed, including interest upon a judgment, shall be deemed part of the amount recovered. For the following or similar items there shall be no deduction in computing such percentages: Liens, assignments or claims in favor of hospitals, for medical care and treatment by doctors and nurses, or self-insurers or insurance carriers.

(4) In the event that claimant's or plaintiff's attorney believes in good faith that Schedule A, *supra,* because of extraordinary circumstances, will not give him adequate compensation, application for greater compensation may be made upon affidavit with written notice and an opportunity to be heard to the client and other persons holding liens or assignments on the recovery. Such application shall be made to the justice of the trial part to which the action had been sent for trial; or, if it had not been sent to a part for trial, then to the justice presiding at the trial term calendar part of the court in which the action had been instituted; or, if no action had been instituted, then to the justice presiding at the trial term calendar part of the Supreme Court for the county in the judicial department in which the attorney who filed the statement of retainer, pursuant to this section, has an office. Upon such application, the justice, in his discretion, if extraordinary circumstances are found to be present, and without regard to the claimant's or plaintiff's consent, may fix as reasonable compensation for legal services rendered an amount greater than that specified in Schedule A, *supra,* provided, however, that such greater amount shall not exceed the fee fixed pursuant to the contractual arrangement, if any, between the client and the attorney. If the application be granted, the justice shall make a written order accordingly, briefly stating the reasons for granting the greater compensation; and a copy of such order shall be served on all persons entitled to receive notice of the application.

(5) The provisions of subdivision (e) of this section shall not apply to an

attorney retained as counsel in a claim or action for personal injury or wrongful death by another attorney, if such other attorney is not subject to the provisions of this rule in such claim or action, but all other subdivisions of this section shall apply.

(6) Nothing contained in subdivision (e) of this rule shall be deemed applicable to the fixing of compensation for attorneys representing infants or other persons, where the statutes or rules provide for the fixation of such compensation by the court.

(f) *Preservation of records of claims and actions.* Attorneys for both plaintiff and defendant in the case of any such claim or cause of action shall preserve, for a period of at least five years after any settlement or satisfaction of the claim or cause of action or any judgment thereon or after the dismissal or discontinuance of any action, the pleadings and other papers pertaining to such claim or cause of action, including, but not limited to, letters or other data relating to the claim of loss of time from employment or loss of income; medical reports, medical bills, x-ray reports, x-ray bills; repair bills, estimates of repairs; all correspondence concerning the claim or cause of action; and memoranda of the disposition thereof as well as canceled vouchers, receipts and memoranda evidencing the amounts disbursed by the attorney to the client and others in connection with the aforesaid claim or cause of action.

* * *

603.5 Sharing of legal fees. No attorney shall share the legal fees received by him in connection with any claim, action or proceeding except with another attorney or attorneys based upon a division of service or responsibility.

* * *

603.6 Compromise of claims or actions belonging to infants. (a) An application for the approval by the court of a settlement of a claim or cause of action belonging to an infant must be made as provided in CPLR 1207 and 1208.

(b) In the case of a claim or demand belonging to an infant, any sum collected by an attorney shall be deposited in a special account apart from his personal account, and a statement of the amount received shall be delivered personally to the duly qualified guardian of the infant or mailed to such guardian by registered or certified mail addressed to said guardian's last known address. But no payment or withdrawal shall be made from such deposit in the said account to the credit of the infant's claim except pursuant to an order of the court after application as provided in section 474 of the Judiciary Law, upon at least two days notice to the guardian.

Index